The Odyssey and the Idiocy Marriage to an Actor

A Memoir

Candace Hilligoss

First Edition Design Publishing

The Odyssey and the Idiocy Marriage to an Actor

ISBN 978-1506-914-35-0 PRINT
ISBN 978-1506-914-36-7 HC

LCCN 2015959748

November 2016

Published and Distributed by
First Edition Design Publishing, Inc.
P.O. Box 20217, Sarasota, FL 34276-3217
www.firsteditiondesignpublishing.com

(Any resemblance to persons living or dead is purely intentional.)

The greatest tragedy is not in death, but to lose one's life while living–never to reclaim or to establish our identity within ourselves. To arrive at the end of life's odyssey and realize that we cannot redeem it, any more than we have a chance to live it all over again.

Amen,

Candace Hilligoss

In blessed memory of

Michelle Cousin

Adjunct Associate Professor of television and film writing at New York University. She was my first writing teacher.

and for

Paul Gillette

Novelist, Producer, Adjunct Professor in the professional writing program and the School of Cinema and TV at the University of Southern California. As a mentor, he inspired and kept me writing at a time when my life seemed to be a running sea of despair and darkness from which there was no escape.

and for

Richard L. Coe

Theater Critic and Columnist for The Washington Post. He insisted I must tell the story with my usual sense of humor about marriage to that actor.

Acknowledgments

I am deeply grateful to Ken Rotcop for his unfailing support that encouraged me to write this memoir. Without him and his Hollywood Workshop, this book might not have existed. Once a week for a few years, we met in the community room of the famous Farmer's Market in West Hollywood. He created a nurturing and inspiring atmosphere for writers that is rare in a tinsel town like Hollywood.

How thankful I am for Tom Weaver and his editorial guidance. He was willing to read 400 bulky pages and to give notes. It was because of him that I made appearances at film conventions, and that an abridged part of my chapter about the cult classic movie *"Carnival of Souls"* was published in the magazine "Monsters From The Vault."

I am indebted to my dear friend, Valedia Sullivan, who generously read an early draft of the memoir, even though for years she has listened to all my stories. Her suggestions were invaluable.

The six illustrations were done by four-time Oscar nominee, Garrett Lewis. He earned accolades as a set decorator for movies such as: *Bram Stoker's* ***Dracula*** *directed by Francis Ford Coppola, Steven Spielberg's* ***Hook****, and Edward Zwick's* ***Glory*** among 39 other films. Had he not passed away, it was his intention to illustrate each chapter. When I was nineteen, I met him for the first time in NY's LaGuardia Airport. I had just arrived from South Dakota. We stayed close friends for many years. When I moved to Beverly Hills, he decorated my apartment with furniture from the movie set of *California Suite*. He made my new home so gorgeous.

And, he was, too.

Garrett Lewis

Prologue

"There's no mother-fucking way, I'm going to pay alimony to a healthy woman. Tell her to get a job!" Richard Forest yelled this at my attorney and me from across a conference table.

Irving Buter, his attorney, put a restraining arm on Richard and barked, "Shut up, big mouth."

Buter (rhymes with cuter) was already annoyed at his client's previous refusal to take his advice. So was my attorney, Gary Zimmerman. The four of us were sweating it out, literally, in a small windowless room off the hall of the Superior Courthouse in downtown Los Angeles on Hill Street.

Southern California was in the midst of an August heat wave that brought the Santanas "Devil" winds. These were desert winds, warned the newscasters, that caused garbage cans to roll down the alleys of Palm Drive in Beverly Hills, the city where I lived.

Throughout six months of negotiations, Buter had assured my attorney Zimmerman that we would settle out of court. "My clients do exactly what I tell them to do," he said.

Zimmerman had told me that our case did not warrant a trial. I was not exactly divorcing an actor in the same league as Kirk Douglas or Clint Eastwood. In fact, there was very little community property to divide as Richard and I had spent most of our marriage renting an apartment in New York.

The only thing to share was Richard's ability to make money as an actor. In the past four years, his earnings from his television appearances had been in the six figures. But right now in the summer of 1980, the Screen Actors Guild was into its third month of strike. The SAG board promised that it would not capitulate to the producers' demands. Richard was now an out-of-work actor who claimed he probably would never work again. His leading man days were over.

All actors when they are between roles are technically unemployed as no play or TV series runs forever. Actors accept that as the norm in show business. They don't lose their agents, managers or their talents, just because a play closed out of town or a television series was canceled. And as all things come to an end, so would the current SAG strike.

"Jesus, what rotten timing for us," Zimmerman repeated like a mantra when the news of the strike hit the papers before our court date.

It was nearly noon, and the lawyers were anxious to finalize everything and go to lunch. Wiping the perspiration from his brow with his forehand, Buter leaned over to Richard and said, "Pay her a thousand a month, and let's get out of here."

"I'll pay for 90 days of support, and that's all."

Buter tried to control himself as he said quietly, "That's not long enough. No judge will agree to that, Richard. You were married too long—twenty years. Trust me!"

"Then I'll declare bankruptcy!"

"You're not going to do that so shut up, big mouth."

I could tell that Zimmerman was masking his disappointment with Richard, who remained so uncooperative. Last June, Zimmerman had assured me that no reasonable man wants to face a court battle. "The closer we get to the trial date, the more likely Richard will back down. Reality will hit him."

That very day, when we arrived at the courthouse, Zimmerman kept up his delusions. "Once we're inside, and Richard takes in the cold atmosphere of the court and the unsmiling judge's face, he'll settle. We'll never go to trial. I've seen many men in the twelfth hour drop this macho facade and come to their senses."

My attorney doesn't understand the psyche, not to mention the narcissistic ego of an actor. Richard needs drama in his life, particularly when he's unemployed and between roles. He will relish standing in the witness box as if he were on stage and projecting to us, his captive audience.

Years ago, a well-respected critic wrote that no man with any brains has ever been an actor. I have to agree. Any man lured upon the stage as politicians are sometimes lured into bordellos, would have his mind almost immediately destroyed by the gaudy nonsense spilling out of his mouth every night.

(I have to step aside here and admit that Richard Forest is not his real name. I changed it, not to protect him, but because he doesn't deserve this much free publicity.)

This is my first life experience at retaining an attorney and preparing for court. I tried to find someone who was not too expensive. Then I was nervous about retaining an attorney who seemed too cheap in comparison with his colleagues. I didn't want to feel like the astronaut who climbed into the spaceship and remembered it was built by the lowest bidder.

Zimmerman, in his upbeat way, had tried to explain to me how California was in the avant-garde of the divorce game. In this state, divorce is called dissolution. Plaintiff and defendant have been replaced with petitioner and respondent. These new terms make it look as if it were a proceeding, not a lawsuit, a less adversarial nomenclature.

As Zimmerman said, "Previously, divorce stated that someone was at fault and could be denied. Now we have 'no-fault' divorce, and that's why Richard has pleaded irreconcilable differences."

In Richard's case, irreconcilable differences meant he had found a twenty-two-year-old girlfriend. Hell hath no fury like a man who wishes to marry a girl half his age. I studied Richard for a moment as he conferred with Buter. Richard was still handsome for someone in his mid-forties. He had just begun to tint his prematurely gray hair. The chlorine from his swimming pool must have affected it, for his chestnut brown locks had a strange cast that resembled menopause red. Perhaps his new young friend didn't notice or care. I reminded myself that she would have been about two years old on the day Richard and I married. I wondered what Richard would have thought if he had known at our wedding that somewhere in the universe, there was a toddler running about who would someday become his second wife.

Zimmerman started speaking as he flipped through his files. "According to our budget, Candace will need around $2,000 a month to live on if she's to keep her Beverly Hills apartment and maintain her standard of living."

"No shit!" Richard said. His face flushed like a sunburn.

"Hey now, I live in Beverly Hills," Buter said, "and I don't need $2,000 a month, and neither does she. Look at her, she could easily make $1,500 a month. Candace, why don't you go to real estate school? It's a six-week course. You get your license, and you can make a million dollars. I know a lady who did that last year."

"Ninety days of alimony would be enough to see you through real estate school." Richard said, nodding.

Buter nodded in unison with Richard. "You've had a free ride for twenty years. You can't expect him to support you forever. Your husband and I want to know what you plan to do to rehabilitate yourself."

I asked, "Isn't the word 'rehabilitation' used for criminals when they're sent to factories to make license plates? Or for drug addicts?"

Buter snapped back with, "What we're asking is, how do you plan to re-enter society?"

"I've never left."

Zimmerman put his hand on my arm as though he could calm us both down. "They want to know how much time you need for retraining in order to support yourself."

"Maybe I could revive my acting career. It was as an actress that I had supported both Richard and myself in the early days of our marriage."

There were rolling of eyes and exasperated sighs from the enemy camp. Richard's attorney turned to mine and said, "She needs to be tested. I recommend that we set up an appointment for psychological evaluation and some vocational tests. That can be arranged at UCLA. I know a shrink over there, who's the best in his field."

My attorney made note of this in one of his files as though it were a good idea. I wanted to ask how a psychiatrist would evaluate me, when my only employment history had been that of an actress? How does one transfer the skills of a middle-aged homemaker, mother of two daughters, ego-booster of the actor-husband into a job market that competes with college grads and their impressive résumés? No one seemed concerned about the impact of the trauma that I was feeling, the grief or the loss of my self-esteem at having been replaced by a younger woman. True, we live in a modern, disposable society where we either throw things away or recycle them, but should a mature woman be treated no better than used Pampers?

Buter focused on me and continued: "No judge is going to put a husband in shackles for the rest of his life to support a wife. Forget any career as an actress; you're too old."

The perspiration on Richard's upper lip seemed to dissolve into a slight foam around his mouth as he said, "Don't let her use my good name of Forest as an actress! Make her use her maiden name! Hell, I've worked damn hard for years to build my reputation as an actor. I won't have her ruining my name!"

"I can go by any name I choose, Richard. Maybe I'll be like Mrs. Patrick Campbell at the turn of the century. Remember G.B. Shaw's favorite actress? She acted under her married surname. If I do the same, critics will review me as Mrs. Richard Forest who appeared in, or the worst performance in the play was given by Mrs. Richard Forest, who is related to the actor of the same name."

Before Richard had a chance to respond, his attorney said, "Shut up, big mouth. She has a legal right to your name. Nothing we can do about it." Then Buter gave me one of those smiles worthy of an executioner before he pulls the switch. "Richard needs to build his career as an actor. He's at a turning point where he doesn't want to jeopardize his reputation by accepting second-rate guest spots on TV any more. One more episode on 'Wonder Woman' or 'Spider Man' and he'll never be considered for better movies with the heavy hitters."

"I swore..." Richard could hardly catch his breath. He began again: "I fucking swore I'd never prostitute my art and do one more "soap-opera" crap to support her. Someone, please give her that message."

Zimmerman and I ignored him. Richard's defense that he was forced to appear in "soap-opera" crap is unsound and dishonest. An actor never disdains anything that pays him money. He is devoid of that aesthetic conscience, which is the mark of the genuine artist. If there were a public willing to pay him enough money to hear him blow a trombone, or to see him strip off his boxer shorts and dance a jig stark naked on Hollywood Boulevard, he would do so without a moment of hesitation.

Buter grabbed his files and stood. "Enough is enough. Zimmerman, as far as I'm concerned, we should report back to Department Two. Maybe we can still get a judge for this afternoon."

The four of us filed into the main assembly room. Richard and Buter went to one side, and Zimmerman and I discreetly sat some distance away. The place was packed with couples waiting to be assigned a judge to hear their cases.

Zimmerman whispered that I was in the appropriate dress for a trial. He had recommended no silk, just cotton. I wore a dingy white blouse that had been through fifteen years of washing. It was frayed at the cuffs and collar. My cotton skirt looked like a left-over checkered tablecloth. My face was naked of any makeup, and my hair was in a ponytail secured by a supermarket's rubber band.

Richard must have received the same kind of advice from his attorney. Richard had owned fabulous designer suits...well, actually he had walked away with many of them from various wardrobe departments. He was often cast as the successful "Mafia lawyer" type on television. But now he wore shiny pants that were too short. This way one would notice his torn socks that draped over his unpolished loafers that had run-down heels. I recognized his three dollar jacket from our New York days when he used to shop in thrift stores on Tenth Avenue. I wondered in what trunk he managed to find that moth-eaten relic of an item.

About this time, two lawyers were before the judge with their clients, an agitated wife who was pointing at her husband, who stood quietly in a well-behaved fashion. She complained, “I’m afraid of him, your Honor. He’s an abusive spouse. Please, please don’t put me in the same conference room with him. He has a violent temper!”

All eyes seemed to stare at the husband, who was well-groomed and pleasant looking. The judge, as well as the rest of the attorneys, I’m sure, deemed her a hysterical woman. He ordered her, “Now, now, be reasonable. It’s a rule in family law that there be a first meeting in a conference room before I can assign you to the judge for the hearing. I’ll let you use conference room ‘A’ that adjoins us. Any trouble with the respondent, you come and report to me.”

She burst into sobs as her attorney led her up the aisle and out of the main assembly room, followed by the husband and his attorney.

The judge resumed his roll-call. Then after about five minutes, there was a gunshot. Zimmerman and I froze, as we weren’t sure what we just heard. A few of the lawyers jumped up, turning toward the double doors where the couple had exited. Another shot rang out. Zimmerman grabbed his chest in reflex then grabbed me. The third shot was fired. “Get down!” he ordered. We both fell into a brace-for-impact position. Some lawyers ducked under the benches. Others were crawling toward a side door.

The security guards, more terrified than anyone as they are untrained to respond to open gunfire, raced through the aisles as if to get out of the line of fire. By now, even the judge had left the bench and disappeared with the court reporter. Someone with a voice of authority shouted for everyone to remain seated and to be calm.

Footsteps ran back and forth in the halls. People were yelling. Richard and Buter managed to step outside the courtroom. After a few seconds, they returned and came over to Zimmerman and me. Buter, in a husky whisper, said, "You’ll never believe this. That woman we thought acted like a crazed housewife? Well, she wasn’t that crazy. Her husband shot her, shot the attorney, then shot himself. All three are dead!"

The color left Zimmerman’s face. Then he asked, "Which attorney got it, his or hers?" Buter snarled, "Hers." After a pause, he added, "What rotten luck! Damn it! This means we’ll have to be continued."

He patted Richard on the back. "How about some Chinese food? Two blocks from here is the best Peking duck in town. My treat."

Zimmerman and I watched them leave. He seemed shaky himself. He shook his head. "I've lost my appetite. Are you hungry?" I managed a weak no.

Soon other lawyers and clients seemed to spring from their hiding places. There was much grumblings over the delay. Now that the police arrived, no one seemed that concerned over the dead people next door. As Zimmerman and I pushed through the crowd, he said, "Maybe by the time we come back, the actor's strike will have been settled. What a tragedy."

"Oh, yes, it's so tragic. That poor woman! And now she's dead!"

"I'm not talking about her. I mean the actor's strike."

"Gary, how can you think about the strike, when three people have just been murdered?"

"Because, Candace, I am your lawyer and, as a professional, I'm hired to protect your interests. These murders do not affect your case. The SAG strike is 1,000 times more important to your case than dead people. My only concern, right now, is to win for you."

"Sorry, I got carried away." I followed him to the first floor escalator. He was mumbling to himself, "If only you'd married a doctor or an engineer...."

If only I hadn't been so naive at twenty as to fall in love and marry an actor with a John Barrymore profile.

> "Paper napkins never return from a laundry
> nor love from a trip to the law courts."
>
> – John Barrymore

ACT ONE

Chapter One

New York–Fall 1958–Twenty Years Earlier

Right after I graduated as an actress from the American Theatre Wing, the president of the school sent me to the Cape Playhouse in Dennis, Massachusetts. In the eight weeks of summer stock there, I saved as much of my salary as possible in hopes this would support me through the Fall season while looking for work as an actress in New York.

Fall came, then it was winter. I was still unemployed. Making rounds of casting agents or producers seemed futile if actors didn't have a theatrical agent to represent them. Wandering on Broadway and 49th Street, I ran into George Lindsey, a student actor from the Wing who carried a copy of the newspaper "Show Business." "Look, Candace, this paper tells you where the acting jobs are. Here's something for you. This week, auditions are being held at the Copacabana for 'The Copa Girls.' You can dance, too, and you don't need an agent for the interview."

Growing up in South Dakota, I learned about the Copa from magazines like the defunct Pageant, Look and Coronet. My girlfriends and I read them in the magazine sections of drug stores and dime stores. We believed every word. We accepted that the Copacabana was the hottest nightclub north of Havana, and that the Copa Girls caused a revolution in show business, that they were considered the most beautiful girls in the world. At clubs like the Latin Quarter owned by Barbara Walters's father, show girls wore silly costumes of feathers and plumes, unlike the Copa Girls who were dressed in Paris and New York couture fashions. The club claimed that the Copa Girl graduates had gone on to be the brightest stars in Hollywood. As of last count there were fifty stars whose stardom began on the Copa floor.

George said encouragingly, "The open-call for girls is this afternoon. Go now!"

"Right now?"

"This is your chance. Think of it this way: it's the best job for an actress. It's a night job, and your days are free for auditions. What could be a better job than dancing in the most glamorous nightclub in New York. You'll be the envy of every actress with thick ankles–what fabulous, unforgettable nights–nights of laughter–nights of excitement—headquarters for stars like Frank Sinatra, Dean Martin and Jerry Lewis, Tony Bennett, Peggy Lee–and you! The list is endless."

Friends and foes back home couldn't understand why I did not have a steady job as an actress. When they graduated from college with a degree in teaching or nursing, they found jobs within a week. My father did not understand it either. However, dancing at the Copacabana and getting paid for it, I could call off the wolves.

I took a Fifth Avenue bus until it stopped at 60th Street. There was an awning with COPACABANA at 10 East 60th. At my age, twenty, this was the first nightclub I had ever entered.

The entrance was quite dark and upstairs appeared to be a lounge. I kept going until I came to a mezzanine that overlooked a small dance floor. White palm trees decorated the background with silk pineapples in keeping with the Latin atmosphere. The Copa Girl in a tropical bonnet (like Carmen Miranda's turban) was the motif painted on each musician's bandstand, on every match book cover, every ashtray, the dinner menu and in every poster along with the name of the current headliner. It was hard to believe that this small room with the tiny dance floor was the most glamorous nightclub in New York. Was it really true that the Copa was filled with fabulous nights of laughter, of unforgettable excitement? It had a kind of cheapness in the style of the decor that was expensive to reproduce. A perfect background for Rita Hayworth in "Gilda" when she sang, "Put the Blame on Mame, Boys."

I waited discreetly as the choreographer Doug Coudy interviewed a couple of girls on the dance floor. When they left, I approached him. "Mr. Coudy, here's my résumé. I've been studying dance with J.C. McCord at the Wing and Nell Fischer who's with the Martha Graham Company."

"I–I--k--k--know them –v-ve-very g–g-good. Come b-b-back t-t-t-tomorrow at t-t-two."

Doug Coudy had the worst stammer or stutter I had ever heard. I said, "T-t-thank you." Oh my, in sympathy I picked up his stutter. It took him a couple minutes of more stuttering to tell me to return in a leotard for the audition.

The next afternoon I came prepared. In case this was going to be a serious dance audition, I kept a pair of Ruby Keeler tap shoes with the tie ribbon-bows in my black tote bag. Coudy had twenty girls lined up. He demonstrated a dance combination. Some of the models tripped. Other girls lost their footing. I realized that those dance lessons of ballet and tap from the age of three through high school with the local dance teacher in Huron, South Dakota, were going to pay off. Coudy asked me how high I could kick. This was easy for me as I could kick over my head in a three-inch heel and maintain my balance.

Late that night I received a call from someone at the Copa who said to show up at two in the afternoon again. Make sure to wear a leotard. This was the finals for the new show's Copa Girls. Once I arrived at the nightclub, I was told to go immediately to the dance floor. As I joined the line of girls, I realized there were just eight of us. This meant we had made it as this season's Copa Girls.

Coudy sat at a table on the mezzanine with Jules Podell, the owner and managing director of the Copcabana. Podell remained stone-faced as he slowly stared at each one of us. Coudy leaned over with a résumé in hand as he whispered each girl's name and credits to Podell.

A Russian Jew, Podell was short and squat. With almost no neck, he looked like the meanest, toughest bull in a pen snorting for a fight. Gangsters wanted to stay on the good side of him. The Copa's cabaret roots started in the twenties as a speakeasy when Prohibition began forbidding the sale of alcohol. This law was a failure since speakeasies quickly sprang up to sell and to supply liquor, making the owners rich. Local law agencies were bribed to look the other way. When Prohibition ended, organized crime didn't want to give up the clubs and the lucrative profits. They needed front-men, legitimate businessmen like Jules Podell to operate the clubs. During the '40s and '50s Frank Costello, one of the Mafia's most famous bosses, and Vito Genovese, top dog in the underworld, were the main muscle and money behind Podell's Copacabana. Costello was considered to be the most powerful and influential of crime bosses in the U.S. He was known as "Prime Minister of the Underworld." Years later Mario Puzo modeled the character of Don Vito Corleone in his book, "The Godfather" (1969) on Costello.

None of this meant anything to me. There were no Italian families in Huron, South Dakota. The first time I heard the word "Mafia," I thought it was the name of an Italian salad dressing. After all, I grew up without television, and this was years before Martin Scorsese, Little Italy's hometown boy, made all his Italian gangster movies.

Before Podell came to the Copa, he operated successful restaurants and other clubs. However, it was the Copacabana that was his lifelong passion. Every night he sat at the same table for the shows. If he wanted something, he tapped his ring on the table. A waiter would come running to him. When Podell heard a comedian do what he considered filthy or risqué material, Podell knocked his ring on the table. The comic could expect a visit from Podell after the show: "I don't want no filth in the Copa!" Podell ruled with an iron fist and watched the kitchen like a hawk. Let a piece of lettuce fall to the floor and you would hear his wrath coming through the basement walls. Serving plates were checked for portions and for appearance. If Podell didn't like it, he sent the waiter to the back of the line to start over. There were twenty chefs and fifteen cooks who answered to him. If a waiter showed a spot on his white jacket, he was ordered to change his clothes. Podell never left the club until four a.m., his closing time.

Coudy passed out sheets of paper to us. "Th-th-these–are the–r-rules." I read that we were never again to enter the Copacabana through the front entrance, but to take the back entrance to the basement along with the waiters and other employees. We were not to stand waiting on the sidewalk in front of the Copacabana. We were to meet dates, parents or other relatives several feet away from the doorway, either on Madison Avenue or on Fifth Avenue.

We were not allowed to join relatives between shows even if they were dining at the Copa. I didn't quite understand the strict rules until a girl next to me whispered, "Podell doesn't want any girl to look like a prostitute soliciting at the Copa because he could lose his liquor license if that happens. Then the Mafia would whack you."

"What's 'whack' mean?"

We were ordered to go to City Hall to have a photo taken (mug shot) for a New York City Cabaret Identification Card. As he clicked his camera, the photographer said to his assistant, "Jeez, the girls are getting skinnier each year." Just before I left, he said to me, "Did you know you look like the actress, Carol Landis?" I shrugged. Recently, there had been a unflattering photo of her suicide in Life Magazine. She was curled around the pedestal of a bathroom sink with an empty medicine bottle in her hand. Her note said, "That she couldn't live without Rex Harrison's love any longer." It was obvious that sexy Rex had dumped her.

Then the Copa girls were also required to get a performer's permit from the New York Police Department's License Bureau. This was to make sure a girl had never been arrested for drugs, drunkenness or prostitution. Did Peggy Lee or Rosemary Clooney have to get a photo ID and a permit? The irony is that in New York you weren't required to do this to buy a gun, but if (God forbid) you tried to work as a cabaret performer without a license, the police might arrest you or cause you to lose your job.

Podell had a strict rule about a Copa girl's hairdo: It must always be worn in a French twist or with a chignon because this style would make us look like pristine ladies. Another girl whispered to me, "Under penalty of death, never let a curl fall to your shoulder."

The upswept hair style was as important as learning the dance steps. The Copa kept an account with Larry Matthews Beauty Salon that stayed open twenty-four hours, seven days a week. Every day before show time, the girls were expected to report to the beauty salon. If your hairdo came apart during a show, then in your breaks between shows you had to go back to the salon to be restyled and coiffed. Because of the 2 a.m. shows on the weekend, a girl could still get her hair done along with airline stewardesses, call girls and drag queens.

I learned that as a new nightclub performer I was required to join the union, AGVA, which stands for American Guild of Variety Artists.

My first question was, "What does that cost?"

"The initiation fee is eighty dollars," someone answered.

"Eighty dollars? Oh, no. What if I never tell anyone I'm working in a club? I'll say I forgot. I'll put on my dumb blonde face."

Another girl said, "They'll find you. The union sends over one of their reps."

"What's the representative look like?"

"He wears a rumpled trench coat. The bulge underneath is a shoulder holster for his gun. His hat is pulled down to his ears."

"What are the benefits in joining AGVA?"

"There are none. No medical insurance, no rehearsal pay."

"You mean I'm supposed to rehearse at the Copa for four weeks and not get paid?"

"Right. However, if you want to stall paying the union, tell the rep that under the Taft-Hartley Act you do not have to join a union until after thirty days."

As if it were his cue, the union rep showed up at that rehearsal and said, "Youse the new goil?"

I nodded. He announced in a monotone, "Youse suppos'ta give the union eighty dollars to become a member of AGVA."

I said with great authority, "I plead the Taft-Hartley Law."

"You'll see me in thoity days,“ he said with equal authority.

*****

Podell paid around $30,000 each season for our costumes. At the time this was considered a small fortune. He felt obligated as the Copa girls danced so close to the ringside tables. He wanted the best quality in fabrics and beads. Our couture costumes were designed and made by Madame Bertha, a tiny Hungarian lady. Each outfit was tailored specifically to our bodies. She asked me to try on a couple of her designs. After an hour, she thanked me and slipped me fifty dollars for allowing her to use me like a house-model. I was so delighted, particularly since I was rehearsing without pay.

Around this time, I found out two reasons why the required age for the Copa girls must be from eighteen to twenty-four. Once a dancer reaches her late twenties, she looks too old under the harsh overhead lighting at the Copa. There were no footlights to flatter performers. The other reason was that on the weekends, the Copa does three shows a night, the last one at two a.m. This requires a physical stamina found only in extreme youth.

Doug Coudy confided to me that the other requirements are: the girls have to have wide shoulders and beautiful legs. Not only was he the choreographer, but he handled the lighting and the sound effects for the shows. He made all the announcements and introductions for the stars. He was considered a mentor to the Copa Girls. We had a very small mirrored dressing room. He often walked in unannounced while the girls were half-naked. I was so taken aback, the girl next to me whispered, "Don't worry, he's gay."

"So what if he's happy?" To me the word 'gay' meant the same as it did to actress Cornelia Otis Skinner, who wrote the play *Our Hearts Were Young and Gay*.

Inside the dressing room was a closet where our costumes were kept. Our dresser, Marie, an alcoholic and a chain smoker, had a mattress on the floor of the closet. Between shows, she plopped on the mattress and went to sleep. We worried that she would set the mattress on fire with her burning cigarette. After her nap, we could smell whiskey wafting around us. We said nothing. She had a dreary job and, at the end of the week, we tipped her. We also kept an eye on her for fear that Podell or Coudy would find her snoozing away with a lighted butt hanging from her lips beneath Madame Bertha's thirty thousand dollar costumes with layers of tulle almost sweeping Marie's face as she softly snored.

Between shows we had a two-hour break. We strolled around Madison Avenue and sat in coffee shops. This routine became very boring. One of the girls, June, and I made a discovery. We happened to explore the Plaza Hotel. There off the lobby was the ladies room with a lounge area fitted with two huge couches. At midnight it was deserted. We both ran for a couch then stretched out on it. We wrapped our hairdo in chiffon scarves for protection, then put our heads gingerly on the armrest and closed our eyes. What heaven! We had at least an hour and a half before the two a.m. show began. The next night we were careful that the other girls didn't see us as we raced in secret for the Plaza Hotel. Our couches were there waiting for us. It was wonderful. Just to take off high heels then to rest our dancing feet upon a soft cushion. This seemed too good to last, and it didn't. After about a week, the Plaza housekeeper discovered us. She yelled, "What're you doing?"

We protested that we were just weary cabaret dancers. She could not care less.

"Get out, you bums! You can't sleep here! I'll call the cops if I see ya again!"

*****

Jimmy Durante starred at the Copa when I began there. I never saw such adoration from an audience until Michael Jackson came upon the scene many years later. Durante would enter with a few steps onto the Copa floor: "Hell-loo, everyone!" For five minutes the audience cheered, applauded and laughed. Then Durante would pull off his felt hat and sing, "Ring-a-ding-a-doo." Again there were five minutes more of cheering, applauding and yells of "We love ya, Schnoz!" As far as an audience was concerned he could do no wrong.

I began to realize my night job was swallowing up a greater part of my day, too. At four o'clock in the afternoon I went to the beauty shop to have my hair washed and set. Afterward, I sat under the dryer for an hour, then the comb-out began. It took another hour to brush and to tease my hair into an elaborate French twist. At six-thirty I would arrive at the Copa to start my makeup. After the two a.m. show was over, some of us would go out and eat breakfast. This meant that I wouldn't be in bed until almost five a.m. Usually I awakened around one or two o'clock in the afternoon. That meant only a couple hours of freedom before I had to start getting ready again, then it was off to the beauty shop.

Once in a while as I entered the club's basement, I passed the Copa's kitchen and heard shouts. Then there were sounds of smacking flesh accompanied by cries of "I didn't do it!" I wanted to look through the port windows in the kitchen door, but what if it were Podell punching out someone and saw me peeking at him? One of the waiters said in confidence that working for Hitler would be working for a nicer man than Podell. Another waiter said that Mrs. Podell's hairdresser claimed that ever since her marriage to this man, she developed a stutter from fear of him. The waiters put up with a lot as they could make more money here than any other club. For instance, one waiter said that during Sinatra's appearance at the Copa, he made enough just in tips to buy himself a new car.

The Copa girls had names like Cindy, Mindy, Jackie and Jeri, who had introduced herself as Jeri spelled with an i. She wanted to sound sophisticated. She was just eighteen, from New Jersey, and was one of two brunettes in the Copa line as the rest of us seemed to be different shades of blonde.

One of the older girls at twenty-three instructed me that Podell gave orders to the mob not to date any of the Copa girls. Last season there had been an unfortunate incident. A mobster fell for a naive eighteen-year-old. He liked sending her gifts, which she would find on her dressing table every night before the show. She kept the presents. Of course she always thanked him. When he decided to ask her out, she apologized as her boyfriend had just returned from a trip.

The mobster went berserk. He ordered one of his mob-soldiers to carve up her face with a razor. Make her scars look so ugly that no one would ever want her again! Podell and his men took him aside and explained that the girl didn't understand the Mafia's rule that by accepting gifts she belonged to him. For Christ's sake, she's a dumb teenager!

Nonetheless, the gangsters were allowed to invite us as a group to dinner between shows at Chickee's Place on the upper East Side. Chickee James was a former showgirl at the Latin Quarter. She had red hair, green eyes and a spectacular figure. However, her days as the most beautiful show girl at the Latin Quarter had ended because she was considered too old at twenty-eight. Audiences didn't want to pay to see old flesh prancing up and down the Latin Quarter's runway.

Instead of her life ending sadly as an unemployed, ex-showgirl, Chickee was now going to be the "front-man" for a legitimate business with this restaurant and bar. Since it was Frank Costello and his guys who invited us to Chickee's Place, they didn't have to obey the rules but picked us up in front of the Copa. They kept a row of shiny black cars with tinted windows double-parked there most of the evening. It was about a ten-minute drive from the Copa to Chickee's Place.

I never realized it at the time, but I was cavorting with the superstars of the underworld. The gangsters always wore black tie whenever at the club and were quite polite to us. They liked to be generous. They said things to me such as, "Sweetheart, you wanna car? We can lend youse anyting you like. Mebbe a Cadillac? Buick? Mebbe a foreign car? A nice goil like youse needs a car. A purty goil shouldn't ride the subway–too dangerous."

When I first heard their accents, these characters sounded as if they were in the musical "Guys and Dolls." I almost laughed aloud at how well they were imitating the cast in that show. Luckily, I caught myself in time. Their accents were real.

Chickee's Place was quite new so it seemed as we were her only customers at the moment. I didn't really want to eat or order a drink. If I did, I might not be able to zip up my form-fitted costume. Chickee was very cordial and very happy to have us as customers. She said to me, "The boys are calling Walter Winchell to tell him to put in his column that my place is where the Copa Girls dine."

We were there not even fifteen minutes when one of the guys signaled to Chickee to come with him. Nearby was an open door to the basement. They disappeared inside, and soon a couple of more men followed them downstairs. Then the yelling started. The first threatening sounds were all male. Chickee raised her voice in defense of something. The Copa girls and I sat at the table nonchalantly playing with our Coca Colas as though we were deaf. I faked a nervous yawn.

There came a piercing scream accompanied by slapping sounds. Smack! Smack! No getting around it. The thugs in their tuxedos were beating up Chickee. I was swallowing lumps of panic. I said to myself, "Feet get me out of here!"

"See you later," I tossed over my shoulder as I sprinted for the front door. I felt as if I were escaping a horror movie. The other girls remained seated as if frozen in fear.

Back in the security of our dressing room, I decided to put on my costume earlier than usual. Slowly the other girls returned. A pale-faced Jeri stumbled inside. She had spent the break between shows entertaining former classmates from New Jersey at a bar on Madison Avenue. She staggered to her dressing table at the end of the room. I had never seen her like this. As she sat strange gurgling sounds rose from her throat. Oh, dear goddess, don't let this become projectile vomiting.

Jeri spelled with an i threw up all over her dressing table. We jumped to our feet. "Where's a towel? A pail? Anything?" Jeri spun halfway around. She pulled herself to her feet then vomited on top of her beaded costume draped across the chair. She was drunker than a hoot owl. She advanced a step toward us. There was that warning throat gurgle again. The girls rescued their costumes and swung them high overhead as Jeri vomited down her front, ruining her French lace underwear. She still had enough left in her to upchuck across the floor before she passed out. Maria grabbed her. We propped Jeri in a chair, then rested her face on the dressing table. Someone found a hand-towel, which we draped over her head so Coudy wouldn't notice if he came inside.

We discuss what to do in the next dance number as we are now seven girls instead of eight. The buzzer sounds. That's Coudy's cue for us to take our places at the staircase. Three of us who happened to be dressed race outside where we see Coudy turning on the special lights for our number. He notices that we aren't all there. We ask him to wait a bit as there's been an emergency. He glares at us as he gives the signal to the orchestra to play the Copa Girls' theme. The three of us hop down the stairs and begin our dance alone on the floor, which has diminished a great deal in size as this is a crowded Saturday night and, if a waiter receives a big enough tip, he'll set up a new table right on the floor.

I see the other girls running toward us as they are still zipping themselves. They fly down the stairs, but they can't tell where we are in the routine. Due to their inexperience, they start the dance at the beginning, but the rest of us are already sixteen bars into the chorus. We bump into one another. There is no room on the floor any more. As I do a high kick, my toe catches a waiter's tray of champagne bottles and glasses that he balances above his head. The bottles flip over, pouring champagne upon startled customers. Waving napkins like flags, waiters scurry to mop up the damage. Some of the drenched people are not happy about it. Dinner plates swim in champagne

Right in front of me, seated at a center table, is Jayne Mansfield. Her head flops back in laughter. She is laughing and crying at the same time. She can't stop to catch her breath and collapses upon her date's shoulder. The orchestra keeps playing over the confusion. If Podell is knocking his ring on the tabletop, no one will hear it in this crowd roaring with helpless laughter.

Later in the dressing room, while we changed into our street clothes, we expected Coudy to enter any minute. Maybe to fire us. He never showed up. Jeri was in a stupor. She'll never know the hell she put us through tonight on the dance floor. This was her first experience imbibing. We learned that she ordered Brandy Alexanders because they were served in a tiny glass and tasted like melted ice cream. She drank about ten of them on an empty stomach.

Marie volunteered to call Jeri's parents since they lived in New Jersey. Certainly, they will have to drive into the city to pick her up.

The next night was Sunday, family night for the mob. Jeri showed up on time, completely recovered. Her conversation was silly and trivial as though her drunken stupor had never happened. She acted reproach less. Recovery is fast when you are eighteen. She did have a slight redness in her face, which made us wonder if she were blushing in secret shame. While we waited in the dressing room for our cue, Coudy appeared. Instead of scolding her or even firing her, he laughed. We were amazed at his reaction. He joked about being pickled, and asked if she painted the town red or something else as inane. She giggled as though there were no consequences to what she had done. She twisted a lock of her hair with her little hand, retreating into a childhood where such gestures looked cute.

Even though the crowds for Sunday were light, we still had to perform to the best of our ability because on one side of the dance floor sat Frank Costello and friends such as Charles "Lucky" Luciano. On the opposite side was Costello's enemy, Vito Genovese, his family and soldiers. (Gangster bosses like to refer to their men in the underworld as soldiers.)

Johnny Mathis was the new star. He stayed at Hotel Fourteen next door where he took an elevator that went down to the basement that opened in an alcove next to our dressing room. He remembered to bring his photograph, which he promised to autograph for me. I was thrilled. This was the first photo I have signed by a star: "To Candy, with Love, Johnny Mathis."

Another gangster called Blacky (because he has a full head of wavy black hair) liked to take a couple of us to dinner at our first break. He was so charming. It was hard to believe he was the same mobster who made the front pages of the newspapers every day because of his narcotics racketeering trial. At the same time I dated a young lawyer who happened to be a New York district attorney. His job was to prosecute members of the mob for their drug dealings.

After the first show, I joined Blacky and another girl. He loved to dine at expensive restaurants on the East Side. He always brought us back in time for the second show. When the break came between the second show and the third one, I raced from the Copa toward Madison and 61st Street where my lawyer-friend waited in a Volkswagen. We would speed away to Second Avenue, looking for a semi-dark French bistro. In the weak candlelight, we had just enough time to enjoy dessert. I was always worried that I might run into Blacky while dating a lawyer-district attorney that was determined to prosecute Blacky for drug trading.

I was turning into one of those night people who sleeps all day and only comes to life at night time. I was totally exhausted from wining, dining and dancing. Finally, I said to my hairdresser at Larry Matthews, "It takes so long to comb my hair in a French twist. Let's do a page boy like Grace Kelly."

That night at the Copacabana, my page boy stayed in perfect place as I kicked or twirled on the dance floor. All of us were seated in the dressing room preparing for the second number when the door flew open. Coudy marched inside and, like a vicious animal, attacked me with, "You-y-you f-f-f-uckin –b-b-b-itch!"

My mouth opened but nothing came out.

He spewed out a torrent of every bad imaginable word, and some I never heard before. He was stuttering or stammering so fast at the cardinal sin I had committed. Not only did I not wear my hair in a French twist but I let it fall, and the hair fell to my shoulders!

I was in total shock. I couldn't speak or move but only stared at him as he ranted on and on. Despite his stuttering, I did understand that I was fired, that this was my last week. Once he exited, a swirl of arms grabbed my hair, shoving the curls into an upswept chignon. Marie found a box of Bobbie pins, and the girls tried to secure my hair with them. A couple of girls were actually crying. My updo looked awful but then someone pinned a costume hat on top of my head. Now it did not seem as messy-looking.

What has happened to the unforgettable, fabulous nights, nights of laughter, nights of excitement, and the feeling that something important is happening to the Copa?

The end of the week came. Coudy showed up in the dressing room. He spoke to me as if there had never been a problem between us. "C-c-can you s-s-stay another week? The girl in training is having some problems with the s-s-s-steps." I nodded. How I wish I didn't need the $90 a week salary or I would have told him to go jump in the Central Park Lake.

Soon one week turned into two weeks, then three weeks. The new girl was probably a model struggling to learn to dance as well as memorizing the routines. Finally Coudy informed me that my replacement was ready.

At last it was really over, and I was sadly gone. Later that month June called me, "Our winter revue ends tonight. The mob guys want to give us a farewell present and, since you were really one of us, you have a present waiting."

"Thanks for thinking of me, but I'm never coming back to 10 East 60th Street again."

June sincerely pursued me. "But you have to have this present. It's gorgeous. It's an ankle bracelet made by Tiffany in gold. The letters hanging on it spell out C-o-p-a-c-a-b-a-n-a."

I didn't really care for an ankle bracelet reminding me of the Copa and asked her to thank the guys anyway. A couple of hours later, my phone rang. An unfamiliar male voice spoke. I said, "Who is this?"

The voice answered, "This is your new Daddy."

I didn't ask any more questions as to who was calling or how he got my phone number. From his conversation I realized that I had touched the hearts of the mob who were genuinely concerned that I had lost my job at the Copa. He made an offer: "How'd ya like to go to Florida? Run a place–a club for us. Youse could be our front there like Chickee's Place."

Am I speaking to one of Genovese's guys? One of Frank Costello's? Or maybe this is Frank Costello! I knew the job offer meant more money than I could ever make kicking up my heels at the Copa. "Well, that's so kind of you. But I don't want to leave New York. I am hoping to study acting with Lee Strasberg. My dream is to become an actress." I thanked "my new Daddy" profusely then thanked him again.

My district attorney boyfriend warned me that if I accepted one of their favors or one job, I would belong to the Mafia forever. I could never leave them. In fact he knew one of their girlfriends who, in order to get away, starved herself until she became so thin and ugly that her lustrous auburn hair fell out. No one wanted her any more. She was free at last but what a price she paid.

The Copacabana's golden years were from the 1940s into the 1960s. The decade of the 1970s brought in discos, and the era of the nightclubs was fading fast. Jules Podell made an economic decision to eliminate the famous Copa Girls. He cut his house band in half. The club suffered as he could not compete with the salaries of entertainers who chose to play Las Vegas casinos. The public could now see performers on television's variety shows without getting dressed up and dining in expensive clubs. Podell had to forget about the posh days when he had a dress code and wouldn't allow men inside if they weren't in a suit and tie.

In 1972 Podell closed the club for the first time during the summer months. He refused to retire as the Copa was his life. Nonetheless, as business at the Copa began to die, so did Podell. He was the heart of the Copa. It is almost fitting that a fatal heart attack killed him one day in 1973. His relatives believed that he simply lost the will to live.

Today's generation will never know the excitement or the compelling romance of a place like the Copacabana. There are no more stars like Frank Sinatra, Sammy Davis, Jr., Peggy Lee, Dean Martin, Nat

King Cole, Rosemary Clooney, and Bobby Darin, who mesmerized Copa audiences with their musical talents.

I never saw Podell smile. I heard that on rare occasions he did smile, especially when he had his picture taken in front of the Copa handing out toys to orphans during the Christmas holiday season. He smiled again when he posed for newspapers at Thanksgiving time giving away turkeys to Mother Bernadette and the sisters for a convent in the neighborhood.

One of the best lines uttered at the Copa was said by comedian Joey Bishop. He was the headliner then and, in the middle of his act, Marilyn Monroe came in and distracted everyone as she was getting seated. Bishop waited a couple of minutes, then said, “Marilyn, I told you to wait in the truck!”

In 1976 new owners of the Copacabana finally reopened the club as a disco and cabaret, but it now was competing with Studio 54 and other disco clubs. New York was a different place than in Podell’s era. There was a new venture to do weekly entertainment of Latin salsa-style music and dance at the Copa. It didn’t catch on with New Yorkers even though the club was doing brisk business as a catering hall for weddings and banquets.

A couple of years later songwriter and performer Barry Manilow was walking along East 60th Street and saw workmen tearing down the front of the old Copacabana. He went inside and stood in the middle of the dust, broken beams and missing walls with palm trees. In the ‘60s the Copa was where he spent his prom night. This was a nightclub that was the epitome of sophistication and fun for teenagers during prom season. Some of the workmen recognized him and folded up the Copacabana awning then gave it to him. What a keepsake! And what an inspiration for a hit song—

"Her name was Lola, she was a show girl...
At the Copa music and passion were always
the fashion. At the Copa they fell in love..."

Copacabana Music by Barry Manilow
Lyrics by Bruce Sussman & Jack Feldman

Candace backstage at the
Copacabana Nightclub in New York.

The "World Famous Copa Girls" with the ten-year-old
niece of comedians Phil Ford and Mimi Hines.

Chapter Two

New York – Springtime

The idea of expressing myself in a letter to Lee Strasberg, the head of the Actors Studio filled me with terror. To think that my development as an actress and, possibly my future success as one, could hinge on a single piece of paper requesting an interview, was too forbidding. I didn't trust myself to undertake this task alone, so I called upon the only professional writer I knew to help me–Mel Brooks.

The previous summer, my roommate, Betty, had met him at a party on Fire Island. For a few days, they had hung out on the beach like a couple of drinking buddies. Newly divorced, he would often drop by to visit us in our two-room Greenwich Village apartment. He said he was a staff writer for The Sid Caesar Hour, along with three other unknowns, Woody Allen, Carl Reiner and Neil Simon. A couple of times when I couldn't come up with the $35 a month rent, he hired me as an extra on The Sid Caesar Hour. Whenever I was discouraged after a day of making the rounds of talent and casting agents, Mel tried to cheer me up. He would leap upon the coffee table in my Village apartment and imitate Frank Sinatra singing, "The Star Spangled Banner." He had done the same routine on The Jack Paar Show but had said to us that Frank's boys had called him after the televised broadcast with the warning, "Frank doesn't mind you imitating him, just don't sing the national anthem."

After we forced Mel to go home, Betty and I would have a splitting headache from laughing at his routines for Caesar and the rest of the cast as he played every part. Mel made extra money as a play-doctor, rewriting the dialogue to help spiff up a new Broadway play that got bad reviews out of town. We worried about his future in show business if the TV show were to be canceled. He had an ex-wife and three kids somewhere. Maybe he'd end up playing drums again on the Borscht Circuit in the Catskills.

Early one evening, Mel came over. He said he would be delighted to help me write a letter that would attract Lee Strasberg's attention. Since Betty knew how to type, she plunked her portable typewriter on the coffee table and waited for Mel's muse to kick in. He dictated a two-page letter for me. I vaguely recalled that it began: "Dear Mr. Strasberg, ever since I was a six-year-old little girl, I couldn't wait to grow up to sing–to dance–to become a great actress." Mel and I ended with this emotional plea: "Please don't fold this letter into a paper airplane and sail it out your window!"

That same week, a public relations firm informed me that the North Carolina Azalea Festival had chosen me to be their Greenfield Gardens Princess, a member of the traditional royal court. In one of those fluky things that can happen to an actress, I found myself traveling by train to Wilmington with the Queen of the 1960 festival, Hollywood film star Linda Christian. Linda and I spent a total of six days together, coming and going throughout the South. She was a native of Mexico and claimed to be fluent in six languages. She also said she had stolen her former husband, Tyrone Power, away from Lana Turner. Her reputation as the hottest tamale to leave Mexico for Hollywood far exceeded her abilities as an actress.

Linda also claimed that she had been discovered by Errol Flynn while she was enrolled in medical school. Nothing she said to me during our trip ever gave evidence that she had attended any institution of higher learning.

I was curious to know if it were true that after her ex Tyrone Power died, she had the nerve to attend a ball dressed as the Merry Widow. What did she do in the bedroom that caused the hearts of so many men to flip flop? That made men willing to pay her bills? She held up her wrist to show off a huge gold bracelet that dangled so many charms that she complained of the weight. She returned it to the jewelry store for a refund, she said, but the man who gave her the bracelet merely bought it again. She had no choice but to wear the damn thing. She was incredibly beautiful and, I thought, very well-preserved for a thirty-five-year old.

Her lifestyle had been immortalized in Errol Flynn's book "My Wicked, Wicked Ways," but she preferred to talk about her two daughters as if she were just a simple Hausfrau.

At Wilmington, we were joined by the rest of the pageant celebrities. The festival king was actor Paul Henreid, on whom I'd had a crush since I was in the fourth grade.

I thought that my reign as a princess meant that I was to be squired around to a few ritzy parties, to be entertained in the fashion befitting royalty. I discovered that I was working my buns off. Queen Linda and I and the current Miss America raced from one festivity to another. We attended the Azalea Open Golf Tournament, a dedication ceremony for the new Azalea Station branch of the U.S. Post Office, a harness race, a variety show at the American Legion Stadium. We climbed aboard the naval vessels at the state docks, attended an outdoor art exhibit at Cottage Lane, went to the airport to watch troops of the 82nd Airborne Division do mass parachute drops, and even sailed on the U. S. Coast Guard Cutter "Mendota."

As part of the Queen Azalea XIII court, we rode for hours in a parade of decorated floats. There were two balls still ahead, where I would be required to dance with the men from the Azalea committee. For my reign as a princess, I received no money, but was given two Ship'N'Shore blouses and a nylon nightgown from JCPenney.

At the coronation pageant, I had a chance to speak with the Master of Ceremonies, Merv Griffin. He said he was a well-known singer and movie actor, but frankly, I was not impressed. I had never heard of him. It was the star of "Casablanca" that had my attention. Later I found myself seated next to Paul Henreid, the king of the festival at the coronation banquet. I couldn't resist introducing myself to this handsome leading man with an accent that blended Austria and Italy.

I whispered to him, "Mr. Henreid? In one of my favorite movies, *Now Voyager*, you did something so romantic."

"Oh, what was that?" he smiled at me.

"When you offered Bette Davis a cigarette, you lit two at the same time."

"You mean like this?" He took two cigarettes from a package in his pocket, placed them together between his lips, then lit them both simultaneously. As seductively as he had with Bette, he gave me one.

Since I'm a non-smoker, I just held it, trying to appear sophisticated. "Mr. Henreid, I hope you don't think I'm too forward."

"I adore forward women."

"Would you mind giving me the same cue you gave Bette at the end of the picture?"

He laughed, then leaning closer, said his line very seriously: "And will you be happy, Charlotte?" He puffed on his cigarette.

I felt the cigarette smoke curling up past my eyes, irritating them. I hoped that it would make them glisten with tears just like Bette's, as I answered with one of the most famous exit lines in movie history. "Oh, Jerry, don't let's ask for the moon. We have the stars."

If there were ever a Kodak moment for me, this was it.

*****

I related all this to Mel Brooks on my return to New York. We spent one spring evening strolling along Sixth Avenue on our way to O'Henry's for dinner. I was still exhausted from my duties as an Azalea princess. I had assumed that by now, some word would have come from Lee Strasberg. "Oh, Mel, I'm so depressed. I expected to find a letter of acceptance for his classes after my trip to North Carolina."

Mel said cheerfully, "It's only been about two weeks. Don't give up yet."

After dinner, we wandered back to my apartment. My complaints continued. Why hadn't I heard from my agent? How would I ever find work again as an actress?

When we entered, Betty was fast asleep on the studio couch with the lights off. If Mel and I were to continue talking, we would have to adjourn to the other room, which was my bedroom. Cautiously, we tiptoed around her and into my tiny room, so typical of a Village apartment. We gently shut the door behind us.

This room looked crowded with a roll-away bed, two small cardboard dressers and one little gingham-covered chair. Next to the bed was the ironing board with an iron perched on it.

"We can talk while I iron. Betty can't hear us."

He sat in the chair.

Since I had been making the rounds all day, I was still dressed in my best clothes, which I wore only for interviews. "Mel, do you mind if I change into something more comfortable?" This line may have been said ad nauseam in B-movies, but unlike the gangster molls in those pictures, I actually meant it.

Mel nodded as I stepped into the walk-in closet, the most luxurious feature of the apartment. Out of sight, I wiggled out of my Playtex girdle. I changed into my Lanz of Salzburg, cotton-quilted robe tailored in a blue Tyrolean print. Its button front ran from its eyelet lace collar to the hemline below the knees. The robe hung in a shape like a penguin and with about as much sex appeal. I'm not sure what Mel expected when I came out of the closet, but he was still sitting patiently, waiting for me. I turned the iron on and faced the ironing board, where I proceeded with this unglamourous chore, while bemoaning my disappointments. "Oh dear goddess, please let Strasberg answer me soon. And please, dear goddess, I need a job to pay for the classes if I'm accepted."

After jabbering for a while, I realized that Mel was not audibly reacting. Since silence was not one of his virtues, I glanced over my shoulder toward where he had been in the chair. To my surprise, we almost bumped noses. He was directly behind me, as close as if we were subway riders squashed together. But my surprise changed to shock. He was standing in a pool of his pants, which encircled his ankles. He had managed to remove his blue shirt and tie, which left him wearing an undershirt and boxer shorts.

"Mel! What on earth do you think you're doing?" Since I had the iron in one hand, I debated whether I should press his face.

Hesitating was my big mistake. I had no idea that a woman in a quilted bathrobe that revealed as much as a spacesuit, poised at an ironing board, could be such a turn-on to a man. Mel flung himself at me with the passion of an eighteen-year-old farm boy on Saturday night after a week of harvesting the wheat fields.

We both toppled over the ironing board, just escaping the hot iron, which landed somewhere on the floor. I screamed for Betty's help, but it was to no avail. I had always assumed that a woman's fierce struggle meant no, not yes. But Mel did not get the message. I scrambled to my feet, but found that the only way to escape his hands was to crawl up on my bed, where I stood, my legs growing weaker and curling under me like rubber-bands. Mel jumped on the bed, pushing me against the wall. My roll-away bed was not built for such activity and did what it was designed to do. It rolled away from the wall, sending Mel and me to the floor. I struggled to reach the door while crying for Betty. The battle grew fiercer in a sea of flinging arms and legs. I pushed, shoved, slapped, hit, pinched and twisted, which seemed only to add fuel to his passions. Arms and legs were locking, unlocking. The armchair flipped over, soon to be joined by the dressers, which opened and fell forward, spilling my clothes across the floor.

Despite the frenzy, Betty never awakened. She claimed to sleep so soundly, that if she ever took half a sleeping pill, you could amputate her leg, and she would never feel it. Tonight was proof that she had not been exaggerating.

Mel never uttered a word. Like a prizefighter in the ring, he saved his breath support to win. I felt my muscles giving out, strength ebbing, but he showed no signs of giving up. I even burst into tears, but it had no effect. Pretending to regurgitate, I emitted the worst retching sounds I could muster.

Mel froze, then quickly backed off. The idea of vomit landing on him squelched his ardor. I staggered out of the bedroom, stunned that my Lanz bathrobe had remained intact, not one ripped button. Mel followed me, but he had completely dressed as speedily as a stripper. He went to the front door, which was near Betty's sleeping head on the pillow. I stayed safely at her feet and yelled over her prostrate form, "Melvin! Are you crazy? How could you treat me like this? I thought you were my friend! Why did you try, what you did?"

His hand was twisting the doorknob as he replied, "Because fifty percent of the time, it works."

> "For an actress to be a success, she must have the face of Venus, the brains of Minerva, the grace of Terpsichore, the memory of Macaulay, the figure of Juno, and the hide of a rhinoceros."
>
> –Ethel Barrymore

Chapter Three

Miraculously, the letter Mel Brooks composed did get Lee Strasberg's attention. After almost a year's wait, his secretary finally called with my appointment at Mr. Strasberg's apartment on Central Park West. I was quite nervous during my interview with him, which lasted forty-five minutes. I couldn't tell whether he was staring or glaring at me. Socially, he was a basket case. When he asked at what age I had decided I wanted to be an actress, I answered nervously, "Six."

Strasberg looked piqued and said in his nasal monotone, "Nonsense. How could a child of six in South Dakota know anything about the theater?"

I felt as if I were running out of breath, so my explanation rose an octave as I described going to hometown movies since I was two years old. I learned everything from the double-features on Sunday afternoons. I wore my hair like Betty Grable, tottered on platform heels like Carmen Miranda, tried to tap dance like Ginger Rogers. Mickey and Judy showed me how to stage plays in the family garage. I learned how to kiss and to slap a guy from Rita Hayworth in "The Loves of Carmen."

At the age of twelve, I put together an act pantomiming Betty Hutton records. For this, I was paid five dollars each time I performed for the Elks, Eastern Star and The American Farmers Association. I finally reached the pinnacle of my amateur career with a performance before the governor of South Dakota at a Republican banquet. The Republicans paid me ten dollars, which made me feel like a professional performer.

Somehow, even though I was rambling, Strasberg interrupted to invite me to join his classes.

*****

On my beginning day as a new member of Lee Strasberg's private class for actors, I slipped into the first vacant seat of a large rehearsal studio above the Loew's Capitol Theater at 50th and Broadway. The butterflies in my stomach were having a nervous breakdown. Then I had a knot in my stomach, so, bending forward, I grabbed onto the back of the chair in front of me for support. The actress sitting in that seat leaned back, pinning my hand in place. My fingertips were entwined in the cable stitching of her Irish knit sweater. By the time I had the courage to untangle my fingers and focus, I realized that she was none other than Marilyn Monroe. The love goddess of the world was pinching my fingers!

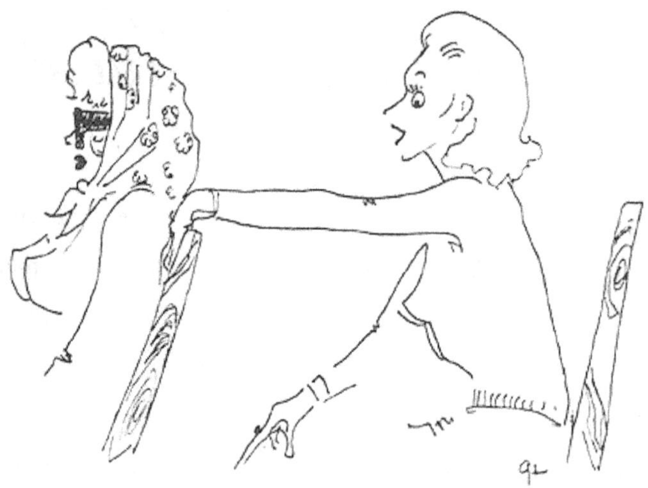

This was one of those times in life when you wanted all your high school buddies to see you, the friends who made fun of you for not marrying the small town sweetheart, for going off to pursue a foolhardy career on the wicked stage. Marilyn had tied a beige scarf around her hair and wore the best disguise of all–no makeup. Not even a smidgen of lipstick. What courage not only as an actress but as a woman! She had on plaid slacks, just like a Scottish lass. To anyone who asked, she introduced herself as, "Marilyn from class." She was at the height of her fame from her movie roles in "The Seven Year Itch" and "Bus Stop" having made millions for the studios.

I had recently finished a summer stock run in which I had played the same roles in "The Seven Year Itch" and "Bus Stop." I had made $150 a week and, after ten weeks of bookings, felt as if I had earned a million, too. This income could last me through four to five months of unemployment in the fall. These were the days when splitting the rent with my roommate meant my half came to $35 a month.

With Marilyn conjoined to my hand, I glanced around the studio. Strasberg sat in the only armchair in the middle of the first row facing the stage. In the row behind me were Dennis Hopper, Joan Hackett, Madeline Sherwood, Nina Foch, Brooke Hayward and Diana Hyland. To my right was the Hollywood contingent: Gloria Grahame, Shepperd Strudwick, Richard Beymer and Tommy Sands. Since classes were held twice a week in the mornings, there were many other familiar faces, Broadway actors currently starring on Broadway.

I had stage fright, and I wasn't even on stage yet. For more than a year, I had placed many calls to this guru without a response. Finally, his secretary had suggested that, in order to be granted a personal interview, I must continue to write Mr. Strasberg letters, as proof of my interest in studying with him. Voila! It had paid off.

Here I was, feeling as if I were just one of the Actors Studio gang, like Marilyn, Nina, Madeline and the rest. Strasberg announced that the new people should meet after class and find a partner for a scene. There were only five of us that waited after class. One of them was Richard Forest. I had barely noticed him in class since he huddled in a trench coat and wore sunglasses to hide his eyes for fear his hangover would be noticed. Now he removed the glasses, and I gazed into incredible green eyes, fringed by black eyelashes that would have flattered Elizabeth Taylor. In fact, like her, he was born in London. Richard liked to boast his father was British and his mother an American–the same combination as Winston Churchill's parents. I was also taken by the naturally curly hair, the cleft in his chin and the Richard Burton voice.

For the next three weeks, we spent every spare moment together, when we weren't working at our survival jobs. Richard was making four dollars an hour at a marketing firm, doing survey research. I had been employed for the spring season as a house-model for a designer in the garment center. As a starving actress, I had to keep starving in order to stay thin enough to model. If my weight went over 105 pounds, I couldn't fit in the clothes. I existed on a menu that no self-respecting prison would serve cottage cheese and water. I complained to Richard how hungry I always was. Everything reminded me of food. My last job was particularly painful. I was the model for 'Murray Hamburger Wedding Gowns.' Every time I called out the boss's name, "Mr. Hamburger," I had hunger pains all over again. I would have been tempted to take a bite out of him, if he weren't so elderly and wizened. He had about as much appeal as beef jerky.

Mr. Hamburger's sample gowns were made with twenty-two-inch waists. This meant that I had to be corseted like Scarlett O'Hara. I could no longer indulge myself in a lunch of cottage cheese and water. Even this tiny amount caused my waist to expand that extra fraction of an inch that made the seamstress mutter obscenities as she struggled to zip me.

By four o'clock in the afternoon, I had a typical Excedrin headache. I was always famished. In floor-length gown and veil, I would pose and twirl in the showroom before the department store buyers, who often complimented me on my white opalescent skin, my pale complexion that rivaled Snow White's in the Disney cartoon. Actually, it was because I was being drained of blood supply by the Merry Widow corset, which was constricting me.

In between quick changes, the seamstress rouged my cheeks, while giving advice in her chain-smoker sultry voice, "Don't you dare faint! Mr. Hamburger will fire you. There are too many models around with naturally small waists."

I learned one of life's hard lessons from her: No matter who you are, there's always someone younger, prettier and skinnier to take your place.

Mr. Hamburger would stick his head between the curtains that separated the dressing room from the small factory where all his slaves were huddled over humming machines, to bark orders: "Make her wear darker lipstick. She looks like a corpse with gray lips."

My salary was $75 a week, far more than that of a typist who was paid one dollar and fifty cents an hour. But this was enough salary to keep me in low-fat cottage cheese and pay the rent.

Richard was sympathetic to the demands of my survival job. He promised me that soon times would change, and we would look back at this memory with a good laugh. We strolled through Schubert Alley, past the Broadway marquees along 44th and 45th Streets. Gore Vidal's play "The Best Man" was there, along with "The Miracle Worker." Up the street was Ethel Merman in the box office hit "Gypsy."

"West Side Story" was in its third successful year. This musical had been a shock. For the first time the boy did not get the girl, and neither one of them was glamorous. How bold of Leonard Bernstein and Jerome Robbins to think that juvenile crime on the scabrous sidewalks of New York could be a smash hit.

For fifteen cents apiece, Richard and I would ride the Staten Island Ferry all night. One could buy Nathan's Hot Dog from a vendor then. On the second level of the ferry, we liked to sit on a bench in the open air, people-watching or studying the sea gulls in flight. We discussed our approaches to acting. I was a graduate of the American Theater Wing, and Richard had studied at the Royal Academy of Dramatic Arts in London. We bemoaned the fact that there were no new American playwrights. Talented writers seemed to have been seduced by Hollywood. "Have you noticed," Richard asked, "how shabby the Off-Broadway season has been? There's nothing but small plays about small people!"

"Oh, Richard, what are we going to do if there are no new playwrights? Where are the new great actors to inspire us? There's a decline in the art of acting; the decline of the actor!"

"God dammit, you're bright. I wish you could have seen my production of 'Toys In the Attic' that I not only acted in, but directed, at the Charles Playhouse in Boston. My actors were playing down to the audience because they thought they were performing in the modern style. These actors wanted to be naturalistic. They said their lines with a mumbling, a dramatic crooning. God forbid they should project loud enough to be heard—reality would fall out of their fuckin' mouths. How can an actor strive for truth if no one can hear the fucker!"

The ferry was carrying us past the Statue of Liberty with all the harbor lights of the city glimmering behind it in the distance. At this hour, the ferry was almost empty of commuters, the moon was spectacular, and the air was fresh and salty. This was a night made for enchantment, the type of romantic evening about the Big Apple that songwriters like Betty Comden and Adolph Green immortalized.

Picking up Richard's train of thought, I added, sounding like a recent grad of a drama school, "Truth in acting depends completely on style. Don't you agree? What is true in Shakespeare turns out to be a lie in any modern American drama. We, as artists, must interpret life through our imagination rather than slavishly copy it. Promise me, Richard, that we will never lose our true personalities as actors, that we will never become one of those cookie-cutter look-alike actors." I said it very seriously. We would save the theater together.

Then he answered like a RADA student: "As God is my witness, Candace, we will never let greed, selfishness for commercial reasons, destroy us as artists. We will fight for the truth, or we will live to witness the extinction of the theater as an art form."

Richard joined me in a pact to revitalize the American theater—now that was togetherness. I soon learned that Richard was never at a loss for words about anyone or anything. He had an opinion on every major actor who was in a prominent Broadway show. If I had thrown out the word, "Hello," he could have done a half-hour analysis on the meaning of it. After circling until the wee hours of the morning, Richard ran out of steam and was quiet for about one minute. It was then the romantic setting began to affect him, too. This was the spring when famous hearts were turning to marriage. Princess Margaret Rose married Anthony Armstrong Jones in Westminister Abbey. Sammy Davis, Jr. married actress May Britt in London, and producer Leland Hayward married Pamela Churchill, the former wife of Winston Churchill's son Randolph, in Las Vegas.

There was love light in Richard's eyes when he turned to me, and I thought he was about to tell me that his lifelong passion was to play Hamlet, but instead he said, "Marry me? I promise to make you very happy."

I was flabbergasted. Not because he was so young at twenty-six, or that he was an out-of-work actor, or that he didn't have enough cash to open a checking account, but because most ambitious young actors had to be free agents. They couldn't afford the domestic accouterments of the usual banker, doctor or baker, who knew where their futures would be in twenty years.

As for myself, I didn't want to end up in a marriage trap like a Doris Day movie. Her character always seemed to give up a career. Her reward was moving to the suburbs and raising babies. I didn't believe that women should forfeit their careers in order to stand behind their husbands.

So I answered Richard, in the only way I could. "Of course, I'll marry you." Deep in my heart, I didn't believe that a marriage would ever happen. I was afraid that if I said no, Richard would be so hurt that he wouldn't want to see me anymore. I might damage that remarkable sensitivity of his that made him an actor.

Richard was thrilled. We left the ferry and immediately went to tell his roommate, another actor, the good news. Richard lived on Tenth Avenue at 55th Street in Hell's Kitchen. There above the "Supreme Glass Shop," we climbed a six-flight walk-up to a railroad flat. Richard's hovel was a floor-through, had five non-working fireplaces, 19th Century gas spigots in the ceilings, no means of heat, and no fire escape. He had sublet this place from other actors who were touring with the Barter Theater in Virginia. The interior decor looked like something out of an "early reign of terror." Bearskin rugs bought at the Salvation Army covered second-hand chairs for plushness. The coffee table was made from a door found on Tenth Avenue atop a garbage can. Painted cardboard egg crates served as lampshades. The burgundy wall-to-wall carpeting had been taken from the lobby of a movie theater just before the building was razed. I thought it all very imaginative.

Richard woke his roommate who upon hearing the announcement, asked, "You're not going to make me move out, are you?" When Richard reassured him that he could keep the place, the roommate congratulated us on our mutual stupidity.

Next we raced to my Village apartment, which was on the third floor. Since Betty, my roommate, always slept in the living room, we woke her immediately. When the door was wide enough to enter, it slammed into the foot of her studio couch. Her first reaction at our news was "Huh?" followed by a disgruntled, "Where are my cigarettes?" Later, Mel Brooks called to say, "You are a big, dumb, blonde pussycat. Marry an actor? It won't last. Actors aren't grown-up people."

Richard and I now sat together in Strasberg's class. Tuesday's classes were for sense memory exercises. Four chairs were placed side by side on the stage facing Strasberg and the class. He called the names of the four new people, which included Richard and me. Sitting in the chairs, we tried to relax completely before we attempted the first exercise: to drink a glass of orange juice.

Strasberg didn't care if you were a star on Broadway or in the movies or if you were Sir Laurence Olivier, the greatest English-speaking actor in history. Everyone had to learn how to drink orange juice. Strasberg developed a series of sense memory exercises based upon his interpretation of Stanislavsky's method for actors. It would take too long to explain to the lay person, but here it is in a nutshell: never pantomime, imitate or indicate but create as if for the first time. Feel the weight of the glass as being half empty or full; is this glass heavy in your hand; is the aroma of the juice sweet or spoiled; is the glass wet to the touch, etc., etc., etc., as the King of Siam once said. This exercise lasts about forty-five minutes.

When Strasberg said stop, the four of us quickly sat up straight as he critiqued us one by one. He told me that I was ready to do the next exercise–sunshine. Then Strasberg told Richard that the orange juice exercise needed more practice. Richard would have to repeat the exercise at the next class.

Later in class, Richard whispered to me his disappointment. "I flunked orange juice in front of forty-two actors!"

"Don't feel bad. I'm sure some Broadway actors in class didn't get orange juice right the first time either."

Next week I watched in class as Richard worked on the orange juice exercise. Strasberg repeated that Richard was still indicating. He would have to redo the exercise for the third time.

Next it was my turn on stage, and I did my sunshine exercise. I'm not sure what Strasberg meant but I threw myself into sunshine with abandon. I felt heat on one side of my body and shivering with goose bumps on the other side. Strasberg was pleased and said that I was ready for the next exercise–pain. Unlike Richard, I felt as if I'm advancing too fast since I still don't understand what to do but am responding instinctively.

Marilyn Monroe asked if she could try the singing exercise. Of course Strasberg said yes; he was in love with her just as much as the movie audiences are. I admired her courage to stand alone and to be this vulnerable in front of many Broadway actors. I hated the singing exercise because one faced Strasberg and the other students while half singing or wailing on each note; only to change when you ran out of breath. It sounded as if an actor were in severe pain, not singing. But this technique allowed the emotion buried inside to come forth in laughter or tears. Marilyn let out a sound, quite soft, but stopped herself. She tried again but stopped. Strasberg said with tenderness, "Marilyn, don't be a critic. There are forty-two people behind me who are your critics." Marilyn sang again then said, "I can't stop my hands from shaking."

Strasberg pronounced, "That's your sensitivity as an artist, Marilyn. Our job here is to channel that sensitivity so that it comes out in the work."

I wondered how well Marilyn would do with orange juice.

A couple of months later, Richard and I find ourselves together on Strasberg's stage. I'm aware that I have graduated to a harder exercise for pain. Richard has rehearsed for so long doing orange juice, I'm sure he'll be fine this time. I work on pain in my side. I cry out! Tears come to my eyes. I fall to my knees, sobbing in pain. Strasberg leans toward me, murmuring, "Let it go. Relax, keep relaxing."

I roll onto my side. I double up and scream. I can feel the silence in the studio. The other actors aren't sure if I have lost control or am in real pain. If that happened, Strasberg would step onto the stage, then slap me back to reality.

Strasberg orders us to stop the exercises. I jump to my feet then sit in my chair. Strasberg praises my exercise. "You show great improvement. Your concentration is excellent. You're ready to do a private moment. Book the time with the class secretary."

It was Richard's turn. Strasberg saw no improvement in Richard's attempt at orange juice. Richard felt compelled to defend himself: "She distracted me." He indicated me. "I kept hearing her moans and–" Richard just committed the cardinal sin: blaming another actor for his poor performance. If he had waved a red flag in front of a bull, he could not have done more damage to himself in front of the class. Strasberg's voice rose with fury. He ripped Richard apart. He tore whatever was left of Richard's ego.

By the time class was over, Richard said, "I couldn't help it. Marilyn Monroe is sitting directly in front of me next to Strasberg. Then you're on the floor crying in pain or something. How in hell was I supposed to concentrate? Fuck it! I'm not going to Tuesday exercise classes any more. I'll stick to scene study on Thursdays."

We went to the office of Actors Equity Association. There were the casting notices for summer stock. Some companies had open calls or cattle calls, where we would stand in line, waiting for an interview and hoping the producers liked us well enough to ask for our pictures and résumés. If I didn't find summer stock work, I'd end up working for Mr. Hamburger again, forcing myself into his wedding dresses for the rest of the summer.

I did have a theatrical agent. He left a message with my phone service about an audition for a new play. "Richard, maybe there might be a part for you?"

"Naw, I've been offered to do stock in Maine for the summer."

He might as well have said the Arctic. Summer stock in Maine was too far away for an industry showcase. We were going to face our first separation. I had heart pangs. Richard was so handsome, so great-looking. At twenty-one, I was drawn to actors because there's something about their energy, their creativeness that always makes an actor so appealing.

Finally we said our goodbyes for the summer. I went on to my audition for a new play, "Turn On the Night," which was held in the director's apartment. I auditioned for a small group of producers, then was told to come back tomorrow. When my agent heard that, he got excited. He's a boutique agent, which means that his office is mostly in his hat, and his phone is one of the public phone booths on a street corner. I explained that the play was a turn-of-the-century comedy with some drama here and there involving a rich widow who makes two Parisian men vie for her love. I complained to the agent, "I don't find the play that compelling." Nonetheless I went back and auditioned a couple of more times.

Then the phone call came that every actors wants to get. "Candace, you got the part!"

"Thank you, dear goddess. Where is the play being done? What stock company?"

My agent said, "You just got your first Broadway play!"

"I did what?"

"And you're the leading lady."

"Are you sure of that? Broadway?"

"Do you understand what it means to be a leading lady in a new play by Jerome Lawrence and Robert Lee?"

I couldn't think fast enough. "Who are they now?"

"Don't you remember 'Inherit the Wind?' Or 'Auntie Mame?' "

The rehearsals were in Philadelphia, in the John B. Kelly Playhouse in the park. This was the Playhouse's first world premiere in ten years of a new play prior to Broadway. I saw my leading man for the first time, Joseph Wiseman. I was taken aback as he must be thirty years older than I. Plus he's scary-looking in that Jack Palance way. A director once said to me that when Palance asked for an audition, he got the appointment.

Audiences know Wiseman as Marlon Brando's enemy in "Viva Zapata" and as the title character in the James Bond movie "Dr. No." My character was supposed to look at Wiseman with desire and longing. But off-stage Wiseman never spoke or acknowledged me. In the play we're supposed to be madly in love. This took a great deal of acting on my part, much more than drinking orange juice for Strasberg.

Ann Roth was our costume designer. (A few years later she won an Academy Award for her designs.) She took me for a fitting. A clerk brought forth a bolt of fabric for her. She grabbed the bolt and flung it in the clerk's face with the warning, "Don't show me this cheap piece of crap again!" Ann turned to me, "What's your waist measurement?"

"Twenty-four inches."

Ann yelled to the sewing team, "Make sure the dresses are for waist twenty-two inches!"

Trying to be diplomatic, I said, "Miss Roth, if my diaphragm is cinched in two more inches, I won't have the room for breath support—"

But she wasn't listening and stepped away from me. Shades of Murray Hamburger wedding dresses, I am back to going without lunch and dining on low-fat cottage cheese and water for meals.

Wiseman and I passed backstage after rehearsal like two ships in the night. On stage he had a melodious way of speaking, which had sounded as if he's almost singing his lines. He crooned like this as "Dr. No," the James Bond movie, where he sounded like a freaky villain. The audience ate it up. It was hard to act as his lover. I can assure you it was a lot easier for Brando to act with him in that Mexican movie. Wiseman's indicating emotion rather than being organic was a style of exterior acting that Strasberg despised. Wiseman said his lines with such confidence that the audience accepted his bizarre speech and behavior on stage.

On opening night the theater was filled with many important New York producers who were interested in the new Lawrence and Lee play. I tried not to remind myself, but this was the biggest break of my career so far. I was like a race horse gearing up for the biggest Kentucky Derby race of her life.

The house lights went down. The play began, and I waited for my cue in the wings of the theater. Just as I was about to make my grand entrance, Jerry Lawrence grabbed my arm and whispered a couple of line changes in my ear. I listened, then quickly went on stage raising my gloved hand for my first speech. Thinking of the line changes, I drew a blank.

In my opening night jitters, not only did I forget the playwright's changes, but it made me forget my first speech in the play. This scene has been played out in so many actors' worst nightmares, and here it was happening for real in my first Broadway role. I, who could memorize a play in three days and retain not only my lines but also the other actors. I stared at Wiseman's face. His burning brown eyes were far more terrifying than when he tortured his victims as Dr. No. For the first time he did what he never did in rehearsals. He really looked at me, dropping his planned reaction. The most real, honest moment he had since we were together was now. He was stuck, too, as he couldn't say his lines until I gave him his cue.

I stood in place breathing hard as I could against my twenty-two-inch corset, trying to remember who I was, where I was, what play was I in? What theater is this? I died a thousand deaths on that stage. This loss of memory never happened before and has never happened since and, because this was theater-in-the-round, there was no stage manager who could prompt an actor. You are working without a net. Besides, what actress would ever forget her first lines in a play on opening night?

I sighed, cleared my throat, said, "Aha, hmm, my, my" for what seemed like eternity while the other actors on stage were trying not to panic. I finally mumbled something and another actor picked up the cue. After the play ended, I hid in my dressing room. There was a knock on the door. My agent stood with his hat (his office) in hand. He had not told me he was coming for opening night. He had a look of mortification on his face. It was no use trying to explain that the playwright threw me with the new line changes. Our relationship was over. We would never speak again.

The next morning Jerry Lawrence, the playwright, approached me and said with a guilty smile, "I hope I didn't throw you with the new lines." I wanted to slowly strangle him to death. If I had a dagger I would have shoved it into his heart and claimed temporary insanity as Lady Macbeth. To this day my fury is still boiling at the memory.

Many years later I was a guest in Jerry's Malibu home. He took me downstairs to admire the drawings done by the famous *New York Times* cartoonist who drew every one of the plays by him and Robert Lee. "Candace, wait until you see your drawing with Joseph Wiseman. It's wonderful." There on the walls were fabulous drawings of Lucille Ball, Angela Lansbury, Fredric March and then came mine in 'Turn On the Night.' This sketch depicted my entire backside while on a stool facing upstage at Joseph Wiseman. Jerry kept repeating, "Isn't it great of you two?" Well, I studied the sketch and, unless I was warned, I don't know if I could have recognized the back of my head. He went on to say that after our play closed out of town, there were many rewrites. Nonetheless, he and his partner renamed the play and tried it out on a college campus somewhere in Minnesota. It bombed there, too, so the playwrights shelved it forever.

'Turn On Night' Opens in Park

By JAMES O'BRIEN

For the first time in its 10-year history, the John B. Kelly Playhouse in the Park is presenting the world premiere of a play prior to its production on Broadway.

"Turn On the Night," a comedy - drama set in the Paris theatrical world of a century ago, is the work of the seemingly indefatigable writing team of Jerome Lawrence and Robert E. Lee.

CANDACE HILLIGOSS endows the comely widow with all the grace, beauty and fire the role requires. Others in the excellent cast directed by George Keathley are John Seymour, Tom Klunis, David Huddleston, Rex Thompson, Francis Compton and Constance Simons.

Special music created by Dr. Roy Harris was effective in setting the scenes.

ERIC BERRY, Candace Hilligoss and Joseph Wiseman (l. to r.) have leading roles in "Turn on the Night," new comedy-drama by Jerome Lawrence and Robert E. Lee which has its premiere Monday night at the John B. Kelly Playhouse in the Park.

A newspaper photo of Joseph Wiseman and Candace in Jerome Lawrence and Robert Lee's try out of a new Broadway play *Turn On the Night.*

At last Richard finished with summer stock in Maine. After my fiasco in Philadelphia with the play, I was back hanging out at my Chelsea apartment. We spent almost every evening together for the next month. Richard still kissed me goodnight at my doorstep as if I were a fragile doll. On one hand I was grateful, he was a gentleman, but on the other hand, I was worried. We were so physically attracted that in the light of other men's behavior, Richard's seemed abnormal. Betty and I discussed my dilemma. If he were homosexual, why would he propose marriage? Usually, my problems with a man were how to keep his hands off of me. Like many young actresses, I had been chased around offices, pawed at by directors who promised parts, received calls from agents who hinted at stardom if I came across friendly enough.

After dinner one night, Richard and I strolled in the balmy dusk of the Village. The streets were crowded with passers-by, but we were lost in our own desert isle in the city. Every time I glanced at Richard, I could see the love radiating from him. Tactfully, I said, "Richard, would you like to make love to me?" We were so in tune that without saying a word, we found ourselves in the lobby of a small hotel on a side street near Gramercy Park. The hotel clerk never missed a beat as he registered us for the night, a couple with no suitcases.

In bed that night in a room blanched in moonlight, we lay awake for hours. Every single minute made us delirious with excitement. I had never felt such closeness, such tenderness as Richard whispered how much he loved me. This joyous spring promised no more lonely summers, no more empty winters, we were together forever, the champion of each other's dreams.

The future was golden, the city was golden, our lives were golden because we believed in our youth that felt as if all sorrow and pain were blotted out forever.

When I touched Richard, I felt the stars and moon were in my hands, sheer rhapsody that would stay with me in one of those immortal times that followed you to life's end. So what if our feelings were just like clichés. Clichés were that way because they really happened when young lovers were in the glow of first love.

"The typical actor, at least in America, is the most upright of men: he always marries the girl."

– H. L. Mencken

THE
LOVING
COUPLE
G.L.

Chapter Four

Autumn 1960

Later, Richard admitted how much he had fallen in lust when we first met. He was smart enough to understand that if he had made a pass at me too soon I might reject him as being like all the others in my life who seemed to chase women for only one reason. He decided to wait until I made the first move. That endeared him to me even more. Gradually, our friends began to inquire when the wedding would take place. Richard and I had no money to speak of so it seemed appropriate to wait until summer stock was over. He had been cast in a Cape Cod tour with June Havoc, and I had a chance to appear in a dinner theater in Washington D.C., where I would repeat my "Marilyn roles." We would marry in September when we could afford to pay for a small wedding.

It never occurred to us to think of how much extra money we needed for a new apartment, some furniture, or whatever else happens when newlyweds set up housekeeping in the marriage trap. As far I was concerned, the wedding wasn't for three more months. Anything could happen during that eternity.

Then Richard asked if he should formally ask my father for my hand in marriage, since we were officially engaged (even if he couldn't afford an engagement ring.) I was playing the part of the happy fiancée, but to involve my widowed father in this scenario meant that this marriage business was serious business. "Richard, I have to explain something about my father. He must never know that you're not a college graduate. If he learned that you never made it past tenth grade, he would shoot you. He does not approve of actors; he thinks of them as no better than carnival performers whom he feels spread diseases. Also, should you ever meet him, you must never, ever let him know that you don't wear an undershirt."

Richard cocked an eyebrow and said, "Surely, you exaggerate. I can understand his hesitations about my being an actor, but what is this about an undershirt?"

"My father says that I should never trust a man who doesn't wear an undershirt. Men who don't wear one are killers, thieves and ne'er-do-wells."

"Where did he get such an idea?"

"There're certain things I don't ask my father."

Once when I was sharing a soda with a young man at the local teen hangout in Huron, South Dakota, my father came by. He yanked my elbow while muttering, “Pal, get away from him. He’s not wearing an undershirt!”

*****

I placed the call to my father in Huron with a report that I had great news. He assumed that I was about to tell him I had a job. He got excited. For a couple of months I had a TV commercial that ran only at one a.m. in South Dakota. Since this was past his bedtime, it meant he had to set his alarm so that he could wake up each night to see it. He imagined that I was about to make the announcement of a career break. There was no way to soften the truth. I said I wanted to get married. For a moment I thought the phone went dead. After a long silence came the expected question of, "What does he do for a living?" When I said, "He’s an actor." My father thought he heard architect. No, I corrected, an *actor*. To the question of what college did he graduate from, I answered, "RADA, the Royal Academy of Dramatic Arts in London." Then the big sixty-four dollar question of, "Pal, where’s he working now?" I had to say that he’s an out-of-work actor. Another prolonged silence. Was it possible he hung up on me?

Momentarily, my Aunt Margie came on the line. "Your father’s told me the tragic news and, as you may suspect, he’s not taking it well." I overheard him half-cursing, half-sobbing in the background. Even though Aunt Margie was covering the phone, I heard her admonishing him as if he were a recalcitrant child. At last she returned to me, "Don’t worry, I’ll have a little talk with him. This is not a real tragedy, after all. Girls do grow up to get married."

Since he was a widower, my father was dependent on his sister. Before I boarded the plane for New York to enroll at the American Theater Wing, he left her alone with me in the waiting room of the airport. Aunt Margie was a woman in her sixties who had never married. She was a maiden lady, as they kindly say back home. She was not a beauty, or even pretty in face or physique. I don’t think I ever knew her to have a boyfriend or, as they say also at home, a gentleman caller.

She said, in a discreetly low voice, that since I was leaving our town for the big wicked city of New York, and would be meeting men, my father wanted her to have a girl-talk with me. "Your father feels it’s time for you to know the facts of life. He’s asked me to tell you about sex! This is the only lesson you need to know. Always say no! No matter what a man wants or asks for, just say no! Take me, for example. I always said no, and there isn’t a man alive who doesn’t respect me. A few years ago, I used to go out with a fella who lived down the street from us. I always said no to him and, even though he married someone else, to this day, if I need an escort to an Eastern Star Dance, his wife lets him escort me–because he respects me. I am a lady, and I want you to remain one, too. Oh, before I forget, don’t ever take a job in show business if you have to take off your clothes–like a stripper. It’d break your father’s heart if you did that. No nudity!”

Aunt Margie let out a tremendous sigh at the duty she had just performed. Then, with her hand clutching a crucifix at her throat, she gave a small gasp. “Oh my, I almost forgot to tell you this, too. Your father wanted me to remind you never trust a man who doesn’t wear an undershirt."

*****

Our summer stock tours came and went, and suddenly I found myself back in Manhattan with Richard. Before I could really be sure, we were having a conference on the East Side with the Reverend Orin Grismeyer at the Little-Church-Around-the-Corner.

At the turn of the century, when the churches on Park and Fifth Avenue refused to marry actors, ministers and priests suggested that actors go instead to the Episcopal Church of the Ascension, a little church around the corner at Twenty-Ninth street that was willing to marry undesirables. Of course, these were also the times when actors weren’t allowed to be buried in consecrated grounds either.

The Reverend was rather surprised and pleased that both Richard and I were Episcopalians. Richard assumed he was because his mother was, whereas I had been confirmed in the church. The Reverend suggested that, for a small wedding, we use the bridal chapel instead of the main cathedral. He also asked us about hiring the church organist for twenty-five dollars. Richard and I reluctantly explained that our budget didn’t allow such extravagance as church music. We would be happy to walk down the aisle in silence. The Reverend appeared shocked. He remarked that he had never officiated at a wedding where there was no music for the wedding march. We insisted that we didn’t mind. The Reverend, shaking his head, said he couldn’t bear to hold our service without music, adding, "I’ll pay the organist myself."

Soon I was taken over by wedding fever and peering through bridal magazines. Mentally, I shelved my self-doubts in the excitement. My father seemed to have grown mellower and sent us a check for two hundred dollars to pay for whatever was needed. Richard and I put a deposit on a cake at a French bakery. He purchased a gold wedding band for me, which cost seventy-five dollars. It was a reproduction of an antique style with garnets set in it. An actress friend of his offered her studio apartment for the reception, a place just big enough to squeeze in our guest list of sixty-five. We’d be wall-to-wall people with no room to sit, but who cared? My roommate, Betty, came forth with, "What the hell? I love a good party and what better party than a wedding?"

If I counted on my fingers, Richard and I technically had only been in each other’s company for a total of six weeks. Summer stock had caused our mutual separation. How well did I know him after this short courtship? How well does one have to know an actor to marry him?

Girlfriends asked if I would be wearing a Murray Hamburger wedding dress. I said, "No, the dresses are too expensive." Besides, I didn’t want to be cinched into one of those gowns so tightly that I couldn’t eat a piece of wedding cake or drink a glass of domestic champagne. I couldn’t even pay for one of Mr. Hamburger’s sample dresses either.

I went up and down Fifth Avenue trying to find a ready-to-wear wedding dress for under a hundred dollars. There was no such animal, and none of the new fall cocktail dresses came in any shade of white. Luckily, at Lord and Taylor's, a saleswoman found a summer sales rack in the storage room. Left over from the spring season was a white brocade rayon dress with jacket, wadded up among the bathing suits and sun dresses. I tried it on. My thrill at the waistline, which fit perfectly, was replaced by my doubts at the sleeves that stopped halfway between the elbow and wrist. "Too short! Oh dear, the sleeves are too short!" I complained.

The saleslady suggested that if I kept my arms bent with the wedding bouquet held high before me, no one would notice the sleeve length. And the price was right at fifty dollars.

Somehow Richard and I were going through our savings from summer stock faster than we had anticipated. The news that my father decided to come five days before the wedding, rather than two, upset us. How were we going to entertain him and to pay for it was going to be a problem. Richard was well-rehearsed to play the part of the dutiful son-in-law. No matter how often my father might ask him if he would like a drink, Richard must answer no, that nothing with alcohol in it ever touched his lips. That was the first test. Second, he must never remove his blazer and reveal that he wasn't wearing an undershirt. Richard had only one blazer to his name, a heavy wool one, which was perfect for a New York winter blizzard, but neither did he own an undershirt, nor did his roommate have one to lend him.

Of course, my father could never see where Richard lived. At sixty-five, Pops might have a heart attack. Not only the six-flight climb, but from a tenement railroad flat that would convince him that Richard was not far removed from the panhandler on the street.

At last the big moment arrived when my father was introduced to Richard in the lobby of the Statler Hilton Hotel. Pops chewed on his cigar hesitantly while looking Richard over. As Richard ran to fetch the bellhop, my father pulled me aside and asked, "Pal, what make car does Richard drive?" In the Midwest, the true worth of a man is judged by the model of car he owns. I answered as carefree and unconcerned as I could, "Richard doesn't own one. An actor in New York doesn't need a car."

This caused my father to remove the cigar for the first time. "Jesus Christ! What kind of a man goes on a honeymoon who doesn't own a car?"

I knew better than to tell him that there would be no honeymoon either. Out-of-work actors don't take honeymoons.

We took my father to the best restaurants, where Richard and I sipped sodas with our dinner. We entertained my father by sitting him in the front row at Broadway shows. Pops was warming up to his new son-in-law. Feeling more generous, he asked Richard if he had ever considered sales for a career. "Listen, son, the show business racket is not a steady thing. How would you like to sell for me? You could be my New York representative. I'll give you some of my samples. Show you how to take orders for me, too."

Richard gave out a long, "Hmmm," as though the idea were a possibility. His ambiguous nods were enough to satisfy my father.

It was autumn, and we were in the midst of an Indian summer. The temperature had reached a muggy 90 degrees. One night while having a late supper, Pops saw that Richard was perspiring profusely in his heavy wool blazer. "Son, why don't you take off your jacket? It's too hot to wear it."

"Sir, as a gentleman at dinner, I don't feel right not wearing my jacket."

"You have my permission, son. Go ahead, I want you to be comfortable. There's no one but us at the table."

My father insisted and reached over to remove Richard's jacket. However, Richard grabbed his own lapels as though he were about to lose his virtue. "Sir, I'm not warm at all! I feel fine, fine, really. Please, believe me!"

Pops was slightly puzzled at Richard's willingness to suffer like this in a heat wave, but gave him his *Good Housekeeping* stamp of approval with, "Son, how about a cigar?" He reached into his pocket and pulled out a couple.

"Sorry, sir. I don't smoke. As an actor, I have to protect the vocal cords."

"Is that so?" My father reached over and gave Richard a slight jab to the shoulder, which meant, "You're okay, fella."

*****

On the wedding eve, I introduced Betty, my roommate and maid of honor, to the best man, Dick Coe, the esteemed theater critic for the *Washington Post*. Dick and I had become acquainted when I had appeared at a dinner theater in Washington D.C., and he had known Richard in his days at the Barter Theater. I knew that Dick, in his forties, would provide an air of respectability that would impress my father. Dick had the kind of manners that gave him entrances to palaces and kings and, even more important, any Broadway producer's office. A theater critic of his reputation would convince my father I had not turned into a beatnik from Greenwich Village.

For my last meal as a single woman, I chose a quaint, three-star Italian restaurant, the Capri, located in the theater district. Betty, Dick and I waited at the restaurant for Richard, who soon arrived with my father. Richard was carrying a huge paper sack with the logo of a nearby men's haberdasher, the type of store that has a permanent sign in the window reading GOING OUT OF BUSINESS SALE.

"Your father bought me some dress shirts," Richard said to me. This prompted Pops to add, "They were two for five dollars. A great bargain! I wanted to give a present to my new son-in-law so I got four of 'em for ten bucks." Richard was a good sport about it as he thanked my father for his generosity.

Everyone had been well-rehearsed as to how to behave around my nervous father. Betty and Dick promised to forego any alcohol beverages, not to discuss anything to do with World War I or II, or the possibility that Senator John Kennedy might lose the presidential election. Dick must not mention that he is a Republican. Small talk would be geared to Richard's bright future as an actor on Broadway.

Dick toasted Pops by raising a glass of ginger ale. "Welcome to New York. Here's to your happy visit and to your new son-in-law, a future star on the Great White Way."

Betty cheered. "Nice to meet you at last. What a terrific and talented son-in-law you have!" She waved her glass of sparkling ginger ale in Pops's direction. Richard and I threw all money cautions to the winds as we ordered the house specials of mozzarella marinara, linguine with white clam sauce, veal pizziaola and eggplant lasagna, truly exotic dishes for a Midwestern father, who was strictly a meat loaf and mashed potatoes man. Dick said to the waiter, "Please, another round of drinks for us. This one's on me." The waiter returned with a tray of bottled ginger ales, which he poured as grandly as if they were vintage Dom Perignon. In this convivial atmosphere, we all toasted one another's health, career success, and many years of wedded bliss for Richard and me.

We were just finishing our dessert of spumoni ice cream when my father, attempting to stand, collapsed and fell to the floor, groaning. I sprang to my feet, almost tripping over him in my haste. "Pops! What's wrong"?

Betty cried out, "Oh my god! Is he having a heart attack?"

Dick immediately came to my father's side. Both he and Richard tried to lift him from the floor. Pops was speaking in dramatic tones worthy of a Shakespearean death scene: "My leg! It's my leg! I can't move it. The pain is killing me! Where's the nearest hospital, pal? Don't worry. My Blue Cross card is in my wallet."

The waiter rushed over with the maitre d'. It took four men to raise my father and maneuver him into position where they were able to half-drag, half-carry him through the restaurant. To say that we attracted attention is an understatement. New Yorkers reacted as if they were extras in a Vittorio de Sica film. Gasping in sympathy, they jumped to their feet and swept their chairs aside to let our parade pass by to the doorway.

Pops made a sign of the cross over his heart with one hand while grasping a cigar in the other as though it were a life belt. "The shirts! Don't forget the shirts!"

I already had the precious package under my arms as we came out onto the sidewalk and into a parked taxi. Richard and I shoved my father inside, then scrambled beside him with the unwieldy sack blocking our view of the cab driver. For a moment, Betty and Dick waved to us with shouts of "Good luck! See you tomorrow! If you need us, we'll be at Sardi's!" They dashed across the street as if they were Death Row inmates making a break for freedom. The cowards did not once look back at us.

I knew them well enough to know that they would head straight for the Sardi's bar, where Betty would down Bloody Marys, and Dick would match her with vodka martinis. We directed the cab driver to the hospital on the West Side. Within five minutes, we were at Roosevelt's Emergency Room. Regaining his composure, my father was placed in a wheelchair. After the resident doctor examined father's swollen knee, he turned to Richard and me. "It's a severe gout attack. Has this man had a shock recently?"

"Well, I'm his only child, and I'm getting married tomorrow." Then I pointed at the guilty party beside me. "I'm marrying an actor."

The young doctor gave Richard a resentful look, which I understood. Professional men in heavy-duty careers, like medicine, usually can't stand actors, who are considered lazy, empty-brained show-offs. They can sleep until noon if they don't have a matinee, then spend the rest of the afternoon at the gym, go for a sauna, lie under a sunlamp, so that they can feel irresistible to women.

The doctor concentrated on the patient's leg. "Mr. Hilligoss, if you're planning to walk the bride down the aisle tomorrow, you'll need to use crutches or at the very least, a cane."

"I'm not going to use crutches or a cane to escort my daughter, Kansas, down the aisle!" Pops almost ate through his cigar in his anxiety.

"Well, my advice then," the doctor went on, "is to go to bed and elevate your leg immediately. Find someone who can administer hot packs to your knee tonight. Maybe by morning the swelling will have subsided enough for you to walk without assistance."

Richard and I glanced at each other helplessly. Then he volunteered with great conviction, "I am more than willing to spend the night putting hot packs on Mr. Hilligoss's knee. If that's what it takes, I'll be happy to do it."

An attendant wheeled my father out to the curb where, once again, we placed him into a cab. He was mumbling something about his regrets that he couldn't enjoy all the bright lights of the city with us. Clutching the package of shirts, Richard got in beside him. The taxi took off. For a few moments, I watched them disappear into the mainstream of Broadway traffic. Somehow, I knew my father would survive, but the question was, would Richard survive playing nursemaid the night before our big day?

For hours that night, I had insomnia. At last, I sat up in bed and turned on the radio to some music. All the demons about the marriage trap raced through my mind. Would I turn into a Doris Day housewife? Then again, maybe Richard and I would have triumphant careers like the Lunts? Or maybe we would be like Jessica Tandy and Hume Cronyn and spend our lives successfully emoting on the Broadway stage between the movies.

I constantly checked the clock to note the time. My roommate still hadn't returned; this was not like her. Betty was not the kind of person who stayed out nights like some party animal, and, as my maid of honor, she would want her beauty sleep. I imagined her being held up or worse yet, murdered, her body thrown into the 42nd Street subway tunnel, the hell-hole of Manhattan. Then I worried about Richard. He had not called once during the night. Maybe an argument broke out between Pops and Richard, who was probably afraid to wake me.

I shouldn't be so pessimistic. Things had been going really well for him and Pops. Soon it was sunrise, and Betty still had not come home. We needed to be at the church by one o'clock. I assumed that someone would call to check on the bride, but oddly no one did. Something was rotten in Denmark–or at the Statler Hotel. I called my father's room. There was no answer. I called Richard's apartment. If he weren't there, the best man surely would be. Again no answer.

I did my makeup, then put on the wedding dress. I sat on the couch with my crystal tiara and veil in my lap. The netting billowed around me like the wings of a giant butterfly. After several minutes of staring at the clock, I realized that it was only half an hour until the service was to begin. If I didn't leave soon, I would be late for my own wedding. The idea of having to walk alone to the corner at Sixth Avenue in my white satin slippers and wedding dress, to stand at the curb to flag a cab, was infuriating. I went to the windows of our apartment and peered down into the courtyard. Charlie, one of my neighbors, was sitting there, painting at his easel. I yelled to him. "Hi there, Charlie! I need your help."

Charlie looked upward and waved.

"Guess what? I'm getting married. Can you find a cab for me and direct it to my building?

The shock of seeing me in my white wedding dress with veil in hand brought Charlie to his feet so fast he knocked over the easel and paints. I saw him run toward the gate for the street. Within seconds he was at my door pounding and out of breath: "Your taxi's waiting. I can't believe you're getting married! When did all this happen?"

I explained to Charlie as much as I could as we ran down the stairs and out onto the street. He helped me into the taxi, carefully lifting my veil, which ballooned like a parachute in the breeze. At last, I was settled. I gave the cab driver the address for the Little Church Around the Corner.

The taxi peeled away from the curb so fast that I didn't have a chance to thank Charlie. After a couple of blocks, the driver stared into his rear-view mirror. Even for a cab driver, who must have seen about everything under the New York sun, he seemed aghast. He snapped his head around to confirm what his mirror identified. "Ma'am? Are you going to the church to get married?"

"Yes, I am."

"You look pretty young to me."

"Yes, I am."

"You're in the prime of life."

"Yes, I am."

"Well then, God damn it, why do you want to get married?"

"I beg your pardon?"

"Take me! I'm married twenty-five years, and it's been hell on earth! Do you want to end up like me and have your life ruined?"

"I really don't think you should talk to me like this on my wedding day!"

"Didn't your folks *talk* to you? Didn't they tell you what a mistake marriage is?" He began pounding the steering wheel for emphasis. "A young gorgeous doll like you can have so much fun! Why throw it away? Ain't you having fun as a single girl?"

"Can't I be married and have fun, too?"

"You're too damn dumb! You don't have a clue what you're getting yourself into. You need help. Tell you what, let's drive around and discuss it."

"Sir, there's nothing to discuss. Just get me to the church."

"Ain't gonna do it. Me and you is goin' for a ride 'til you come to your senses."

I felt beads of perspiration on my face as the self-doubts about matrimony came over me. If a guardian angel wanted to prevent me from getting to the church, why would she send a cynical cab driver from the Bronx to give advice like a marriage counselor? What if I did stand everyone up at the church? My father might really have a heart attack. This kind of shock could give him such a bad case of the gout, that maybe he might never walk again! How would I ever face our friends? Richard would be so humiliated, he'd never speak to me, never want to do scenes with me for Strasberg's class. Why didn't I check my horoscope in the paper this morning? I was in a predicament that went beyond anything that was portrayed in Doris Day's movies. What would a nice girl like Doris do in this situation?

We were driving on streets in the opposite direction of the church, heading toward the Hudson River. Now that I knew my cab driver was a certifiable lunatic, I began to get scared. My legs trembled. I envisioned the headlines in the *Daily News*, KIDNAPPED ON HER WEDDING DAY. I had read that when in the presence of a nut case, remain calm, talk in a soothing, ladylike voice.

"Please, if you don't mind, sir, if you'd be so kind, I wish to go to the church. Right now. My father's waiting to—"

"I'm talkin' to you like your *father*! Listen to me! We ain't goin' to the church!"

Dammit! It was forget ladylike, forget soothing, forget sweet Doris Day. I rolled down the window, leaned out and screamed. "Help! Help me! Someone help! I'm being kidnapped! Kidnapped on my wedding day!"

That did the trick. He spun the cab around, then drove like a maniac back to the East Side, cursing me the whole distance. His middle finger was puncturing the hot stuffy air around him as he yelled over my screams, "See if I care! Go ahead, stupid! Ruin your life!"

Twenty minutes later, the wheels of the cab scraped the curb as we lurched to an abrupt stop before the church. "Here we are, stupid! You owe me thirty dollars!"

Technically, this should have been a dollar and a half ride but, after our detour, the meter read seven dollars. "What kind of thug are you, to gyp me on my wedding day?"

It was then that I caught sight of Richard grasping one arm of my father, while the best man, Dick Coe, held the other. They were coming along the sidewalk toward the church. Seeing me, Dick ran for the cab. "Darling, how much is your fare?" He took out his wallet. The driver yelled, "Thirty dollars!"

I argued back, "Dick, don't pay it! He's cheating me! Stealing from a bride, and in front of the Lord's house! Thief! Thief!"

There was a moment of mass confusion as Dick offered the dollar bills through the open front window, and I shoved his hand aside, while the driver grabbed for the money. Dick became frazzled. "Forget it. Whatever the man wants, he can have it. Don't upset yourself today of all days."

I stumbled from the cab, feeling as if I had been riding in a steam bath. Between wind and perspiration, my hairdo collapsed. After chewing my lips, all trace of Revlon's Passion Pink was gone. Richard didn't seem to notice as he rushed to me with a bridal bouquet of white and peach roses. "I've never seen a bride more beautiful in my life. Sweetheart, you take my breath away."

But the moment my father noticed me, he burst into tears and tripped, about to fall to the sidewalk. Dick raced to his rescue. "Mr. Hilligoss, do you want your cane?"

My father pulled himself together and said rather grandly, "I don't need a cane! Not for Kansas's wedding day."

Richard took me aside as we entered the church. There was a hum of activity from the chapel as the waiting guests had been seated half an hour ago. We quickly walked toward the private office where we were to greet Reverend Grismeyer.

"Where've you been, Richard? No one called me!"

"I'm sorry. Your father had us so worried, Dick and I couldn't think straight. I haven't been to bed. I spent the entire night at the hotel, putting hot towels on your father's knee. Just when I thought he was asleep, and I could sneak in some shut-eye, he'd come alive and tell me to bring more hot towels. I was in and out of the bathroom, dipping and wringing out towels in the sink. Before I knew it, the sun was up."

"Oh, you poor dear, how terrible for you!"

"That's not the worst part."

"What else could possibly have happened?"

"Your father kept insisting that I make myself at home and take off my jacket. I said that I was fine with it on. Finally, after a couple of hours, he said he'd like me to try on the new shirts. He wanted to know if they were the right size. I assured him that they were, but he would have none of it. He had to see me in a shirt, because he said if it didn't fit, he was going to return all of them and get his money back."

"Oh no, what did you do?"

"I said to him that I had a confession to make. His eyes narrowed, and he asked me, 'What do you mean by a confession?' I explained how embarrassed I was that I was not wearing an undershirt. I couldn't believe it! This look of complete horror flashed across his face. I used every bit of my actor's training as I made up the excuse that last week I had sent my undershirts to a Chinese laundry, and they had lost them. Your father hesitated, then asked, 'A Chinese laundry? One of them foreign places?' I said, 'Oh, yes, a foreign place,' then he grew quieter. I could see he was deciding whether I was telling him the truth or not. The suspense was killing me! At last, he said, 'Son, I can see how that might happen to a person. It's okay. Go ahead. Try on the shirts.' "

"Darling Richard, you're so clever, so brilliant. And I love you so much."

We entered the office where the Reverend had us sign our marriage certificates. Soon my father and Dick joined us. I asked them, "Has anyone seen Betty?" Before they could answer, the door opened, and she ran in, apologizing, "Sorry, I'm glad I'm not too late."

"Betty, what happened to you?" Even though I was annoyed, I was grateful to see her.

Betty's breathless words rushed out in a torrent: "Well, after Dick and I went to Sardi's, we decided to go to the Oyster Bar at the Plaza Hotel. Then we went across the street to the cocktail lounge at the Hotel Pierre. After I left him, I went to visit a friend, where I passed out on the floor. When I came to, it was morning. I realized I was late for my hair appointment at Charles of the Ritz. And you know how Karoj always runs behind anyway. Thank goodness, I had the foresight to bring my dress with me. I changed at the salon."

The Reverend asked if we would bow our heads for a moment of silent prayer. I think he realized there was a great deal of tension in the air and wanted to calm us. After a couple of minutes, he instructed us how to proceed into the chapel. He said to my father, "Mr. Hilligoss, after you bring your daughter to the altar, I will give you a nod. That is your cue to leave her, to step aside and to join the other guests in the front pew."

I could tell from Pops's blank eyes that none of this was sinking in as he appeared to be in a state of shell shock, the way he had once described himself as a corporal in combat in World War I.

We filed out of the office and took our positions as the organist began to play. Betty preceded me and began the slow wedding march down the aisle. Father held onto my arm tightly to support himself so that he wouldn't limp. From the back of the chapel, we saw Richard and Dick take their positions before the altar. Pops and I began to do our shaky version of the two-step march. Richard and I had invited not only our close friends and my former boyfriends, but our theatrical agents, too. We included my acting teachers from the American Theater Wing. Despite my protests, Richard wanted to invite Lee Strasberg: "Why shouldn't we ask the sucker to come? If it weren't for him, we'd never have met." But Strasberg's secretary replied in the negative, saying that he never attended these kinds of functions.

At last the moment came. We made it to the altar railing before the Reverend, who nodded to my father, standing between Richard and me. But Pops seemed paralyzed. He stared back at the Reverend, who waited politely for a few seconds. Thinking that my father missed his cue to leave the altar, the

Reverend gave a deeper nod that was almost a bow. Still no reaction from Pops. Rather than embarrassing my father, there was nothing the Reverend could do but to begin. During the entire ceremony, Pops remained between Richard and myself. I had a funny thought that somehow I was marrying my father, too. He mouthed the vows right along with us. As Richard placed the ring on my finger, he had to reach across my father. When we were pronounced man and wife and could kiss each other, Richard and I almost planted one on Pops's cheeks instead.

After about twenty minutes, the service was over. The guests applauded and cheered us as everyone raced out of the church into the sunshine. The church bells chimed. One of the ushers took my brownie camera and posed our bridal party near the shrubbery. Pops started to cry at the idea that my name would no longer be Kansas Hilligoss.

From the churchyard, everyone relocated to our friend's studio apartment for the reception. We had the traditional cake and paper cups filled with New York Taylor champagne, candy mints and Planter's Peanuts set about in saucers. It was late afternoon, and I didn't want to leave what we then considered a great party, but my maid of honor and a few of the guests indicated that it was time for Richard and me to be alone.

Before I knew it, we were out on the sidewalk with a waiting taxi. A hail of rice landed on Richard and me while close buddies encircled us. As the taxi carried us away, I looked around and saw Pops lying on the front stoop, his hand massaging his knee.

"Bye, Kansas! Write me soon, pal!"

Our friends seemed to have lost interest in the bride and groom as they crowded around him. Dick came forward with the cane but Pops, out of pride, still refused to accept it.

The last picture of the most important day in my life was my father lying in a crippled heap on the stoop of a New York brownstone. What a way for him to say goodbye or for me to bid farewell to a widowed father and to my life as a single girl. It was too much for me. I burst into tears.

Richard was terribly hurt. "Why are you crying? I thought brides were supposed to be happy."

By the time dusk appeared, I was in control of myself. Richard and I changed our clothes and put on our blue jeans. An actress on tour had lent us her apartment on 85th Street for two weeks. That gave us fourteen days to find our own place. Richard was in a quandary as to what we should do if we couldn't find a rent-controlled apartment that was affordable. I suggested that I could move back with Betty, and he could do the same with his roommate on Tenth Avenue. Richard was appalled. He vowed that no matter what, we would never live apart.

For our first meal as husband and wife, we went to the Horn and Hardart Automat on 86th Street in the Yorkville section. We placed coins in slots like in Las Vegas, only we "won" sandwiches instead of money. We carried our trays to a window table, somewhat removed from the rest of the patrons. We ate watching the city come to life in the darkness outside.

"How much money have we got left?" Richard asked. I opened my purse and emptied it on the table. Richard took out his wallet and did likewise. Together, we counted out what we had left in the world. Between us, it came to fifteen dollars and eleven cents.

Richard said, "I'm not worried, are you?"

I shook my head. Why would I worry when we were so rich in love, in youth, in talent?

Impulsively, Richard grabbed my hand and pressed it against his lips. He said, "I wrote you a note. It's something I want you to keep in case we're ever separated." He gave me a small piece of folded paper.

I opened it and read: "Dearest Sweetheart, I never dreamed I could love someone as much as you. When I'm alone at night, I play music. My mind transposes into reflections of you. Each melody is the surprise of your spirit, so rain-drop fresh, so tender like your understanding. The soft notes become your lovely eyes in quiet light. Your spirit is with me forever. I love you, Candace."

I felt myself choking up. This was the first love letter I have ever received. In our private world, we lost any awareness of the noisy Saturday-night diners at the automat. We leaned across the sticky table and kissed each other with great passion. Richard murmured over and over, "I adore you. You're the love of my life."

> "Heaven be thanked, we live in such an age
> when no man dies for love, but on the stage."
>
> – John Dryden

GET ME TO THE CHURCH...ON.....
HELP!!!
TAXI
TAXI

Chapter Five

Return to 1980—Beverly Hills

"Meredith is the love of my life," Richard said, while facing me in my Beverly Hills apartment. A place he had picked out and for which he had signed the lease before moving our two daughters and me from New York to join him in California. "The girls can only benefit from my loving relationship with Meredith. I want them to live with both of us so that they can understand what real love is."

How familiar his words sounded, I thought. He's like an old song now out of sync. I couldn't resist prying, "What does Meredith do?"

He informed me that Meredith was a librarian who was working part-time. At twenty-two she had just graduated from college in the spring. She intended to start her master's degree in library science in the Fall at U.S.C. "She's brilliant," he added, "much smarter than I am. She speaks French and reads constantly."

Richard doesn't speak a word of French, and the only books he reads are the ones optioned for movies. In fact, he is a high school drop-out, who has a peasant's awe of diplomas. Even quack doctor certificates impress him.

Since this had been my week to share our daughters, he had come over to pick them up. The girls, fearing a potential family argument, had bolted outside the apartment.

Richard was about to leave. "Meredith and I are going to spend the day at the beach with the kids."

There was an air of benevolence about him that was raising suspicious hairs on the back of my neck, particularly because we were scheduled to meet in divorce court again in a few days. I followed him out the door then down the stairwell to the sidewalk.

"Candace, I've talked to your landlord, and he wants to sell this building. I told him I'd be interested in buying it. So why don't you sell your farm property, use the money for the down payment, and I'll pay the mortgage for you."

"While we're in the middle of a divorce, you're suggesting that I sell my grandmother's inheritance of a homestead farm—use the money to buy this building. In a sense, I'm to give you money for a deposit. What on earth are you proposing?"

"Well, we'd be partners, like a business deal. I'd pay the monthly mortgage."

Now I understood Richard's behavior, why he was being nice in the midst of the animosity of a divorce. For years, he had wanted me to sell my homestead farmland back in South Dakota. The year before, in New York, against my farm agent's advice, I had accepted an offer from the U.S. Fish and Wildlife Service to execute an easement on my farm for waterfowl rights, a contract in perpetuity that could reduce the value of any future sale. Richard needed the money for a chance to go to Hollywood before he was too old to face the cameras as a leading man. His idea of financial help was to use this easement money to purchase a Dodge Surfer van, which was now parked at the curb in front of my apartment with Meredith, the librarian, waiting in the passenger seat and our teenage daughters in the back, amidst scuba gear and picnic paraphernalia.

I had my first glimpse of the "other woman," if you can call a "hippie" girl of twenty-two a woman. Meredith was a petite brunette who wore her hair in two long braids to her waist, rather like Pocahontas. She looked like a leftover flower child in a long, gauzy Indian skirt and wide-leather sandals that made her feet resemble a Roman gladiator's.

"Richard, I don't know if I want to sell my land yet. And how could I depend on you to pay the mortgage? You're an out-of-work actor!"

He glowered at me. "I've just offered to buy this building for you. You could live here rent-free. I'm being generous, and you're being foolish. Well, I tried my best to do the right thing by you. No more Mr. Nice Guy. Tell that to your attorney."

As Richard drove away, I thought maybe he assumed that because I had in the past used whatever money I earned for him, I was dumb enough to keep doing it while he was in the process of divorcing me. Obviously, he understood what happens to community property when one commingles funds, and that explained the pretense of being Mr. Nice Guy.

*****

At 8:30 AM the following Monday, Gary Zimmerman met me outside Department Two in Superior Court. After we were seated inside, I whispered to him, "Any more wives shot since we were last here?"

"No, no, we're safe."

"Everyone here seems so calm after the woman's husband went on a rampage with a gun."

"Don't worry, that's water under the bridge," Gary said. "For a while the guards made us open our briefcases before we were allowed in here, but that stopped after a week. Now the guards are back to their usual state of indifference."

After the preliminary roll call, he asked me, "By the way, does Richard own a gun?"

"He owns two."

"You never told me." There was a sharp edge in his voice.

"You never asked. Where should I have put guns on my list of community assets? Somewhere between the dishware and the bedding?"

My attorney never answered as he was already on his feet reporting to the judge along with Richard's attorney, Irwin Buter. After a few minutes, Gary returned to me. "Well, we were assigned to a female judge, but Richard exercised his veto and turned her down. He doesn't want to be heard by a woman. He's afraid she'll be prejudicial toward you."

"What about me with a male judge? Can I veto that, too?" Naturally, Gary couldn't or wouldn't answer my question.

"What's this mean, Gary?"

"It means we've probably blown the whole morning. We'll have to wait around for another judge. We may not get up before this afternoon."

"Richard still intends to ask for custody of the girls."

"We can't agree to that. You know that's a ploy to get out of paying you alimony."

"But I was married for twenty years."

"If you don't have kids at home, the judge will tell you to find a job. You're free to do so without children."

"What about my standard of living?"

"Too often judges feel that if a man has a new wife and family, he shouldn't be penalized by supporting the old one."

"How did that come about?"

"James Hayes, a member of the California Assembly, who authored the first no-fault divorce act in the United States. He used it to get rid of his first wife of twenty-five years. She's on welfare now. He's remarried, of course."

"But Gary, shouldn't the court recognize that a husband can't have it both ways? He can't have his wife remain at home as a housewife while he feathers his own nest in the world. Then just because he doesn't need her services any more, deprives her of income. That's cruel and inhuman."

"Did you really think that just because you're before a man wearing a black robe, you'll find justice?"

"The only community property I have is the intangible property of my husband's career. Richard's ability to earn money is my only asset."

"California judges don't consider a husband's career to be a community asset. Don't be so naive as to expect the courts to be concerned about the economic turmoil of older women; they aren't. No court is going to reward you for your devotion to your spouse or family. Right now, your husband's whining that he'll never work again. His leading man days are over. You've been a SAG member. Tell them to settle this strike or it could go pretty bad for us in court."

"What's the best I can hope for?"

"Half of all women in long-term marriages are awarded no alimony at all. Because you have no community property of note with this actor, a judge may be more considerate. Alimony is based on the court's judgment of what the husband can afford. And yours happens to be an out-of-work actor! We can pray, but expect the worst."

After lunch, Gary and I were stopped in the doorway of Department Two by Richard's attorney. Irwin Buter pulled mine aside and mumbled something in his ear so I couldn't hear. Richard remained at the end of the corridor as if to avoid us.

Gary came over to me, then mumbled in the same tone, which meant the other side wants to negotiate now. "Candace, they want to ask for a continuance."

"Huh? What for?"

"Richard just learned he got a commercial."

"How can he shoot one during a SAG strike?'

"He's doing it under the other union–AFTRA. We'll agree to the continuance as long he pays your rent. The more he works as an actor, the better it looks for our case."

Perhaps the gods were on my side after all. Maybe with this postponement, the SAG strike might end before our next court date.

A few days later, Richard phoned to remind me that one little commercial does not a career make, and even though he was also going to New York to revive his part on NBC's soap opera, *Another World*, I should be aware that he was contracted for just six weeks. He was lucky that soaps were done under the auspices of AFTRA. After that gig ended, he would be an out-of-work actor again.

One night, I saw Richard's new commercial four times on network prime time. At $250 a clip, that's a total of $1,000 during the commercial break for a single show. Since the SAG strike was still on, television was into reruns. That same week, I counted seven guest appearances by Richard. There may have been more. As my attorney said, "Richard's face is all over the tube. He's even competing with himself by appearing on two networks simultaneously."

A week later, I was at the movies in Westwood near UCLA. There was Richard on the big screen in *Little Darlings* as Tatum O'Neal's father. Down the street, he was playing Diane Keaton's husband in the movie *Reds*, directed by Warren Beatty.

When Richard's agent answered a subpoena, the statement from his bookkeeper revealed that while Richard was unemployed, he earned more than $100,000 in commercials and community property residuals from television guest spots. Gary was elated at the discovery. "Richard's caught on to Hollywood's system of double bookkeeping. He claims in court he has no income, but the subpoenas of his unions show he's still making money."

Both of our attorneys instructed Richard and me to attend a family clinic for guidance. Each attorney wanted to be able to convince the judge what good guys we were in regard to who would better deserve custody of the children. Richard and I found ourselves sitting side by side in a cubicle, with no windows, at the children's clinic of UCLA. This was the office of a resident psychologist, Dr. Rhoda Hicks. Above her desk on the wall, she had Scotch-taped a variety of scrubbily, scrawly children's drawings. Even though at twenty-six she had neither married nor had children, she considered herself an authority on child psychology. She wore Levis, Mexican boots and chandelier earrings that swung back and forth, brushing her shoulders. If this was a fashion statement, I had no idea of how to interpret it.

"My wife—I mean Candace and I," Richard said, quickly correcting himself, "plan to share the girls this summer."

Dr. Hicks cooed, "Oh, I'm so pleased to see you're planning and structuring your family's activities. How do you feel about it, Mrs. Forest?"

"I'm looking ahead to a fun summer with our daughters. I have no animosity toward Richard about sharing the girls."

Dr. Hicks gave us one of those practiced smiles that belong in institutions that cater to the insane.

The tension between Richard and me was like a ticking bomb. However, Dr. Hicks was programmed to interact with children, not actors. She carried on: "I think it's so wonderful that despite the fact that you two are proceeding with the divorce, you're able to put aside your problems and come together for the sake of your daughters."

Gritting my teeth, my head nodded along with Richard's in polite agreement. The psychiatrist then suggested that next time we report to a special divorce clinic, located in Santa Monica. She would call the clinic to set up an appointment.

Together, Richard and I marched out to the hospital's parking lot. I turned to him and said, "Since the girls are staying at your house, I want to remind you that next week, on my birthday, you're supposed to deliver them to me for brunch."

"Fine, that's fine with me," he said. "What time is brunch?"

"Around noon on Saturday."

"That's out of the question. It's too late. You have to do brunch at eight, Saturday morning."

"Richard, I don't understand. The girls are still in bed at eight. They prefer brunch at noon, when they're awake."

"But I have to be at home. I'm cooking a turkey for a picnic. Noon's when I have to start my turkey in the oven."

"Can't Meredith help you?"

"She doesn't know how to cook yet."

"Can't you leave her a note? Turn oven on. Put turkey in pan, put turkey in oven, baste turkey. Surely, if she's the brilliant librarian you claim she is, she can check out a cookbook."

"Fuck it! I try my best to get along with you, then you have to stick the dagger in."

"Oh, fuck you back, Richard, I'm not having brunch at eight in the morning, so you can run home and give your girlfriend a cooking lesson on my birthday."

"Fuck your birthday! Fuck it! I've had it!"

Richard's purple veins were throbbing in his neck as he leaned across the hood of a parked car and hollered at me. The "fuck you's" were going back and forth like a rally of gunshots. Years ago, I had tried to curb my husband's use of this four-letter epithet. But it was as much a habit with him as nail-biting or coke-snorting was to others.

A station wagon filled with children came to a stop in front of us. The driver jumped out, then ran over to Richard. "Excuse me, sir, but are you Richard Forest, the movie star?"

We straightened up as Richard stood at attention, cleared his throat and, in a dignified voice, answered with a slight English accent. "Why, yes, I am, sir."

The driver thrust forward a torn envelope and said nervously, "Wow! Do you have a pen?" The man turned to his wife and kids in the station wagon: "Hon, you're right. He's a movie star–right here in the parking lot."

Fumbling in his pockets, Richard couldn't find a pen. I can't count the number of times that fans have asked Richard for an autograph without it occurring to them to provide a pen or paper. As it happened so often in the past, I opened my purse and brought forth a ballpoint. Richard grabbed it and signed the autograph so the man would go away. The man was quickly back in the station wagon, driving off with the star-struck wife and kids leaning out the windows, pointing at us as if we were on display in a zoo.

I decided to say the worst thing I could think of to Richard. "I saw your movie-of-the-week recently. What's happened to your acting?"

"Something's wrong with my acting?"

I gave him the worst zinger of all. "It's become PREDICTABLE!"

This is one of the most dreaded critiques an actor can receive–like being called a ham actor.

"Did you say *predictable*?" Richard grabbed the hood of the car as if to prevent himself from dropping to his knees.

"Yes, it's predictable. A friend of mine told me that once you've heard one Richard Forest line-reading, you've heard them all."

Richard's voice was a husky whisper. "Was your friend in the business? I mean, were you around anyone that counts?"

"No one, just us civilians."

"Thank God." He ran back to his car.

As part of our agreement, we met at the Santa Monica divorce clinic for further counseling on how to cope with children in a divorce. This time, we were given an office with two therapists, a man and a woman. Just like Dr. Hicks, neither of them was married nor had children. Both looked young enough to be the other's prom date. It cost fifty dollars a session to have these kids listen to us. Afterwards, we would end up in the parking lot, denouncing, accusing, screaming and shouting every known accusation we could dream up. Several hundred dollars later, our "his and her" therapists came to the astute conclusion that we should never park in the same lot again. For once during the divorce, Richard and I agreed. We shouldn't have to pay an expensive clinic bill for a diagnosis as simplistic as theirs.

Late that afternoon, I treated my neighbor Gertrude Walker to dinner at Joe Allen Restaurant where we could sit in the patio under the shade of a tree. She was the first friend I made in Beverly Hills. We met on a corner where she and I were both dropping manuscripts in a mailbox. Gertrude, said that as a professional writer, she was curious if I were a writer, too, judging by the fat manila envelope in my hand. From then on our friendship blossomed. She was in her seventies, petite, but made up for it in a deep husky voice that was an octave lower than that of Mae West with whom she toured in ingénue days.

Gertrude told me that years ago during the heyday of Republic Studios, she had set the record for having written the most screenplays while under contract to them. "I got my big break, Candy, when World War II drafted all the male writers. Studios were forced to hire female writers. I also became a staff writer at Warner Brothers, the greatest studio for film noir."

When she asked what happened to me, I regaled her with the tale of my arrival to Beverly Hills from New York with two daughters and a dog in tow. On the third day, a strange man knocked on my new apartment door. He handed me a paper and said, "You've been served." I said, "Served what?"

"A divorce summons." He disappeared.

I went into shock as the realization came over me that Richard tricked me into leaving a rent-controlled NYC apartment to move the family to California. He had plotted this out very carefully. Before our move, he had been living temporarily with his aunt in Pasadena. According to California family law, he needed only six months of residency for filing a divorce. He used the bills for his private phone line installed in Auntie's house as proof he fulfilled the requirement for California.

"Jesus Christ, that's horrible," Gertrude said. "Listen, Candy, take notes, write this court stuff down. The best revenge is to tell this story."

"Oh, Gertrude, another boring tale about a middle-age woman getting divorced. Who'd want to read it?"

"Trust me, I know story. Forget writing about the Dakotas and the Dust Bowl. This is the story that's gonna take you across the finishing line. This one is the winner!"

"But I don't know how to end it. There isn't one in sight. However, not to change the subject, but I have a favor to ask of you."

"What's that, Candy?"

"My attorney wants me to find three witnesses who would be willing to testify as to my talents as an artist, acting or writing."

"Oh, you can count on me. I love a good courtroom scene."

*****

It was now August, and nearly a year had passed since I had been first served with a divorce summons. My, how time flies when you're divorcing in the midst of a SAG strike. At the courthouse, Gary Zimmerman said that Richard's latest complaint was that he owed a tax bill of some thirty thousand dollars. That's why he was so broke; besides that, he was once again an out-of-work actor.

We had to wait until the afternoon to be given the next available judge, Harry Shafer in Department Seven. We made our way through a crowded hallway. Lawyers greeted one another jovially as though they were arranging tennis matches at the Beverly Hills Hotel. The glum faces belonged to their clients, who drifted about waiting to be summoned.

During the lunch hour, while I was in the ladies' room, a woman rushed in, sobbing. It was not a good sign of coming attractions. I had a sudden memory of the day when a very pregnant me had been wheeled through a maternity ward only to be forewarned by women in labor, screaming for mercy. It was one of those rare times that I said to myself, "Feet get me out of here!" I wanted mine to do just that immediately!

Gary prodded me toward Department Seven as Buter and Richard marched behind us. At that moment, strange giggles broke out from a circle of women who were conversing in Spanish. They pointed at Richard. Two of the women broke away and came over to him. "Senor? Are you star of *Another World*?" Buter laughed and asked them, "You think he's someone famous?" His tone indicated that he was impressed by their recognition of his client.

Richard cringed as the women surrounded him, waving pencils and scraps of paper. I could tell he was mortified. Generally, he loved to have fans ask for his autograph, but I knew that since he was in his court appearance wardrobe, which made him resemble a homeless beach bum, he did not appreciate the acknowledgment. I watched as he scribbled his signature that was as legible as chicken scratches.

Gary nudged me. "Is that what you call star power?"

"Call it stud power. We're talking soap operas here. An actor is only as good as his storyline. Richard has starred on eight of them; he's been married seven times, gone to prison three times, murdered once, been killed twice but, somehow, he's always been revived so that he can come back to the arms of the newest leading lady who always looks as if she's Miss America pressed under glass. I've lost track of how many women he's made love to in the afternoon."

At last, Gary ushered me inside Department Seven. I knew that Richard was following close, as I could hear him hyperventilating. Judge Harry Shafer was most intrigued he had a soap opera star before him and an actor who had guest starred on a number of night-time series, too. From the bench, he held out his arms toward us. "Through these portals, all the stars eventually come to see me."

Richard was not amused and remained expressionless.

(Later, we found out that Judge Shafer, a veteran of the Battle of the Bulge, had aspirations of writing screenplays. Gary learned that the judge was collaborating with screenwriter Delbert Mann. I'm convinced that everyone in Hollywood secretly harbors fantasies about being in show business.)

Richard, as the Petitioner, went first in the witness dock. He swore to tell the truth, the whole truth and nothing but the truth so help him God. Then he lied. I whispered to Gary that I assumed since Richard was under oath that he was committing perjury. Gary spoke into my ear, "The judge doesn't care because Richard's the one with the money. He can't pay alimony if he's in prison. You're the one who has to be purer than Caesar's wife."

There was a moment of interruption. A court clerk came to Judge Shafer with a phone in her hand. The judge took the call. The attorneys tried not to show their irritation as our hearing was put on hold while the judge made a date for golfing at some local country club.

(I thought judges were supposed to be like Judge Hardy in the Andy Hardy movies.)

When Gary cross-examined Richard, he showed that the out-of-work actor had generated enough income to purchase two houses, put up $42,000 to build a swimming pool, buy a Honda motorcycle, take a female companion on a vacation to Mexico and Europe, enroll one daughter in an expensive private school, pay $8000 for her horse, plus $400 per month for stable bills, pay for riding lessons and the vet and lease a Volkswagen diesel Rabbit for her.

Though Gary stressed that I had given money from the government's easement on my land to Richard, the judge decided that this was not an investment in my husband's career, but only a loan without an IOU, to be interpreted legally as a gift. How many wives who gave money to help their husbands would insist upon a promissory note?

Gary brought up the fact that Richard, without my knowledge, had borrowed against the cash surrender value of his life insurance policy, a policy that I had paid for with my own private funds; that he had closed out a New York bank account and transferred the funds into a secret account in Brentwood; and that from the date of Richard's deposition, Gary had no accounting of these funds. Richard claimed that he had spent $21,500 to pay community debts, yet still had no evidence to present at trial.

Judge Shafer glared scornfully at Richard, "Don't you have books or receipts for any of this?"

Scratching his head, Richard answered, "Of course I have paperwork as proof."

"Well, where is it?"

Richard held up an old yellow manila envelope, the same kind he used to mail his glossy photos. As he did so, loose papers slipped through a tear in the bottom, scattering hither and yon.

Buter grabbed his head and went to the rear of the court, cursing to himself, "What did I do to deserve this?"

The judge leaned over his desk staring at the mess of papers on the floor. "Mr. Forest, how do you expect me to examine this disorder?"

Shrugging, Richard said helplessly, "It's tube city, folks. We're all going down the tubes here."

The judge checked the time and decided that he had had enough, and since it was 4:30 in the afternoon, we should adjourn until the morning. Gary and I left Department Seven together. We rode the escalator to the street. He said sympathetically, "If you were married to just another businessman, the judge would not have spent this much time hearing our case. He's obviously impressed by actors. I've decided that you better contact your expert witnesses for the hearing tomorrow. Make sure they can testify as to your talents as a screenwriter. Have them call me tonight as soon as possible. We're going to have to convince the judge that you're pursuing a viable career as a screenwriter or whatever. Don't forget to bring a screenplay, too. I may need it as evidence."

"I feel like I'm on trial for murder."

"It's not much different. If you were a murderess, the procedure would be pretty much the same."

At the street level, Gary and I separated. Within a few minutes, I had my Chevette out of the parking lot and onto Hill Street. I drove to Wilshire Boulevard where I stopped at a traffic light. Pulling up beside me at the same light was Richard on his Honda motorcycle. In his helmet, goggles and leather jacket, he looked like a member of Hell's Angels. His jaw was clenched as he concentrated on the red light, seemingly oblivious to everything around him.

Keeping my composure, I rolled down the window. "Richard! May an asteroid fall out of the sky and strike you dead!"

Pretending not to notice me, he flinched, then revved the engine as if to drown out anything I might say. I was undeterred. I wanted to sound as sophisticated as Noël Coward as I shouted, "Liar! Liar! Pants on fire!"

The signal changed to green, and he roared off.

"Remember what happened to Pinocchio! You'll ruin your Barrymore profile!" I wanted to ram him with my Chevette, but it was no match for a speeding motorcycle.

"When you think about it, what is acting but lying?
When I was small, I lied all the time. I like to
think I was just practicing my profession."

– Sir Laurence Olivier

Chapter Six

At my arrival for day two at the Superior Court, I brought my houseguest, Joy McGinnis, who had arrived the previous night. Joy, also a former actress, lived in our old apartment building on 110th Street in Manhattan. A year before, she had been a veteran of her own heartbreaking divorce. She had arranged her summer vacation to spend a couple of days with me after a cross-country tour. It had been virtually impossible to contact Joy, to warn her that after many legal continuances, her visit with me would coincide with my divorce trial. Here she had planned to tour Disneyland, and the Getty Museum, and now found herself traipsing through the hallowed halls of a divorce court.

Outside Department Seven, Judge Shafer's domain, Joy and I bumped into a waiting Richard who, looking like an imitation of Bert Lahr in a burlesque show, did a triple-take upon seeing our ex-New York neighbor. Richard blurted out, "Joy! What are you doing here? Are you here as a character witness or something? Are you going to testify against me?'

"Really, Richard," she replied, "I'm not here to testify against you. I'm here to be supportive of Candace."

The three of us entered the courtroom. Richard and I took our places again at a long table before His Honor as the two attorneys joined us. Soon Richard took the stand to resume his testimony.

I turned to acknowledge Joy, who was sitting in the back of the courtroom. Come wintertime, this event would be wonderful fodder for her New York cocktail parties. She gave me a slight wave of encouragement. To my consternation, I noticed that there were several other spectators. A couple of them I recognized from the day before. One was an elderly gentleman with a cane across his knee. He had a continually bemused look. When he saw that I was staring at him, he tipped his baseball cap as if to show he was cheering for my side. I did a quick head count of the house, as they say, and realized that if this were an off-Broadway show, we would have a hit on our hands.

I nudged Gary. "We have an audience! Why are these people here? Who gave them permission to attend my divorce hearing?"

Gary replied, "Our American justice system allows citizens to attend trials."

The gathering of American citizens suggested a show business atmosphere, rather like the days when folks in the Old West showed up to witness a county hanging. Only the bailiff appeared totally bored as he sat at a desk with one foot perched on an opened drawer while reading the *Los Angeles Times.*

Judge Shafer's courtroom was a clone of all the others off a long hallway. The room was bleak, with gray institutional walls and without one portal of light to remind us we were in sunny California. The air smelled of the staleness of recycled air-conditioning.

On the witness stand, Richard's expression seemed impassive, conveying the solemnity of an accused man who knows he is the righteous one. I had seen this look, this posture of rigid grace many times. In fact, for the better part of one year, Richard starred on CBS's *Young Doctor Malone*, portraying a resident doctor involved in an adulterous affair with his patient's wife. In a great climactic scene Richard had pushed his patient in a wheelchair off the roof of the hospital. The TV ratings for the murder trial saved the show from being canceled that year.

Gary resumed questioning Richard about my inheritance, which he had used to purchase the brand new Dodge Van. Although the judge now said he considered the funds I provided as a gift to my husband, Gary wanted to include this vehicle as part of our community property.

Richard slid his hand through his hair as if he could not believe the insolence of my attorney. "I'm an out-of-work actor. Because of the worst SAG strike in history, I have no means of keeping Kentucky Fried Chicken on the table for my children." Then he held his palms upward as he gazed out at his captive audience, his old and possibly new fans. As though they were the jury, he pleaded, "My only other vocation is that I'm a scuba teacher, a NAUI-certified instructor. During this long stretch of unemployment, I've been giving diving lessons. Of course, this is freelance work. It's not even as steady as part-time, but I still need this van to carry scuba tanks for my classes!"

I thought back to last year in New York, when Richard called from California to say he had bought a van. I was appalled. At the time, he explained that staying with his dowager great-aunt in Pasadena was becoming unbearable. "Honey, you know how ornery Aunt Dorothy can be. It's fuckin' hell commuting from Pasadena to LA on the freeways during rush hours–pure torture. That's the time of day I meet casting directors. With the van, I can camp out near the beach at night."

"Oh, Richard, you could be mugged, robbed. My God, you're in the land of the Manson family."

"Sweetheart, don't worry. I'm careful. I always park within sight of other tourists' trailers. And you know how therapeutic the sound of the ocean is for me. The pounding surf helps me sleep at night. At the beach, I don't have to put up with Aunt Dorothy. Her nagging upsets my ulcer, and I can feel the old blood pressure rising."

I remembered how choked up I felt as Richard described the loneliness of the nights he spent cramped in a borrowed sleeping bag in the back of the van; the hardship of washing out his drip-dry shirts and shorts in public restrooms; the way he would hang his dripping laundry on the door handles and radio antennae in hopes that the underwear would dry in the ocean breeze. "Often, honey, the morning dew settles in, and I just have to drive to auditions in wet clothing."

The idea of my actor-husband in damp underwear and pants meeting producers after a night spent in a sleeping bag nearly tore me apart. My living alone in New York with our two young daughters was nothing compared to the sacrifices my husband was making to stake out a Hollywood career that would better our lives. Many days, I would miss him so much. I tried to call his private phone in his aunt's house. He was never there. It seemed impossible to reach him anymore. How does one call a public beach at midnight?

As I listened to Richard tell the judge why the van was so important for his livelihood as a scuba teacher, I wished I could have driven it through the courtroom. After moving to Beverly Hills, I had finally gotten a glimpse of this van with its blue psychedelic panels, which matched the blue-and-black shag rug on the inside. There was a wet-bar beside a couch that opened into a bed with just enough room for a couple, which I later learned Richard had used for himself and his nymphet, the USC student librarian.

When you consider it, a van with a wet-bar and pull-out bed is a perfect place to carry on an illicit love affair. No one can spy on you through the dark-tinted windows. There's no telephone or answering machine to interrupt lovers, no clues from credit card slips bearing a motel's name, no unexplained cash withdrawals from checking accounts.

I had no idea that the entire winter Richard was secretly seeing Meredith, secretly sleeping with her or rather screwing her in his new love-wagon at the beach bought with my inheritance. I would never have suspected that a young girl could have found Richard so irresistible that she would be willing to sleep with him in a van parked on a public beach. Did she wash out her undies at the local bathhouse, then hang her bras to dry on the van's radio antennae, too? I tried to imagine what it must have looked like to have his and her underwear blowing in the sea breeze as innocently as a ship's pennant.

My father must be rolling over in the grave, cursing in his father-knows-best voice, "Jesus Christ, pal! From the day you married that actor, he never fooled me with that cockamamie story about some Chinaman losing his laundry. You should have listened to me, Kansas. I warned you never to trust a man who doesn't wear an undershirt!"

Then I heard my name called. It was my turn to take the stand. I felt a kind of panic and anxiety accompanied by a visceral queasiness. This was not supposed to be my life. Somewhere in the world, someone else was living the life I should have led. Although, my attorney had prepared me for this horrific moment I still felt unrehearsed and shaky as I took the oath.

I looked over at Richard's impassive face with his eyes shamefully downcast as if he knew he was committing the ultimate betrayal. I wanted to cry out to him, "Richard! How could you not love me after twenty years? Is it because I'm middle-aged now? Is it because I sometimes slept in curlers and long flannel gowns? Or was it that Christmas when I was too tired to bake the traditional apple pie and bought petit-fours instead? You were so furious, you refused to speak to me as I served oysters-on-the-half-shell, turkey with sage dressing, mashed potatoes and fresh green beans plus cranberry bread. Or maybe it was the opening night party at Sardi's as we waited for the reviews for the Broadway play *But Seriously,* in which you had your first co-starring part with Tom Poston and Richard Dreyfuss. I drank two Bloody Marys on an empty stomach, and later I was in the ladies' room, puking up my guts, which meant I wasn't at your side when the producer read aloud that the critics panned the play. He announced that your opening night just became the closing night. Or maybe it's because you're just plain crazy. Otherwise, you would understand that no girl in your life can stay twenty-two forever."

I realized that love is not like a leaky faucet. I can't turn it off at will, can't stop loving that man who had been an important part of my life for twenty years. Richard was like a casting director when he tells you that you're over the hill, too old to play the role of the wife any more. As an actress, you've been replaced by younger and prettier flesh. The heartbreaking question is, "How do I survive the pain, the loss of love, the loss of family?"

Richard never once raised his eyes, but kept them glued to the prim court reporter as his attorney grilled me. Irwin Buter sneered at my past career as an actress and claimed I was too old to pursue that profession or anything else in the arts. However, he seemed to believe I was the right age to work as a sales girl at the May Company, or to be a car hop at Dolores's Drive-In or to drive a taxicab in Los Angeles. I couldn't recall ever noticing a female cab driver, but that made no difference to Buter.

"Mrs. Forest, have you ever written anything that sold?"

"So far--not yet."

"Well, what makes you believe that your screenplays are any good?" Buter's question did not conceal his contempt for me.

"The merits or talents of a writer are not always rewarded by a quick sale. Take Emily Dickinson. During her lifetime, she only sold two poems out of the hundreds she wrote."

"You think you're as good as Emily Dickinson?" Buter's question was really a sarcastic statement.

"I don't know yet. Only time will tell."

Judge Shafer turned to me. "I didn't know Emily only sold two poems. That a fact?"

"Yes, your Honor." I had no idea why this poetess flashed through my mind at that very minute, only Freud would understand, as I'm not a writer who even dabbles in poetry in any form.

Buter attacked my acting ability as an actress, by trying to show the court that my salary in the 1960s revealed a meaningless career. He laughed at the figures of $175 a week in repertory theater, even though I interjected that Richard was only making thirty-five dollars a week as a waiter. There was also the five hundred dollars a week for my tour in *A Streetcar Named Desire.* I emphasized that, at the time, it seemed to be a small fortune to my husband and me. I attempted to explain that this salary translated to about $1500 per week in the 1980s.

An hour later, Gary began calling my three expert witnesses, who had waited patiently in the hallway. At Buter's request they had been asked to sit outside instead of in the courtroom so that they would not be influenced by any of the testimony. First came a Hollywood producer, who testified that he considered my screenplay to be the best script since *Ben-Hur*.

Next was a story editor from a small production company, and she echoed the producer about my talents, and explained why she believed I should continue a career in the entertainment industry.

My last witness was my friend Gertrude Walker. The judge seemed rather intrigued by her as she peered up at him from under a black picture-frame hat. Her thick lenses magnified her soulful brown eyes, making them appear twice as large, and Gertrude twice as saintly. One would never guess that this senior citizen claimed that if her past love affairs were laid out body to body, the carnage would stretch from the hills of Beverly to the hills of Hollywood. She often said, "I've done everything twice and hated it."

When asked to state her name, she said, "Walker."

The judge asked, "As in Nancy?" referring to the comedienne Nancy Walker.

"As in Johnnie," Gertrude snapped back.

The judge fell in love. He leaned toward her. "Would I have seen any of your movies?"

"Well, your Honor," Gertrude said with a slight edge of modesty in her baritone, "I wrote *The Damned Don't Cry* for Joan Crawford. It was the first film ever to be done about Virginia Hill and Bugsy Siegel."

The judge almost applauded. "Did you ever meet Virginia Hill?"

"Several times, your Honor. I used to sneak away to her hiding place in the desert. We were both threatened by the mob. I changed my phone number so often I couldn't remember it. The studio hired bodyguards while I was in my office on the lot."

The judge went on. "What about Bugsy?"

"Had dinner with him several times on the Strip. What charisma! Quite handsome and a better dresser than Cary Grant. Bugsy had the most vivid blue eyes. He could charm the pants off anyone. I told Virginia that he could have parked his shoes under my bed any time."

Richard and Buter glared at her and the judge. I could tell from their reaction that they could barely believe a temporary ceasefire had been declared, so that the judge could listen to inside gossip about Hollywood. He asked her about Garbo. Gertrude had interviewed her for Photoplay magazine. After more urging by the judge, she also told him that one of her screenplays had been optioned by Bette Davis and, later, Humphrey Bogart.

By now, Buter was pacing at the side of the room and emitting tiny snorts like a bull impaled with a picador's lance. Richard, his face drained of color, rapped his fingers impatiently on the table. The only person who was smiling, along with the judge, was my legal advocate.

Indicating me, the judge asked her, "Do you think she's talented?"

Gertrude smiled at him. "Your Honor, she could be another Edna Ferber, another Anita Loos. But a writer needs time to develop. It would be a criminal waste of Candy's talents if she were forced to spend that precious time as a waitress or a shop girl."

The judge glanced at me with renewed appreciation. Then he jotted down some mysterious notes on a pad in front of him.

At last, the judge, straightening up, excused Gertrude. As she left the stand and proceeded up the aisle, he called out to her. "I have a great idea for a book. I could use a collaborator. Would you be interested?"

"Of course, your Honor. Just give me a jingle any time. I'm in the Beverly Hills directory." She flashed him a smile that showed off her $10,000 capped teeth, then tried not to totter on her three-inch heels, which she had worn out of respect for me. Usually, she wore an old pair of Keds.

After Gertrude's testimony, I was optimistic for the first time since the trial began. Gary whispered to me that Gertrude was a terrific witness. If this were a play, an audience would have burst into applause at her exit.

The judge declared a short recess while he retired to his chambers. Gary thought that we would soon receive our judgment and said that His Honor had probably made up his mind yesterday after the first forty-five minutes of the trial.

In half an hour, we were called back and resumed our positions in the trenches. Judge Shafer said, "The Court finds that irreconcilable differences exist, which have caused the irremediable breakdown of the marriage."

Richard was nodding as though to encourage the judge to continue in the same manner.

The judge pronounced, "An interlocutory judgment of dissolution of the marriage is granted."

More nods from Richard as his breathing became heavier. We could hear him hyperventilating. The judge went on, dividing up our paltry household goods, with Richard keeping the new van. Then the judge added, "The Petitioner's future has got too many problems. His career could end at any time. Who knows what can happen in show business? So with relation to Respondent's support, $1250 a month for two years, then reduced to $650 a month until she remarries or he dies."

Richard lurched forward in his chair, his hands flung to his throat as if he were about to strangle himself. I was thrilled at this small amount, better than what I anticipated. Buter jumped to his feet with a question about the legal fees. At the mention of fees, Gary rose, too.

"His contributive share is going to be $3000, payable at the rate of $300 a month on the first."

"But your honor," Gary protested, "her bill is now $10,000. She's not working. She has only forty-six dollars in her checking account."

Going back to my fifth grade math, I calculated that when I first came to court I was forty-six dollars ahead in my checking account. Subtracting Richard's share of my bill meant I was now seven thousand dollars in debt! In my entire lifetime, I had never bought anything on credit, had never owed any amount this exorbitant. Had I won the battle and lost the war? The happiness at the victory of being granted support was short-lived with the news of what I now owed my attorney. The first important lesson in jurisprudence was struck home. No matter which side prevails, it is the attorneys who actually win.

Ignoring Gary's plea, the judge stated, "Joint legal custody of the minor child is awarded to both parties as she's fourteen, but the older one is seventeen so I won't bother about her, as she soon will be eighteen. Since the children are living with the father, I award physical custody to Petitioner with rights of reasonable visitation to Respondent. The two of them must confer on all decisions regarding the daughters."

In a matter of minutes, we were leaving the court. Joy and I joined Gary on the sidewalk. He said to me that he would prepare the proposed decree, and that after two years, I had the right to modify the step-down to $650. "Believe me, by that time you'll be remarried and won't remember all this shit."

"Gary, after what I've been through with this actor, there is no man rich enough to sacrifice my liberty for."

My mouth was so dry, my lips stuck together. I wanted to ask about the seven thousand dollar bill, but before I was able to speak again, Gary had darted across the street to the parking lot. Lawyers seem to have a sixth sense when it comes to that moment a client wants to discuss a reduction of legal fees.

My advocate, my knight in shining armor, once said that there are some clients who are and will always be just clients. But I was different, he said. He thought of me as a dear friend. What does friendship with a lawyer really mean? Do we ever do lunch? Do we chat once a week to catch up on old times? Am I ever invited to his house for a barbecue, to meet his wife, three children and shaggy dog? Joy and I both agreed that a lawyer's idea of friendship lasts as long as his retainer. After that's gone, and there's no more money in the till, the clerical staff never again offers you even a glass of water.

Early that evening, Joy, Gertrude and I went through the classified ads, searching for a more affordable place than my apartment in Beverly Hills. The irony was not lost on us that Richard had purposely moved me from a rent-controlled New York apartment to a place in California that he knew I could never afford to keep by myself.

We sat around my dining room table as the setting sun dropped behind the Beverly Hills Tennis Club. I had grown fond of this apartment that overlooked the alley and the tennis courts. From my windows, I felt as if I had a balcony seat for the celebrity tennis matches. I had often seen Johnny Carson play (not bad), Walter Matthau (so-so), Neil Simon (poor). One could forgive Simon because he grew up on the sidewalks of Brooklyn, where the closest thing to tennis was stickball that the kids played in the streets. However, he made a lousy neighbor. I had often run into him while walking the family terrier. My "hi there" or "good afternoon," had been met with a scowl, shoulders hunched, as he made a wide circle around me and the pet before ducking into the club.

Returning to my two friends, I said, "Since the judge gave us joint custody but with Richard getting physical custody of Tina, what will people think? They're going to wonder if I was a bad mother, aren't they?"

"Your friends know better, and who cares what your enemies think?" Gertrude said. Then she added, "Deep down, your husband is very shallow."

Joy said, "Look at it this way: This is the first time you've had any freedom to yourself since those girls were born. Let Richard find out what it's like dealing with teenagers. Besides, you can't compete with Santa Claus who owns a house with a swimming pool, gives each girl her own room for the first time. Now he's even given Jennifer a new car."

There was a great deal of truth in what Joy said. As much as I wanted my daughters to live with me, they would never consent or leave all the perks that came with Richard's new house.

"Joy's right," Gertrude said. "Put your energy where it belongs–into your career. You have two years to become rich and famous. Why don't you dust off your tap shoes? Maybe go back to acting."

"I always loved your screenplay," Joy said. "I think you should continue writing, develop it into a novel."

Gertrude chimed in, "If she wrote one page a day, then in two years she would have 730 pages." Her penciled eyebrows rose, making her eyes look like a wise owl's.

We were interrupted by the phone. I answered it and, of all people, it was Richard. "You'd better find a job. Better do what the court says. Get rehabilitated!"

I slammed the receiver down as my friends looked at me with curiosity. "Guess who that was? Can you believe that Richard was mimicking his attorney by using that obnoxious phrase, 'get rehabilitated?' How am I supposed to do that?"

"Take a lover," Joy said.

"Take a much younger and richer lover," Gertrude said, grinning at the suggestion.

To which I thought–well, now, maybe...

"Have patience with the jealousies and petulances of actors for their hour is their eternity."

– Richard Garnett

Chapter Seven

My girlfriends were adamant that I find a new man. There had to be a few good men left in the world. If only I were Jewish, they insisted, every synagogue has singles parties that are better than any matchmaking service. Maybe I could crash a Jewish event.

In the meantime, Richard called me with a barrage of threats. "Get rehabilitated! The court ordered you to get rehabilitated!"

My girlfriends chorused back: "Forget him. Get a lover!"

Between my friends and Richard, I decided to begin my rehabilitation by looking up an old boyfriend. I read in *Variety* that he was in Los Angeles shooting a TV pilot.

THE FORMER FLAME

Before Richard entered my life, I dated another actor, Hal, whom I met when we were both doing plays at the Cape Cod Playhouse in Massachusetts. It was easy to track him down. He suggested that we have lunch together at the Polo Lounge. If anyone has ever read a Jackie Collins novel, she has described this place at the Beverly Hills Hotel ad nauseam. It's the watering hole for her hookers, gigolos, studs, housewives, husbands and all the rest of her dopey characters traipsing in and out of the Polo Lounge. The hotel's bungalows are filled with divorcées who don't want their indiscretions publicized. The young pool attendants look as handsome and virile as any leading man even though their uniforms are flamingo pink T-shirts with nurse-white shorts.

At the entrance of the Polo Lounge, I spotted Hal right away as he was seated in the "Marilyn Monroe booth" known to be her favorite for it faced the doorway and anyone who entered. Hal rose and tendered an ingratiating smile as he stretched out his arms to me. "Candace! Candace, how are you after all these years? You're still a beauty. You ought to be in the movies."

"Well, put me in one. I won't stop you." I laughed. The air reeked of Calvin Klein's cologne. I fought back the desire to sneeze as I put a chaste kiss on his cheek. In the passing years Hal had lost his waistline and most of his hair, all of which he said made directors cast him as grandfathers. "Christ, the last TV show I played the leading lady's father. I was only a year older than she was."

I knew what an ego blow this meant to Hal, who was actually just forty-eight years old. "At least you're a working actor, you're—"

He interrupted, "What'd ya like to drink?" He signaled to a waiter.

"A mint frappé." This is the safest alcohol drink a girl can order since it's mostly slushed ice.

"A mint frappé for the lady," Hal said to the waiter, then pointed to his glass. "Make this a double."

The waiter bowed then removed a couple of empty glasses. It seemed that before I had arrived, Hal had time to enjoy himself. From my sniff test, he was into vodka. This was a taste he hadn't cultivated when I first met him in summer stock. As a struggling young actor his drink of choice was a beer to go along with a meal of pretzels.

However, tonight I decided to see Hal a few times as if to rekindle some of the old magic. But I soon learned that he started every morning with a vodka cocktail, claiming it was a real eye-opener. By noon his tongue was slurring and, "Candace, Candace," turned into, "Constance, Constance," then it dissolved into, "Connie–Connie, where art thou?" He broke into tearful sobs as Connie was the name of his last wife. "You'll never guess what she did. She went to her high school reunion in Idaho. Ran into her old boyfriend and fell in love with him all over again. She never came back, wanted to spend her life in Idaho with her soulmate. Maybe you should go to a high school reunion. Maybe you'll fall in love, too."

"Sorry, Hal, been there, done that. No such luck."

A couple of months later after our Polo Lounge meeting, we were enjoying lunch when Hal's agent called to tell him that his TV pilot was not picked up by the networks. It was a crushing blow that even vodka couldn't cure.

"I'm so sorry, Hal. There'll be other roles."

"Yeah, God closes one door so that a window opens. Somethin' like that. Right, Constance?" His words trailed off into a whimper. He was so drunk he didn't even realize his own drunkenness. The poignancy and attraction I felt for him slipped away with each glass of vodka he poured himself.

He claimed the letdown of what had been a dazzling career was driving him crazy. Friends attributed his madness to the effects of alcohol. However, I soon learned his apparent bouts of insanity came from his premature baldness. He bought every hair preparation that could possibly restore, regrow, paint or whatever that was known to mankind. This was new for me. Richard's thick, wavy hair was one of his attributes. He had even been reviewed as that hirsute actor. (That made us run to the dictionary to find out if hirsute was okay or had he been panned.)

Hal would part his hair on the far side of his head in order to comb it back across his bald pate. This attempt at camouflage didn't fool anyone. If he stood in the wind the wrong way, the ends of his hair would fan up like a peacock's tail.

For a while we dined at Chasen's or the Bistro Gardens until his secretary informed him he was in danger of going broke. From then on, his best offer was a box of popcorn for dinner and a movie. His budget still seemed to allow him to slip in a few bottles of vodka. He was incapable of understanding my complaints since I was really a teetotaler.

"Hal, I don't really like men who drink. They look weak. I like strong men."

"What are ya talking about, Constance? I'm strong. Feel this!" His tone was pathetic as he flexed his arm but it fell to his side like a broken appendage.

"That's not what I meant." I said dispassionately.

"Connie, Connie, Connie, Candy, come over here, gimme a kiss." He screwed up his face into a silly grin.

I did not answer. If he could look into a mirror to see his bloodshot, swollen eyes or his lips trembling as he sipped his next drink, he would understand my feelings of disgust. Every redeeming quality he used to have in his youth was now gone. It was time for my rehabilitation to move onward. I simply could not be entangled with a drunk actor after spending twenty years with an actor who was a serial cheater.

THE YOUNGER MAN

My divorce lawyer convinced me to try to have fun for a change. He suggested, "You must go to the Coronet Theatre on LaCienega Drive. There's a musical playing to small but sold-out houses. You'll enjoy it." I agreed, and it was entertaining. At the end of the show, members of the audience wandered into a bar next door. Not wanting to go back to my empty apartment, I went along with the crowd. After ordering my usual, a mint frappé, I looked around and locked eyes with Michael, who was strumming a guitar. Before I could ask, "What song are you playing?" He was at my side serenading me. He was extraordinarily handsome if a bit on the short side. His green eyes were gleaming, and his singing was obviously professional.

I asked, "Are you a performer, a musician, an actor?"

"I'm all of those–and more." He winked as he strummed his guitar and waited for my approval.

"You're very good. Do you appear in cabarets?"

He shook his head no and smiled. "I was just on Broadway in *Grease.* I quit to come to Los Angeles. I wanna be in the movies."

"Do you have an agent here?"

"I'm signed with William Morris." He answered very impressed with himself.

"Congratulations." I did not want to burst his Broadway bubble by telling him that the William Morris Agency can be the death of a young actor's career. It cost them nothing to sign up young thespians and leave them on a shelf so as not to compete with their stable of rising stars.

Gradually the noise in the bar receded as people left. We were left alone. We couldn't stop staring at each other. The bartender dimmed the lights to a pale orange glow. We were cast in a luminous aura as the shadows shimmered across the burnished bar top. We were falling head over heels with infatuation against this fake background.

How much younger was he? Maybe ten years, maybe fifteen and, god forbid, maybe twenty! Every word, every phrase, every interplay, he gave no hint as to his real age. How relative was age anyway? He reminded me so much of a very young Richard before he became jaded. Michael had the enthusiasm, the energy and the same dreams of eventual stardom as any other budding actor.

Michael and I spent the next day together, the following week and the following months. In the mornings he would demonstrate his T'ai Chi exercises. After that he would meditate while doing yoga. At first I did not understand what this Oriental fascination meant to his generation who were considered to be leftover flower children from the sixties. I decided it did for him what Freudian analysis had done for my peers.

In the afternoons Michael would check with his answering service. Surely by now the William Morris Agents would have left word about an audition, an appointment, an anything.

"No one called," he said as if there were an explanation.

I couldn't placate him as this kind of dutiful effort was worn out years ago. We went to a garden restaurant for lunch. The setting was made for romance but that was quickly set aside when he said, "I've been living for months on unemployment, but my checks stop in two weeks." He leaned across the table, running a hand through his hair as he gazed longingly into my eyes. He said in almost a whisper, "Candace, I don't know what I'll do."

His question hung in the air. It was like a bad phonograph record that I've heard too many times. Was it possible that he thought I was a wealthy divorcée from Beverly Hills? He had no idea of how tenuous my lifestyle was, that at any moment it could be swept away by Richard and his lawyers.

The waiter approached us. I stared at the menu as though I couldn't make up my mind. "I'll have a glass of water and a plate of plain spaghetti."

Michael said, "I'll have water, too, and an order of plain toast."

The waiter gave a sigh of irritation. He knew there would not be much of a tip. Who but an unemployed actor would order food that was less than prison fare?

Another dismal week passed for him. Michael couldn't understand why a big, international agency like William Morris couldn't find him a job in anything, an audition for anything, even a walk-on in anything.

"If I go to New York, maybe I might get my part back in *Grease*. If I hang around LA, I'll run out of money. Tomorrow's my last unemployment check." There was real despair in his voice.

This was like a posthumous chord struck in my heart. He looked pathetic in his worn-out shirt, his faded jeans, his unkempt hair, his silly guitar at his side. I wanted to tell him that if he had taken all the hours of yoga, T'ai Chi, strumming his out-of-tune guitar, and calling his agent and, instead, used the time to knock on casting directors' doors, showcasing in workshops and so forth, he might have found work as an actor after all.

"Oh, Candace, I guess we have to say goodbye."

"I guess we do, dear."

Where was the reckless, romantic, John Travolta-like man whom I thought swept me off my feet a few weeks ago? I tried to recapture the feelings of romance but they eluded me. Mentally I had dressed him up like a store mannequin. Without his props, he was empty, vain like most self-involved actors.

"Candace, did you know they're showing *The Graduate* on TV tonight? That's the movie with Dustin Hoffman and Anne Bancroft."

"Really?."

"Kinda reminds me of our affair."

I flinched. I didn't consider myself quite old enough to look like his mother.

"Why do you look so unhappy? I think it's terrific to be compared to Anne Bancroft."

He held my hand in his damp one like a schoolboy as he said, "Will you write to me?"

"I'm not good at correspondence."

"Do you think we will ever see each other again?"

"Well, Michael, we may meet some day, but I don't think we will ever 'see' each other again."

THE OLDER MAN

It was obvious that developing relationships was a waste of time. My real purpose was to sell a screenplay I had written. This was *Dakota Ashes* a story of star-crossed young lovers set against the Dust Bowl days (the early thirties) in a small Midwestern town. A friend introduced me to a producer who was looking for a project. He was quite enthusiastic. "I have a connection with William Morris. The vice-president is an old friend of mine. We lunch together at the Friar's Club. He knows a good script when he sees it. He's not like those kids in the agency who think they're agents. Hell, they only got jobs because their fathers were in the business."

The producer made an appointment for me to call the vice-president of William Morris. This is the agency I can't stand. The vice-president answered the phone with some charm. "I've read your wonderful screenplay, *Dakota Ashes*. It reminded me so much of the filmmaker Renoir. The depth, the pathos, the beauty...."

I kept waiting for the "but."

As if on cue, the vice-president said, "*But*, I already have three love stories about Sitting Bull, and I haven't been able to sell one of them."

"Ah, sir, there are no Indians in my screenplay."

The phone went dead. I waited in silence for a few more uncomfortable moments when I heard some dull stammering: "What–what did you say–what–what was the name of your script?"

"Never mind." I hung up.

A new literary agent insisted that I meet a director who had read my script. A meeting was set up at my favorite restaurant, Joe Allen in West Hollywood. He was waiting for me at a table in the corner. I waved to him, "Hi, Mr. Mann."

"Please, call me Danny."

Daniel Mann had just finished directing for television *Playing for Time* with Vanessa Redgrave. He was known as a woman's director because three of his actresses had won Academy Awards: Shirley Booth in *Come Back Little Sheba*, Anna Magnani in *The Rose Tattoo* and Elizabeth Taylor in *BUtterfield 8*. His film credits were endless. He was small in stature with a sound of Brooklyn in his voice but when he said, "Your script is like William Inge crossed with Tennessee Williams...both of whom I know very well," he became very tall, his pale blue eyes as stunning as Paul Newman's.

Years earlier, during the McCarthy hearings, and at the time he taught acting at the Actors Lab, he was almost caught in the web of Hollywood's blacklist. He heard that the FBI was investigating him by enrolling secretly in his class. He said to them, "If anyone here is a member of the FBI, all I ask is that you're good actors."

He explained that there was now another form of blacklist and that was age discrimination. He was on the threshold of seventy and, though he felt he was at the top of his game, he was passed over for younger, inexperienced directors.

There was a chance for his comeback. A team of Israeli men wanted to invest in movies with him directing. Rent had been paid on a Sunset Boulevard office. Phones were installed. The first movie he wanted to direct was mine, *Dakota Ashes*. He said that Shirley MacLaine had a book she wanted adapted for film. He considered that as his second project for this new company.

Many meetings took place where people talk a lot and shake hands enthusiastically. It was quite a heady experience for me meeting Israeli movie backers.. A movie sale would rescue me from the jaws of divorce lawyers. Just as the second month's rent came due for the Sunset office, Danny received an international call from a French banker. It seems that this Israeli team defrauded not one but ten banks out of money. They were now fugitives on the lam in Europe. Danny asked the French banker why he was informing him, a movie director living in Malibu. The banker said that their detectives traced the man from Israel, who used Danny's stolen credit card number at a Parisian hotel and restaurant.

As quickly as the dream of producing *Dakota Ashes* began, it ended. This meant I was back to square one. I have always been attracted to brilliant, talented men. Danny was no exception. However, there was the problem of age as he was almost thirty years older than I was. Most of the week he liked to breakfast at a delicatessen in Beverly Hills. Before his usual bagel and lox arrived, he would empty an envelope of pills on the table, saying, “If I didn’t take these, I’d be dead. These pills keep me alive.”

He liked to eat at hospital hours, breakfast at 6 a.m. and dinner at 5:30 p.m. More than once, he looked at me regretfully and said, “If only I were fifty again.”

Robert Redford announced that he was starting Sundance Institute in Utah to develop new writers who weren’t part of the Hollywood scene. The guidelines stated that a writer could bring a team if his or her screenplay was chosen.

“Danny, want to be my team? If I’m chosen, all our expenses are paid to stay in Utah while we workshop my script.”

“Sure, I’ll go with you.” He gave me his résumé, which I put along with an application and the first ten pages of “Dakota Ashes” as part of my required submission.

Within a month, a letter came from Sundance requesting the entire script of “Dakota Ashes.” Early that spring there was a phone call from Salt Lake City. A voice gave me an appointment to meet with Redford’s advisor for the West Coast, who was the head of the UCLA film and theater department. I had so many mingled emotions, I didn’t know whether to shriek, cry, laugh or plan my summer wardrobe for sitting on the Utah mountaintops with Redford and Daniel Mann.

I sat in the UCLA office waiting my turn in suspense. Soon a team of four young, earnest-looking men left their meeting with the department head. A secretary nodded for me to enter.

An elderly, gray-haired man gave me a cordial smile as he said, “You’re the only applicant who filled out our form in personal handwriting.” I smiled at him helplessly as I did not know how to use a computer at this stage in my life.

"However, just five screenplays were chosen for the finals from the West Coast. I have read some others that were about farmlands in the Midwest, but yours is the best one.” He perused Danny’s résumé then said in a voice of admiration, “Why, this director has more credits than Sydney Pollack."

I knew that Pollack, a close friend of Redford’s, was going to be at Sundance this summer supervising the workshop. After a few more questions, the department head reached for my hand, squeezing it. "You’re the one I am going to recommend to Sundance."

I raced home and called my friend Gertrude, who was elated. She thought we should celebrate but I said, “I have to wait for one more letter, the last one that announces I’ve been selected. But with UCLA’s recommendation, my chance looks pretty good.”

Two weeks later, *the* letter arrived. I tore open the envelope. It was a great rejection letter thanking and praising me at the same time. The powers that be at Sundance hoped that next year I would try again. If I did a rewrite of “Dakota Ashes,” I could think of submitting it another time. Dreams faded in this semi-tragic news. The thought of registering at one employment agency after another instead of a trip to Utah this summer was depressing.

Danny asked me to give him a ride to a dental surgeon. He was going to have all his teeth pulled. He wore a small bridge but decided to rid himself of the remaining problem teeth.

I held his hand as the surgeon extracted the teeth one by one. I started to look at what life was like with a man old enough to be my father. Most men at this age brought a baggage of problems with pleading ex-wives, whining grown children, and being an out-of-work director was as bad as being an out-of-work actor. What was I doing here? Holding the hand of a toothless genius. I did not want to be an old man's darling or his nurse. This was not the life I was supposed to lead. As great an artist as he was did not negate the fact that he had the frailties of a senior citizen. Gertrude advised that single men that old are constantly taking pills or are serious drunks: "Don't waste what's left of your youth on old men." She was right. The infatuation ended.

THE BLIND DATE

Tina, my youngest, teenage daughter, ran into my apartment with the news, "Guess what I found you? A date with a wonderful man!"

"My dear, this sounds exciting. Tell me more."

"I delivered your rent check to the Levine Management Company. Just as I was handing it to a secretary, I saw through an open door behind her, a very attractive, middle-aged man sitting at his desk reading a paper. I asked her if that was the boss, Joe Levine. She said it was and, when I asked her if he was single, she said yes. So I walked into his office, introduced myself, and explained that I was on the lookout for a terrific guy for my mother. At that point, I took out your picture from my purse and flashed it at him. He smiled his approval. I told him that you are not the kind of woman who goes to bars or clubs to meet men. He immediately said he, too, was not the type of man who hangs out at bars. He asked how he could meet you. I suggested the cocktail lounge at the Four Season's Hotel, right here in Beverly Hills"

"What exactly does he look like?"

"He's not too tall."

"You mean he's short."

"He's not real short, maybe five-foot-eight. Mr. Levine has a great deal of gray hair and wears black-rimmed glasses, like a Cary Grant type."

"You mean he looks like a short Cary Grant?"

"Yeah, mom. But the best thing about him, he is not an actor! In fact he told me he hates to go to movies or plays. My guess is he just likes to sit around making money buying real estate."

The following night I found myself going on the first blind date of my lifetime. At least the scenery was beautiful in the Four Seasons Hotel. As I entered the lounge quite nervously, I could see a few men standing at the bar. I knew immediately, that the shortest one with silver-gray hair and glasses, smoking a cigarette must be Joe Levine. He gave me a smile of recognition so I advanced toward him. We shook hands. He offered to buy me a drink so I ordered my usual, crushed ice mint Frappè. Joe took out a piece of paper and drew a line down the middle. He handed me a pen then said, "You list on one side your favorite things, and I will do the same on the other side." I thought this was so cute and so imaginative of him. I listed: French food, music. I was about to write laws of relativistic quantum field theories, but thought better to stick with conventional things like: window-shopping, dancing, walking on the beach and other generic hobbies. Joe listed his fun ideas, and we learned we were very compatible. (What a fabulous start for a romance.)

After a couple of hours filled with many laughs, Joe asked me if I would like to join him and his two sons for dinner the following Saturday night. He explained that on the weekends, he always had his sons visit him. "I have one daughter from a previous marriage who often drops by on her way to a meeting of Alcoholic Anonymous."

By this time, I noticed that Joe had filled up an ashtray with more than a dozen burned-out cigarette butts. It was obvious he had a nicotine addiction, but I overlooked that as he seemed to be a devoted family man. So I decided it would be a nice way to get to know him better if I accepted his invitation. "Thank you, Joe. I would enjoy having dinner with you and your family next Saturday."

Tina was elated that I was going to see Joe Levine a second time. "He's so perfect for you. He's the right age. He's rich. He has manners." Then she said to me in surprise, "Do you realize that next Saturday is Valentine's Day?"

"No, what should I do about it?"

She said, "Listen mom, you have to do something special for Valentine's Day. You can't show up at his home empty-handed."

On Saturday morning of Valentine's Day, Tina and I decided we would bake homemade cookies in the shape of hearts. It took us half a day of rolling out cookie dough and baking. We made dozens of heart-shaped cookies as I reminded her that we needed to make many for his three kiddies. We covered them in red frosting. Then Tina went to the drugstore and found red wrapping paper and a couple of huge baskets. In the afternoon we decorated the baskets with the red paper and cellophane topped by bows of red ribbon. We packed the two baskets until they were almost overflowing with cookies.

"Oh, mom," Tina said, "I can't wait to hear how impressed Mr. Levine will be."

"I bet this is the first time a date has brought him home-baked cookies for Valentine's Day," I said as Tina and I carefully loaded my car with our red baskets of goodies. I turned to her, saying, "I feel a little like Red Riding Hood." We both laughed.

Joe's condo was in a very nice residence of Santa Monica. I rang the doorbell to a three-story-building and waited with the baskets under each arm. Soon Joe appeared in casual clothing, an open shirt revealing three gold chains. I really don't care for men who wear more jewelry than I do. As he came closer to me, he seemed to have shrunk a couple of inches since we met at the Four Seasons. Why would a short man wear Mexican huaraches? So unflattering and so unsexy. I slumped so I wouldn't seem so tall.

"Hi there. Come this way," he said as he opened the gate for me. I followed him, still balancing under each arm, my baskets. As he opened the front door of his condo, I stepped inside, then trying to peer through the cellophane of my baskets, I was able to maneuver more stairs, as he led the way. I was taken aback that he didn't offer to assist by carrying a basket. He seemed more interested in lighting a cigarette. Then, I saw a kitchen counter top. "Here, I brought you and the children some cookies," I offered as three boys appeared. They were around twelve; one of them was a friend who was also staying the night. They looked with indifference at the baskets, then took off somewhere. His daughter, Miranda, came into sight and politely introduced herself. She said, "I'm so sorry, I can't stay. I'm on my way to an AA Meeting." As she left, I noticed that she, too, was smoking a cigarette.

I glanced around a large living room area filled with the kind of modern furniture you might find in a doctor's office, lots of chrome and glass everywhere plus black leather couches. There were a number of original artworks, hanging here and there. The one I disliked the most was a self-portrait of Andy Warhol that covered one entire side of the dining room wall.

Joe, puffing on a cigarette, announced, "I have made dinner for the two of us."

"What about the children? Their dinner?" I asked.

"They ate a long time ago. They're downstairs, playing video games."

I noticed that Joe was a chain smoker as everywhere I glanced was an ashtray, the size of a killer dog bowl, spilling over with cigarette butts. He opened the oven and brought out a dish filled with potatoes, which he poked at with a fork, then said, "Perfect. They're done." Then he went to a balcony where a preheated grill was blazing. He tossed two small steaks on it. "This won't take long. May I pour you some wine?"

"Oh, that would be nice," I said, as he filled my glass with an inexpensive California wine. Then I added, "Is there something I can do to help here?"

"I've got it handled." He said, while lighting another cigarette. He forgot he had a burning one in an ashtray in the kitchen area.

There was no vegetable or a salad. This was a sign to me that he was not much of a cook. "What did your children eat?"

"They had Chinese food. I grabbed something at a takeout. They love to spend weekends with me as I always let them eat Chinese or Indian food."

We continued on with a very, bland conversation in which he explained how often he has to be out of town as he oversees a great deal of property. "In fact, tomorrow I have to fly to Arizona. You'd love my flying machine." He gave a short laugh and said, "Why don't you come with me?"

"I can't do that. I have a temp job."

"Ah, that's too bad," he said, then he trotted off to retrieve the steaks, plopping them on two plates. As he came back, he said, "I'll get the potatoes for us." He then added the potatoes.

We sat at a long, narrow dining room table. I faced Andy Warhol, who didn't bring anything of interest to the place, except made me wonder what his painted profile cost Joe. The potatoes were dried up and almost impossible to cut without sawing them in half with a knife. The steak was burnt to a crisp, too. I thought if only I had ketchup or a steak sauce, maybe I could find the meal more edible. Struggling to chew a bite of steak, I felt myself slipping down in my chair. To my horror, I saw my foot rising over the opposite side of the table, where Joe began to nibble on my toes. (I had no idea I was so limber.) He was getting a mouth full of Christian Dior pantyhose. I gasped! "What're you doing?!" I dropped my fork then grabbed the edge of the table so I wouldn't slide to the floor. I was amazed how quickly he had removed my shoe, and I had never felt it.

"What's the matter?" he said, shocked at my reaction as if the most natural thing to do was to nibble on a woman's toes at the dinner table. His whole countenance changed. He was insulted at what was supposed to be erotic, and I was not responding likewise to him. "Why, are you so cold?" he asked haughtily, still gripping my foot.

I squirmed helplessly. "Joe, I'm trying to eat dinner, which you so nicely fixed for me. I don't feel it is appropriate behavior for you to act this way—while we're eating—to take a hold of—please release my foot!"

He did, then he pulled himself together by saying, "I have ice cream for dessert."

"No thanks," I said, hoping he would suggest eating one of the cookies I brought for Valentine's Day. Instead, he wanted me to see some more of his artwork, which was in the balcony overlooking the living room. He lighted another cigarette as he showed me around the balcony, which had a built-in banquette that stretched the length of it. None of his modern art was that impressive. He opened albums filled with photos of his children, whom he adored. He wanted to sit close to me, leaning against my shoulder as he started to breathe heavily. He even relinquished his cigarette at this stage.

Obviously, this was going to be another uncomfortable moment between us. Then I was saved by the pitter-patter of little feet below with cries of "Where are the cookies? Can we eat them now?"

Quite annoyed at the interruption, Joe jumped to his feet, then hurried downstairs to help the boys. I ran right after him as this was a perfect excuse to get away from the balcony and the banquette couch. Joe tried not to show his annoyance that the kids grew hungry for cookies. They tore at the cellophane. I pulled apart the ribbons. I ate a cookie myself, turning to Joe, I said, "Wouldn't you like a one, too?" He shook his head, no, and lit up another cigarette instead.

Noting the time from a clock on the wall, I said, "Joe, I didn't realize it was so late. Almost ten o'clock. I have to go. I don't like to drive a long ways, at this late hour."

"Why, can't you take a taxi home?" He said, trying to sound charming.

"Oh, I can't leave my car behind in Santa Monica. I need it in the morning–for my job." Picking up my purse and jacket, I headed for the front door. He escorted me to my car, parked on the street. As I sat inside the Honda, starting the engine, he leaned through my opened window. He said, "I'd like to–like to—" For a minute, I thought he was finally going to thank me for the cookies, instead he said, "May I touch your breast?"

I stepped on the gas pedal so hard, I don't know how I avoided decapitating him. In a fury, I drove back to Beverly Hills. Once I opened my apartment door, Tina was there to greet me. "How did he like the cookies? For Valentine's day?"

"Tina, the only thing he said as I left was, may I touch your breast."

"I can't believe he'd do that. Be so disgusting!! He seemed so nice. The perfect blind date like Cary Grant. Does this mean you won't go again—on a blind date? If I fix you up?"

"Well, let me think about it. I can say this, I'll never bake cookies again. I must have looked as naive as little Red Riding Hood. Only this wolf was a chain smoker."

THE PICKUP

Weekends at The Saloon in Beverly Hills were bursting with the "singles" crowd. Lines of giddy girls formed around the tables. Men of all shapes and sizes trailed after them. There was so much laughter, chatter, coughing and singing that I strained to hear what my girlfriend Greta was telling me. She had convinced me to come tonight. "Let's go somewhere. Have fun for a change. Why sit home on Saturday night, America's date night?"

Greta was a tenured professor of acting at Cal State, Fullerton. She and I knew each other from our days as actresses at Arena Stage in Washington, D.C. She had never married. Still she had not given up hope of finding a potential mate.

Jostling through the crowd, two young men made their way to us. Luke, a long-legged guy, spoke to Greta first. I could tell from the way Greta laughed, playing with a straw in her drink and the wiggling of one foot, she was interested. Luke's friend sat next to me. "The name's Sonny," he smirked as he fingered an unlit cigar.

"And what do you do, Sonny?" It was an inane question but I didn't care. At least I didn't ask what sign he was. He was like a Troy Donahue type. His face was too tan, his hair too sun-streaked for an indoor job.

"I design jewelry," he said with a vague wave of his hand.

He was like so many men who claim professions of sales rep, marketing, realtors, entrepreneurs, careers that never were ever going to happen. Greta whispered in my ear, "I want to give this man a chance," as she nodded in Luke's direction.

Luke bent over us. "I'm house-sitting for a friend. It's a great place. I have to take care of a couple of pets. Why don't you two come with Sonny and me?"

Greta rose to her feet. "How far away is the house?"

"Just a ten-minute drive from here. Real close," Luke said, offering her his arm.

I knew that if I didn't agree to go, Greta wouldn't go either. However, if this were a chance for her to meet someone, I shouldn't be so selfish. What did a couple hours matter? The four of us walked outside. As the valet pulled up in Greta's car, I attempted to get in with her. Luke blocked my way, saying, "I'll ride with her. You ride with Sonny so he won't be alone." Luke jumped in beside Greta and, before I could protest, Greta drove off. I was left with Sonny, who pointed to an old automobile. "My car's parked at a meter."

I was conflicted. What kind of jerky name was Sonny for a real man? His car was a beat-up old Chevrolet. The jewelry design business must be really bad. I'm not that gullible. However, I didn't want to leave Greta alone with some stranger, so I got into Sonny's car.

We drove behind Greta's car for just a block when Sonny spun a quick right. He sped toward Sunset Boulevard. "Sonny, this is not the right way. Stop this car. I want to get out right now!" My protests seemed to make him drive faster. Of course there wasn't a soul walking on the sidewalk in Beverly Hills, no one I could yell to for help. Certainly, he'd have to stop for a red light, and I could jump from the car. But the light was green as he sped across Sunset Boulevard then onto another dark street. Houses became a blur as he gunned the car onto Franklin Canyon. With no street lights, the canyon road loomed ahead as if we were ascending into a black void. He never said a word. The pompous smile frozen on his face was frightening. The greatest terror I have ever felt overcame me. I was living the worst nightmare of every woman. For the first time, I felt that my life was truly in jeopardy.

In the darkness, he seemed to know his way as he drove in circles until we reached the top of the canyon's mountain. He parked the car. His lips parted in a sneer as he grunted, "You know what's going to happen, don't you?" There was no mistaking his intentions. Hanging onto my purse, I pushed open the passenger door, then leaped as far as I could. I knew from the shocked look on Sonny's face that he never thought that I would have dared to jump into unknown blackness, that I would rather fall down the side of a mountain than let him lay a hand on me.

I landed on my hands and knees in a gully. I scrambled to my feet. Despite wearing three-inch-high heels, I quickly climbed a small hill of brush and cactus. Glancing over my shoulder, I saw in the flood of the headlights that Sonny had stepped from the car and was trying to see where I went. "All right, turkey, you can come back! Come back, you turkey!" These were not words of encouragement.

I crawled inside a cluster of thorny bushes, pulling the branches about me as camouflage. I could hardly breathe at the thought that Sonny might start on foot to search for me. After about five minutes I heard his car start then drive slowly away. I knew to stay hidden. After a while, Sonny returned. I could hear him calling from his car, "Okay, turkey. I'll take you back!" He had a small spotlight attached to his car beside the driver's window. He shined this light slowly across the side of the mountain, then up and down. I flattened myself at the root of the vegetation. The light crossed a few feet over me as Sonny moved the spot back and forth.

Cautiously, he drove away with his spotlight scanning both sides of the road. Rising up, I was able to see the last vestige of light as it flickered out in the distance. Yet I waited a few more minutes, worried that Sonny might return a second time.

I began to hike along the dirt road. Far below were the lights of Los Angeles showing me which direction to go. I debated whether to take off my high heels as it was torture to walk a long distance in them. I took off the shoes, but soon put them back on as the gravel road was filled with too many rocks and pebbles.

At one place in the road it narrowed to a single lane. When I peered over the side, the drop-off was like peering down from the top of a building. If Sonny came back, I couldn't jump over the railing without falling several stories into sharp boulders strewn on the hard earth below. I'm trapped! Trapped! I ran until I started gasping. I had to reach civilization before Sonny found me.

A fork appeared in the road. Which way do I go, to the right or the left? Then it occurred to me that this area was known as Rattlesnake Canyon. In the darkness, I would be unable to spot a snake. I might step on a rattler. I started to run again, stumbled, then fell to my knees, which were bleeding. I noticed that my hands were raw and bloodied. There was an unfamiliar sharp pain inside my chest. I felt the strong palpitations. What if I had a heart attack? Who might find me in this godforsaken place? I rose shakily.

In the sliver of moonlight I spotted faraway the outlines of a ranch house and a barn. But there were no lights in the house–no sign of life. It looked like the pictures of the place where Charles Manson once lived. I chose to go the opposite way and kept running until I felt pavement underneath my feet. That was a good sign. Up ahead I saw lights coming from a couple of houses. One house had children's toys in the front yard. I raced up to the front door. I knocked and knocked.

Finally, I heard footsteps. Then someone peered through the peephole in the door. I heard her gasp, "What do you want?"

"Please, help me. I've just escaped from–I mean, could you call a taxi for me?"

The girl answered, "I'm just the babysitter. I'm so sorry I can't let you in. People have to be careful in these times."

"I understand. Please call a cab. I need to get a ride."

"Okay, I'll call a cab."

I sat on the stoop for several minutes until I saw a cab slowly approaching the house. I went to the street, flagging him down. After I was in the cab, he said, "Lady, are you in trouble?"

I caught my reflection in his rearview mirror. My wind-blown hair was upside down covering my face, which was streaked with blood and mud. The entire front of my red dress was covered with dirt and broken twigs. My shoes were torn and the heel on one was broken. No wonder I scared the babysitter.

As best I could, I explained to the cab driver what happened without looking like an idiot who accepted a ride from a stranger who turned out to be a rapist, maybe a serial killer. Once I was home, I saw my phone blinking with a message. It was Greta waiting for me at the house with Luke. She left a phone number as I was to call her immediately, which I did. As I told her about the terror I had just been put through, she was shocked. Then I heard her repeat the tale to Luke, who took the phone from her and said, "If I ever meet that bum again, I'll beat the shit out of him!"

The next day Greta called me to say that after our phone call, she went right home. She lost interest in Luke since it was his friend that took me on the midnight ride from hell. What were two women who were paragons of virtue thinking?

A year later, I was dining with a date in the same restaurant, The Saloon. Through an open door to the bar, I spotted Luke and Sonny making the rounds of single girls. Scenes of the horrific experience rushed back into my mind. I felt as if I couldn't catch my breath. I called for the manager, then I launched into the humiliating story of that dreadful night. I expected him has to throw out these two creeps. The manager replied, "Sorry, I can't do anything. If you had filed a police report, I would be able to kick them out."

I made my date leave with me by exiting through the kitchen's back door. If I ran into Sonny and Luke, I might create a scene, scream out invectives of every kind, yell a warning. Watch out for Sonny. He's a rapist!

"When man is a brute, he is the most
sensual and loathsome of all brutes–"

– Nathaniel Hawthorne

Chapter Eight

Sometimes I reflect upon the halcyon days where it never occurred to me that someday I might end up divorced. I can't help but remember Veronica Lake, a divorce veteran, and her advice. Her words haunted me as I was making appearances in divorce court.

I met her after my first year at the American Theater Wing, and before I knew Richard. I was cast in a summer package of "Idiot's Delight" with Nina Foch and Robert Webber. For those who are unfamiliar with the term "package," it means that the three of us are the starring players while the smaller parts are cast with the local actors in each theater in which the producers have booked our touring play.

It soon became clear that Robert Webber thought I was a little brainless blonde cast to entertain him offstage. Nina was pleasant toward me but rather annoyed that her leading man was on the make for me, the ingénue, whom he invited to dinner every night (instead of her).

Dining with Webber always ended with, "How many dinners is it going to cost me before you say yes?"

Our tour made it to Cincinnati when Webber buttonholed me. I pleaded, "C'mon, Robert. It's a-half-hour to curtain." His answer was to pick me up and toss me in a swimming pool. I just had my hair done. I was so furious I wanted to charge him at Actors Equity, but that is not politically possible when, as a new union member, you are in the middle of Ohio, and he is the star. The director of our play said, "If you say no to Webber, he'll hate you. If you say yes, he will still hate you. He has no affection for women as people. They're only sexual objects. Take my advice for the rest of the tour, keep saying no."

By the time we arrived in Hinsdale, Illinois, Foch and Webber weren't speaking to me. Webber would try to make me feel worse at rehearsals by coming over to Foch whenever I was near. He whispered just loud enough for my benefit, "Hey, Nina, I've rented a car. After the show, let's go into Chicago. We can see some hot nightclubs. I know a great restaurant for us."

During rehearsals at the Hinsdale Theater, I asked the stage manager if he knew of a place for me to stay that was near the theater. I didn't want to be at the same motel as Webber and Foch. The stage manager made a phone call on my behalf. "I found you a room with our show's current star. She's rented a house for her cast. It's just two blocks away."

He drove me to a typical Midwestern two-story house with a big yard and a porch wrapped around it. Waiting behind the screen door was a petite woman in Bermuda shorts. As I took my suitcases from the car, the stage manager said, "There's your landlady."

I carried my belongings up the stoop. The woman said, "Hi, I'm Veronica Lake."

After I introduced myself, she said, "When the stage manager called, he asked if a Candace Hilligoss could live with me. I said, 'Sure, but what is it?' She laughed, then said, "Let me help you." She picked up my suitcases and together we climbed to the second floor.

I tried not to show my surprise as I would not have recognized her as Veronica Lake. Her wavy, natural blonde, shoulder-length hair was gone. The world-famous peek-a-boo style, Veronica's stock in trade, was cut short. Not since Samson's haircut had chopping off one's hair ruined a career as much as Veronica's had. In the summer humidity, her fine, limp hair held no memory of curl. She wore no makeup to hide the freckles on her face. Her eyelashes were the same color as her hair, a silvery, natural blonde that belongs to most Nordic descendants. "Michael, come here and meet Candace Hilligoss."

A boy about twelve appeared. I knew immediately he was her son with his pale hair and eyelashes, the same freckles across his nose and his small bone structure. He held out his hand: "I'm Michael DeToth." As I shook hands with him, I was aware of a mischievous gleam, a red spark in his eyes.

I described to Veronica my tale of woe with Webber and Foch. She laughed. "He used to beat up his first wife. Forget him, come over to the theater tonight and meet the guys in my cast. I've got four actors and a director living in this house. You and I are the only females."

I felt as if I were back in South Dakota living in a grand old rooming house where the boarders are one big happy family. After I unpacked, I ventured around. Veronica had posted little signs everywhere. In the bathroom, the sign said, "Scrub the tub after use." In the hallway was "Make your beds before leaving." Downstairs in the kitchen, the sign above the sink read, "Do your own dishes."

On the kitchen table was a plate with a sandwich. A little note attached to it read, "Candace, eat this then come backstage and meet everyone." Veronica was just like a sorority house mother. How lucky I was to be living with her for the next two weeks.

Later I strolled around the neighborhood. What tranquility, how peaceful, just like a setting from a Thomas Wolfe novel. After living in Manhattan with its stifling subways, fighting the rush hour crowds for a bus, and the constant noise, I felt so calm with the serenity of this suburban town.

I went to the theater. The marquee was lit with Veronica Lake's name in lights and below that was the Broadway comedy "Fair Game." As I entered the stage door, there seemed to a ruckus taking place. Stage hands were running around.

An actor leaned out of his dressing room, "That fuckin' kid, if I get my hands on him, I'll kill him!"

Another actor came to the stage manager and, using Veronica's real name said, "Where's Connie? Why isn't she here? It's almost curtain time."

The stage manager said, "She promised she'd be right back."

This actor said furiously "My wallet's missing, too."

When I asked what had happened, I was told that Michael had been seen an hour ago rummaging through the dressing rooms. It was obvious that he had stolen their wallets.

The first actor yelled to no one in particular, "I'll never tour again if the star brings a fuckin' kid along!"

Soon it was curtain time. Over the squawk box, we could hear the audience starting to get restless, which meant their impatience was growing. The director was pacing and checking the time on his watch. There was still no sign of Veronica Lake.

As if on cue, there was the sound of police sirens. Outside the stage door, a sheriff's car rolled to a stop. Veronica almost fell out as she thanked the sheriff. The stage manager yelled at her, "Connie, hurry, you're forty-five minutes late! What's happened?"

She yelled back over her shoulder as she raced into her dressing room. "Michael's run away! The police are looking for him now!"

This distraught mother in her maternal panic had to change immediately into her costume. She didn't take the time to bother with hair or makeup. The curtain was going up and, Veronica Lake, the star, was in the wings ready to make her first entrance to applause from an audience filled with her fans. The enthusiasm of the crowd settled down to watch a famous movie star carry on as a devil-may-care comedienne in "Fair Game."

After the show, Veronica returned to the police station. She wanted to wait until they found Michael.

In the morning I left for rehearsals of "Idiot's Delight" with the new actors from Chicago. When I was through rehearsing, it was almost six. Once at home I was filled with trepidation. But there was Veronica in the kitchen, calmly making dinner. "Wanna eat? I made enough for both of us." She went on to explain that Michael had hopped on a train. The police picked him up riding a boxcar into the next state. "Candace, don't look so worried. Michael's safe with the cops. They'll bring him home later."

Within a couple of days, life in the boarding house returned to normal. A disturbed Michael hung about the house. I felt so sorry for him. "Michael, I don't have an alarm clock. I'll give you a job. Wake me up in the mornings at eight-thirty. I'll pay you a dollar a day." For the first time since I met him, he looked so happy to be wanted, to be given responsibility. From then on every morning Michael, still in his pajamas, would rap on my door until he heard my voice.

During the days when we rehearsed "Idiot's Delight," Veronica and her cast sat in the theater and watched us. If the actors didn't have plans to commute to Chicago, there was nothing much to do in Hinsdale except come and watch our rehearsals. In a week, Veronica's play would leave and our play would open at the theater.

Most of the time her cast and I would hang out in the kitchen after the show to gossip, talk about that night's audience or how big the house was or the reviews from the Chicago critics. Were they influenced by the standing ovations Veronica usually received on her first entrance?

Then one night the actors and the director of her play left Veronica and me alone as they sauntered off to bed. They bid her, "Goodnight, Connie."

"Veronica, why does everyone call you Connie?"

Little did I know what I was in for but she took my cue. "My real name is Connie or Constance Ockelman." She poured herself a small drink of Scotch then sat opposite me at the kitchen table. "I was born in Brooklyn, spent my high school years in Florida, and at Villa Marie Convent in Montreal. I enraged all the nuns at the stunts I would pull. A priest molested me. I am no longer a Catholic.

"At that time, my family lived in Florida. My mother insisted I enter the competition for Miss Florida. I won first place. You would've thought my mother won. I lost the crown when the judges found out I was underage at fifteen. My stage mother leapt upon the idea that her beautiful daughter belonged in Hollywood. So my mother, stepfather, cousin and I made the automobile trip from Florida to Hollywood. I spent my first year there killing time. My mother enrolled me at the Bliss Hayden School of Acting on Wilshire. I began lessons convinced that I would not become a movie star. We were taught stupid stuff, like balancing a book on your head while walking."

The hour passed from 11:30 p.m. to 12:30 a.m., and Veronica had just reached the age of seventeen, when producer Arthur Hornblow Jr. changed her name from Connie to Veronica Lake. At the time she said she burst into tears for Veronica was her mother's name. Of all the goddamn names in the world to choose! She went on to explain how her hair accidentally fell over her left eye in a screen test. Many of the stars had gimmicks and so she had to have one, in the nicest sense of the word. Her shitty hair became hers.

The clock on the wall ticked 1:00 a.m. as she described her first husband, an art director at Metro. She was seventeen when she fell in love with him. She talked briefly about their daughter and then a baby boy that lived only two days after birth. Her husband couldn't stand it when fans called him Mr. Lake. He joined the army, then went to divorce court to accuse her of being an unfit mother, more concerned about her career than her daughter. But she was now a commodity called a star, a name, face, and reputation that would draw paying patrons into the movie theaters. She said, "I was pursued by some of the most eligible men in Hollywood and even across the seas. And my parties were popular. Everyone wanted to be invited."

In the wee hours of the morning, she regaled me with stories about Alan Ladd and their successful pairing in movies from *This Gun for Hire* (He died in her lap) to *The Blue Dahlia*. I learned more about Alan Ladd than anyone else would want to know. His wife-agent was always on the set behind the camera. At the end of each scene, Alan would look at her instead of the director. If she gave him a nod, he insisted on a retake. Nonetheless, Veronica thought he was a marvelous person.

Then in her odyssey, she covered World War II, and the fact that in two months of touring for the war effort, she made three million dollars war bond sales. She even auctioned off locks of her hair to the highest bidder. Six curls sold for $150,000.

Veronica took a long sip of her Scotch. I was still nursing a lukewarm cola (the ice cubes had melted a while ago). I noted the time on the kitchen clock. It was about three o'clock. I was amazed at the constitution of this five-foot, two-inch actress. She might as well have imbibed orange juice instead of liquor. Her eyes were still bright, lake blue (her description). Her voice and diction were as clear as when she spoke on stage. She never once repeated herself as she reached back into her private past with the tale of what she had to do to survive a dreadful stage mother and Paramount executives who overworked and underpaid her.

It was at this stage in her life that she became the gay divorcée. She said, "Hollywood was a land of swingers; however, I'm not a big swinger. I was enjoying the single life when I filmed "Bring on the Girls," which had a lasting impact on my life. I met my second husband, Hungarian director Andre DeToth."

Just mentioning his name made her pour more Scotch. She swigged it down. "He was the nemesis of my life." If she structured her life as a script, this would be the moment in the plot when the character's life changes forever. "I'd never been close to a Hungarian before. He was quite handsome and dashing and—sadistic. There were scenes at home where he'd belt me in the mouth, then offer me a carving knife to cut out his unworthy heart. I didn't accept the invitation. I made a lot of mistakes in my life. I want you to pay close attention because I'm going to teach you a valuable lesson, one that your mother never knew."

She described a marriage that began like a bed of tulips with two fat incomes. Andre was thrilled when she gave birth to a baby boy, Michael. They lived on a Chatsworth farm filled with animals, guest cottages and live-in servants. They even owned a plane loaded with ten thousand dollars worth of amenities. Then Andre started turning down films as not being good enough for him. She learned that she was pregnant again just as the debts were piling up. "Then my mother sued me for support. In her suit she claimed lack of filial love and responsibility. She wanted back pay of seventeen thousand dollars and payment of five hundred per week for life."

"Oh, Veronica, this must be the worst thing that's ever happened to you."

"As a matter of fact, it's gonna get worse. That's why I want you to be careful of the man you choose to marry."

After the birth of her second daughter, they went deeper into debt. That's when she started to drink. Her husband's theory about life was, the less you had, the more you should spend. Their creditors became impatient. Somehow she was no longer in favor in Hollywood. The only buoy was a bottle of Scotch. They declared bankruptcy after the tax officials seized their home to satisfy unpaid taxes.

Veronica rose to her feet, the glass of Scotch in hand. "I didn't want to go through the grind of playing sirens in grade-B movies. I wasn't psychologically meant to be a picture star. At the age of twenty-eight, I walked out of Hollywood."

"Now this is it. The worst thing you've ever done. Right?"

"Wrong, Candace dear. I signed joint income tax returns with Andre. Wives are expected to do this in order to lower the taxes. That was the biggest mistake of my life. He owed the IRS a million dollars, which he didn't have any more. So the government is after me to make the tax payments. I'm a fugitive now. If I live to be a hundred, I'll never make that much money."

"I don't quite understand."

"Well, it's this way, my dear: The IRS wants to attach my salary if they can find me. I'm on the run for as long as I live. That's why I tour in plays. The legitimate stage is my best place to hide. I'm never in one place long enough for them to catch me."

"What about Andre?"

"He's frequently hiding out of the country–Mexico or Hungary. Let me tell you what that Hungarian beast did to our son." She emptied the Scotch bottle into her glass. "When I was having difficulty with Michael, I decided he needed some discipline that a man, his father, could provide. I sent Andre a telegram to pick up his son at the LA Airport. Andre greeted Mike at the airport, then booked him on the next plane back to New York and said goodbye. He crossed the country twice in one day. What brutal rejection my kid must have felt."

Sunrise was creeping over the treetops as Veronica talked about her third husband, the songwriter who never made much money from his tunes even though he wrote for Mabel Mercer. That marriage lasted about three years.

I heard footsteps on the stairs. The actors were waking up. When I looked again at the kitchen clock, the time was nine and, in half an hour, I had to report to the theater for a dress rehearsal. I felt exhausted after Veronica's odyssey of her life. Her fragile beauty was untouched by the realities of life she had lived through. She reached for my hand, squeezing it. "Candace, you're so talented. If I had what you have, I might not have left Hollywood when I did. Oh, hell, you're so young, you don't even understand or know what you have."

The next day Veronica offered to do my laundry since she had free time in the afternoon. The last night she and her actors were in Hinsdale, she decided to entertain with a goodbye party in the backyard. She barbecued the biggest steaks I had ever seen. I gave her a beautiful blue silk scarf as a parting gift.

When the day came that she and the rest of the cast were leaving, she said to me, "Call me in New York. You'll need this code so I'll know you're not the IRS. Let the phone ring twice, hang up, redial, let the phone ring once, hang up again, then the next time you dial, I'll answer."

Now I was the only one living in this huge house. A couple of days after Veronica left, there was a loud knocking on the front door. I opened it to an irate man wearing a white apron and jacket. "Is Veronica Lake here?"

"Who are you?"

"I'm the butcher who's waiting for Miss Lake's payment. She left a charge for ten pounds of beef steaks."

"Oh, I'm so sorry. I believe she's gone back to New York City."

Before he turned away, I could see not only the anger, but the hurt and disappointment in his eyes. I was embarrassed for Veronica. How could she stiff a small-town butcher?

A week later the "Idiot's Delight's" tour ended. Robert Webber and I were on the same plane going back to New York. He refused to speak with me. He wouldn't even make eye contact. I felt as if I were in high school and the in-crowd's hunk was giving me the cold shoulder.

Once I settled in my apartment I called Veronica, careful to remember her code for the phone. When she answered, she invited me to a party in her apartment on Ninth Street in Greenwich Village. She told me she had two maids catering for her. I brought a date along and both of us were taken aback with the scene at Veronica's. It was as if you crossed Sally Bowles in "I Am a Camera" with Holly Golightly in "Breakfast at Tiffany's."

Basically the place was only two rooms with a Pullman's kitchen where two hefty black maids took up most of the available space. Guests were sitting on boxes or the floor as there were only a couple of chairs in the living room. Veronica passed around a bowl for a collection to pay the party's expenses. Actually, it occurred to me she was raising rent money. She whispered to me that she had used her savings from summer stock to send Michael to military school in Connecticut. She pulled me aside and added, "A friend of mine is in town. I'd like to fix you up with him. I know he would like you. He's staying on his boat moored in the Hudson."

"Does he have a big boat?"

"Pretty big."

"Well, what's his name?"

"Ari Onassis."

I was speechless.

"Candace, this man has the power to change your life. Don't waste your youth on unemployed actors."

Intuitively, I understood. But when I thought about Onassis, his big fat belly came to mind. I had just gone through a crazy scene with playwright Sidney Kingsley who wrote boring social dramas like "Men in

White" and "Dead End." The big difference between Onassis and him (besides a big fortune) is that Kingsley has a hump in his back. He interviewed me for his new play. He sat in a winged-back chair as if he were some kind of royalty receiving commoners. He wore thick lenses, which magnified his dark eyes. He smacked his wet lips back and forth as he ignored my questions about his new play and, instead, inquired if I would be interested in modeling for his sculpture class. I pleaded that I was much too thin to be a sculptor's model.

It was late in the afternoon, a perfect time to insist I join him for dinner next door to his apartment on Central Park South. It would give him a chance to explain the new play of his in which he was also a producer. With the lure of acting in a Broadway play, I was led into a restaurant.

The trouble with dinner is that I'm expected to provide the dessert. I left Kingsley on the street with a brief thank you and the excuse I had an early audition in the morning with the head of Fox Studios. As I headed for the entrance to the subway, these are the words from a prominent American playwright who shouted them to the world on Fifty-Ninth street: "Don't you know that one night with me will do more for your career than any audition for Fox? If Lana Turner had acted as stupid as you, she'd have never been a star!"

I explained to Veronica that I could not handle Onassis. I'm not that sophisticated. I'm just a small town gal from South Dakota.

In the coming fall weekends, she took me pub-crawling with her and a couple of friends. I chewed on my mint frappé's crushed ice as everyone else belted down vodka or gin. She loved to hear jazz, especially as sung by Peggy Lee and Mabel Mercer. I was fascinated with this madcap lifestyle of hers. Once she said to me that if the people knew that Veronica Lake was at the club, and they looked our way, I'd be mistaken for her.

At dinner in an expensive Japanese restaurant, she leaned toward me and said, "I have some great news. They want to make a film about my life. It's going to be called, 'The Peekaboo Girl'."

"How wonderful for you," I said.

"I told the producers I have the perfect actress for the role. I want you to play me."

Again she made me speechless.

"We both have the same cheekbone structure. The same blue eyes, blonde hair. I also told them how impressed I was with your talent."

"Veronica, I'm overwhelmed."

"Tomorrow, I'm lunching with William Inge. He has a new play for Broadway this season. There's a part that's right for me. There's also a role for someone to play my younger sister. I'm going to ask him to meet you."

I could hardly go to sleep that night. Could her luck have really changed? Was it destiny that brought us together? A week went by, and she had not called me. I waited another week and still no phone call.

By the third week, I decided to call her instead, making sure to dial the code. But the phone never rang. Instead a robot operator answered with a recording that this was not a working number. I was stunned.

I said to my roommate, "Maybe I should just go to her apartment. Knock on the door." While I was mulling this over, I happened to buy a *Daily News* from the corner newsstand. Just as I flipped to the second page, the headline said "Veronica Lake Evicted from Apartment." I stumbled and almost fell off the curb. There was a ghastly photo of her belongings piled on the sidewalk. There was a sub-heading about the IRS swooping like vultures to confiscate her possessions to be sold at public auction for delinquency of income taxes.

I never saw her again. A year later I ran into an actor who had toured with her. I complained that she never kept in touch with me. He said, "She doesn't want you to see her again. Doesn't want you to know her whereabouts."

"Why, why? Please, tell me."

"If you promise you won't go and look for her."

"I promise."

"She's a cocktail waitress in an East Side hotel. She lives in a cheap room there."

"Do they realize that she is the former movie star, Veronica Lake?"

"Her employers know her as Connie Ockleman."

Now I really understood what Veronica meant when she said that her life and future were ruined forever by her divorce from Andre DeToth, the community debt, the joint income tax of a million dollars. The IRS would devour her until nothing was left but her famous cheekbones.

Twelve years later Veronica succumbed to acute hepatitis. By that time I had a family. My two daughters on rare occasion would catch one of Veronica's movies on television. They would always comment, "Look, there's the lady who used to do your laundry."

Richard showed me the obituary notice in the paper about Veronica Lake's funeral at the Frank Campbell Mortuary on the East Side. He said, "Maybe you should go." I thought about it but then decided that I didn't want to have a memory of her lying in a casket.

Much later, I learned that her son Michael DeToth was the only person who came to the funeral. He tried to persuade his father to lend him money for his mother's funeral. His father called him obscene names for bothering him. If I had known that her friends, her husbands, her two daughters or her mother would not show up, I would have gone for Michael's sake.

That same year a biography of Veronica came out. The author interviewed her mother, who convinced him that her daughter was not the delicate creature who stirred male filmgoers into sexual fantasies, but a paranoid schizophrenic and an alcoholic by the age of seventeen. Mother wanted to have Veronica put away in an institution but was afraid she would be accused of ruining her daughter's career. (Mom was really afraid she'd kill the golden goose that supported her.)

If she were as mentally disturbed as her mother claimed, Veronica would not have been able to leave us a legacy of more than thirty-eight movies, eighteen television shows plus the three years of performing on stage, including a national tour of *Peter Pan*.

A few more years passed, and there was a rumor that Veronica's ashes had been stored on the mortuary's shelf for four to five years as no one paid the mortician's bill. Eventually, her urn of ashes ended up for sale in an antique shop on Madison Avenue. What would Richard have said if I came home with Veronica's ashes? Actually, he might not have cared. He does have a sentimental side.

Veronica fell into my life for a few memorable moments like the sister I never had, the mother I lost in childhood, then just as quickly was gone.

> "Waves and actors are much alike. They come
> for a little while, rise to separate heights
> and travel with varying speed and force and
> then are gone, unremembered."
>
> – Louise Drew Barrymore

ACT TWO

A playbill photo of the future husband and Candace in a new play in Canada, a month before their wedding.

Chapter Nine

A year has passed since I saw my attorney, Gary Zimmerman. Feeling like an unwanted houseguest, I made an appointment with him as Richard had his manager put stop payments on my alimony checks.

"Oh, my god," Gary said, a bit irritated. "I'll file a Writ of Extension for the sums owed you--against the Petitioner. Where's the bum now?"

"He's in the London production of "The Little Foxes" with Elizabeth Taylor. One night he collapsed. The doctors there did a dangerous procedure–cardio angioplasty."

"Your ex is finally working again, then he gets sick. I'm so sorry."

"Here he's at death's door, and he rises from his hospital bed like Lazarus, makes transatlantic phone calls to the bank–to stop my support payments. Just think if he had dropped over dead, the last person he'd thought of would be me."

Gary said, "Sometime after we left court, Richard went back for a post-decree action for Retention of Jurisdiction Spousal Support."

"Does this mean he wants me to support him if I make lots of money?"

"Yes."

"Even though he's living with Meredith, the librarian."

"Yes. I'm surprised at your husband. I thought he was more macho than that."

"Gary, I realize now that even with my office temp jobs, I'm never going to make my expenses when my alimony steps down to $625. My rent is more than that. I still owe you money, too. I'll have to go back to family court."

"Our firm can't take you as a client any more. We're much too expensive."

My stomach dropped. "What'll I do?"

"I met an attorney in court recently. He was representing the other side, but I thought he did a good job. I'll give you his name. He's not a Beverly Hills attorney. His office is in Santa Monica." Gary scribbled the information on a piece of paper.

As Gary escorted me to the door, he said, "By the way, Irwin Buter tells me that Richard discharged him. He can't afford Buter's fees anymore."

*****

In a few months I was in Santa Monica consulting with Marc Bradfield who was pleased that Gary Zimmerman referred him. He informed me that most of his practice was criminal defense but he was knowledgeable about family law, too. "I shall be pleased to undertake your representation. I'd like a retainer of $1000."

I wrote out a check as if it were no more than ten bucks and gave it to him.

"This is a non-refundable fee. My base charges will be billed monthly. All services rendered will be at the hourly rate of $150. I have also found that in order for a proper client-attorney relationship to exist and be successful, my charges are to be paid promptly on the first of the month."

"Is that all?" I asked as if that were surely the end of the lecture on his billing practice.

"Oh, I may require court costs to be paid ahead by you. I also reserve the right to withdraw from your representation at any time should my fee not be paid."

"When will you file my Spousal Support Order?"

"I'll write a letter to your husband's lawyer first. We'll request that the alimony be kept at $1250 a month for a couple more years."

"That's a waste of time. Richard doesn't care about his lawyer, he does what he wants."

"Well, I want to show the court that we tried to settle. We're required to show the effort."

I knew that was a bunch of crap but kept my mouth shut. So far the thrust of Bradfield's consultation was his legal fees. There was no mention of his experiences in family court, who the judges were now, or what my chances were with a second appearance. I was learning that the world of jurisprudence was a playground for male chauvinists. My first clue: the reception areas in the law firms. Ever notice the magazines? They range from *Field & Stream* and *Popular Mechanics* to *Sports Illustrated.* Not one subscription for a gender-free *Time* or *Newsweek.* God forbid there should be a *Vogue* or a *Good Housekeeping.*

Bradfield said, "I'll be gone for a couple of weeks. My wife and I have planned to go to Spain. In the meantime, my secretary will send you a written arrangement. This way there will be no misunderstanding of my fees."

My intuition was screaming, "Get away from this jerk. He represents criminals, not women in jeopardy." My common sense fought back: "Where will you go now? Trust Gary Zimmerman who referred him. Can a criminal lawyer be that bad for a former ex-wife?" As I left Bradfield's office, I saw his next client, who should have registered for Central Casting with his thug face and build. Obviously he was not here for family court. Guys like him should have stamped on their foreheads "Surgeon General's Warning to Women."

I returned to my Beverly Hills apartment with a sense of relief. My spirits soared. At least I had a lawyer again, Marc Bradfield, a protector and champion of my cause. Actually to believe that is like believing in Santa Claus. I made a note in the calendar of this meeting on October 29.

The weeks went by then months. Not one word from the new attorney. I had spoken to his secretary a couple of times, and she had fobbed me off with, "We haven't heard from the court yet." It was now the end of March. I knew from Gary Zimmerman that once a lawyer files papers in family court, a date is given for 30 days hence.

By the end of March, I finally reached attorney Bradfield on the phone. He said, "Mrs. Forest, I had an accident skiing in Spain. I broke my arm."

It had now been almost four months of waiting for this legal eagle, and he was pleading sympathy for his broken wing. I wanted to yell, "Did you break your mouth, too? Attorneys dictate to secretaries, and your secretary never mentioned anything was wrong with her arm. Any idiot knows that secretaries type up the complaints, not the lawyers."

When I reported to Gary about Bradfield, he was genuinely shocked and apologized. He told me to write a letter asking for my retainer back and, if I didn't get it within a week, I should file a complaint with the State Bar of California. Zimmerman also called Bradfield. My retainer was refunded within a day of receipt of my letter. However, by this time Bradfield's letter had reached Richard. Furious, Richard's answer was to file an Order to Terminate Spousal Support. His new attorney was Steve Lande from Sherman Oaks, probably cheaper than his Beverly Hills lawyer.

Richard was home from London, *The Little Foxes* having ended its run. Before he could spit out the words, "I'm an out-of-work actor," he was cast in NBC's *Santa Barbara* another daytime soap. During this busy time for him, he also married Meredith. He called to give me the news with the excuse that after living with her for two years, he wanted to show respect for their relationship. Should I have congratulated him on his wedded bliss? Or tell him he could count on me for a salad bowl?

Jennifer, our older daughter, said, "The week he married the librarian, he had his house painted. The sun shone for his wedding. But it rained on his new paint job, ruining everything. Since the painter cost more than his wedding, Dad wishes the weather had reversed itself." As the kids said, "That's oh so, so typical, so uncool of him."

I was lawyerless again, like the ex-husband's boat without a rudder. Where do I go? My friends pointed out that on Pico Boulevard there was a small building with a sign above the door: *Women's Legal Clinic.* For twenty-five dollars, a woman could have a consultation with an attorney. I made my appointment with Carl Leibovitz. He looked about seventy with smoky white hair and explained that he had been in family law practice for thirty-five years. Definitely not the type to go skiing. He perused my file. "I can't believe what Bradfield did to you. It makes me angry to see what some lawyers do to their clients. In five months he never filed an order for you. That's a disgrace. I can understand why you're upset."

"Mr. Leibovitz, you're an answer to a maiden's prayer," I said, quoting my mother. "What a godsend you are. I'm so relieved finally to meet someone who knows what to do." Then I asked him that sixty-four dollar question, "Would you take my case?"

Leibovitz hesitated with a couple of pious sighs and hmms. "Well, I believe I can be of help here. Since you joined the clinic in order to see me, I will only charge half of my usual fee." He beamed with a benevolence worthy of a priest. "For seven hundred fifty dollars, I'll take your case. We'll file an OSC. Do you understand what that is?"

"Certainly. I'm quite familiar with an Order to Show Cause."

"I'll need to subpoena the Petitioner's three unions–find out his earnings so far. It'll lower costs if you can type up the subpoenas."

I was happy to comply. Once again I came home feeling elated with the new attorney, a senior citizen who knew the ropes. I took out my portable typewriter and typed on the forms that Leibovitz gave me. I thought they looked very professional.

However, Leibovitz did not agree with me. He thought the subpoenas were the worst typed ones he had ever seen. Since he insisted he didn't want to spend money on his legal secretary, he had no choice but to send out what he considered to be inferior-looking subpoenas. Supposedly, because of my sloppy paperwork, I had put his reputation at risk with the three actors' unions.

Two weeks later Leibovitz asked me come to his office to sign papers. I showed him Richard's Order to Terminate Spousal Support. Leibovitz reared back in his chair as if I'd flung a snake at him. "What's this?"

"It's Richard's OSC. I just received it yesterday," I said casually and professionally.

"This is a new wrinkle. Oh, my, my–I–I–I–I," he began to sputter. "I mean, this is going to be a lot more work for me."

"Why? There's a court date already. Richard's attorney filed for it. Right there on the OSC. See, it says May 24."

"Oh, my, that's a short time," he said in a voice of doom.

"Now that I have signed my OSC today, what's the problem? We still have three weeks to prepare."

"I–I have to check my calendar. There may be a conflict. I might be out of town."

I knew the old man was bluffing me. Once again I found myself stuck with a Looney Tunes character. After a few days I left messages for him at his office. He never returned my calls. I filed a complaint at the Women's Legal Clinic. No one there had seen Leibovitz since I had. I was on the verge of a panic attack. It was a race against time for me to serve Richard my new OSC before the twenty-fourth of May. I knew from his behavior that Leibovitz had not done this.

Gertrude suggested that I find a female lawyer right away. Some of my friends thought this was a great idea. Surely a female lawyer would be more in tune with an ex-wife on the verge of losing her support payments.

Through a recommendation I found Susan Goldstein in Beverly Hills. She was from New York and, at age thirty-five, had a lot of spit and fire as they use to say. When I showed her my files and, she saw the petitioner was Richard Forest, she shrieked, "Was he on *Another World*?"

"One of his many soap operas," I answered.

"I can't believe it. In high school we raced home every afternoon to watch Richard Forest on *Another World*. I'll call my mother tonight and tell her. She'll never believe this." She visibly blushed, all her legal sophistication reduced to a giggling fan.

The same old warning bell was going off in the back of my mind. I reminded myself that I was on my fourth attorney. I can't go around throwing thousand dollar retainers upon lawyers like they were business cards. Susan was decent. She did write Leibovitz that she could not find any conformed copies of Order to Show Cause filed on my behalf. Therefore, she requested that he return my retainer of seven hundred fifty dollars.

Of course he ignored her and, of course, I filed a claim against him in the Small Claims Court of Encino. The night before our scheduled appearance, an attorney representing Leibovitz called with an offer of a hundred dollars as settlement. I said no.

The offer was increased to one hundred fifty dollars. I replied that money was not important to me. It was the issue of a lawyer taking advantage of a woman, representing that he was for women's rights by meeting them at the Women's Legal Clinic. I restrained myself from shouting into the phone, "I want to see the wheels of justice grind slowly over Leibovitz's crooked body."

The next morning I waited outside the Small Claims Court for my friend, actor Johnnie Collins, who was driving in from Agoura to be my support. Leibovitz arrived with a young attorney who appeared embarrassed to be there. Both men carried large black briefcases, which they clung to tightly as though they were filled with treasures (files of evidence) to be displayed later.

When Johnnie came, he apologized for his appearance in jeans and a T-shirt as the lawyers and I were suited up in courtroom attire--all black like a death in the family. Within a few minutes, the doors of the courtroom opened, and a woman ran out.

Johnnie grabbed my arm. "Oh my god, it's Agoura's dog catcher. Is she the judge?"I reassured him, "No, no, she's probably the case before mine." I explained that the proceedings in Small Claims run about fifteen minutes to a half hour. Here a plaintiff and defendant do not need to have a lawyer for representation. That's why Leibovitz looks so silly with an attorney accompanying him.

The four of us trooped inside. Johnnie was the only other person sitting in the auditorium as the attorneys and I took our places at a table in front. The judge was in his chambers. Leibovitz and his attorney immediately pulled a couple of books from the shelves at the side of the room. They engaged in one of those private attorneys' moments of "Aha! Here is the precedent for our case," as they pointed to certain pages in one of the books. Leibovitz jabbed his fingers up and down, then held up his index finger in a signal of triumph. His eyes squinted in contempt as he glanced over at me.

I sat expressionless. We were in battle now. Even if the enemy is old and shapeless and has a pouch resting on his belt, I gave no reactions. I pretended to stifle a yawn as I let my fingers tap randomly upon a sheaf of papers before me. When I glanced back at Johnnie, his face was already shiny with nervous perspiration.

The judge entered and, after the usual protocol, asked me to begin. I testified about Leibovitz's failures, an OSC never filed in court and no Proof of Service filed upon Richard. In a nutshell I wanted my retainer of seven hundred fifty dollars returned, money to pay a new attorney, Susan Goldstein, for what he hadn't done.

Leibovitz went berserk and jumped to his feet. He yelled over and over, "I will not have my reputation ruined here!" He paid no attention to the young lawyer at his side whose mouth opened wide like an O in speechless horror.

The judge in a nice way tried to assure Leibovitz that he would have enough time for his side of the story: "Don't interrupt her."

I held up my calendar and read aloud the number of times I had tried to call Leibovitz, and he had not answered. I read Susan's letter asking him for proof of what he did as she could not find any kind of discovery.

Leibovitz defied the judge's order not to interrupt me and argued fiercely. The judge pleaded with him to back off, to wait his turn. Leibovitz did not care as he wanted to impress the court with what he had done, even though he had health issues, even though he was paid so little by me.

I decided that since Leibovitz was interrupting me I would do the same to him when it was his turn. We went back and forth with our complaints. The judge asked for order but gave up as he covered his eyes with his hands. The judge then pronounced, "Do you realize the time we have spent here? It's more than two hours. Mr. Leibovitz, why protest this? As a lawyer you'd make more money than seven hundred fifty by spending the same amount of time at trial."

"It's not the money, it's my good reputation!" Leibovitz pressed his hand over his heart, his voice shaking. His attorney winced noticeably.

The judge said, "I'm going to give Mrs. Forest a judgment of Five hundred dollars plus court costs of twenty dollars and fifty cents. Mr. Leibovitz can keep two hundred and fifty dollars."

"Why, when he did nothing but almost damaged my case?"

The judge ignored me. It was the end of the day for him, and he wanted to run away. Leibovitz's flabby chest was bulging out in protest as his attorney led him from the courtroom.

I went to my friend Johnnie. He looked faint and asked for water. As I put my arm around him, I felt a slight tremble. He had no idea my trial would take so much out of him. He turned down my offer of lunch or a snack as he just wanted to go home to bed. He whispered, "The idea of food is making me sicker."

Naturally, Leibovitz was not going to honor the judgment against him. He didn't know that I already had an attorney, Susan Goldstein, who then sent a letter informing him of the embarrassment if I had to retain her office in order to execute on this small judgment. He immediately sent a check payable to me but asked that I file a Full Satisfaction of Judgment with a conformed copy to him. Never in any handbook for Small Claims Court is there a request that losers file again copies with the court of a FSJ.

More paperwork, more legal fees—it just never seemed to stop. Susan asked me to arrive a few minutes before Richard came to her office for his deposition. I asked her if his attorney Lande was coming. She said, "No, it's not Lande. His attorney's name is David Stitz." Stitz was now number three in Richard's batting lineup of attorneys. I was ahead with Susan being my fourth attorney. So far seven lawyers had been involved in our dissolution proceedings.

Susan made herself appear as attractive as possible: high heels, and a pretty, red silk dress. I was well aware that she couldn't wait to meet her TV idol, Richard Forest.

The minute Richard arrived with Attorney Stitz (rhymes with pits), Susan couldn't stop smiling. Her dark eyelashes heavy with mascara were fluttering. What happened to my edgy, smarty-pants lawyer? She looked like a Jewish Southern belle ready to swoon.

David Stitz had about as much personality as a funeral director. His complexion was gray, the result of sitting too many hours under artificial light. Even his hair was gray, what remained of it. His face was drained of any humor. He was the only one who didn't exchange a smile as we began Richard's deposition.

Susan went through all the preliminary explanations so Richard would have no misunderstanding, etc. etc. etc. I listened to Richard, fascinated to learn that he owned five new cars, one Suzuki motorcycle and a 53-foot Hutchins twin-diesel diving vessel. Then I remembered that the girls told me Richard couldn't sail this boat from City Island in New York and bring it through the Panama Canal as the boat was judged unseaworthy. He paid ten thousand dollars to have this tub shipped by truck across country to California. He didn't list this anywhere on his expense declaration.

As Richard mentioned that he spent eighty-four thousand dollars on the boat, I thought I would howl in outrage. Did his wife, the librarian, know this? Richard's idea of decorating a home was somewhere between a swap-meet and a second-hand store. He further explained that he intended to use the boat as a charter as he was a licensed Coast Guard operator. He also said he taught scuba diving.

Mentally I was adding up the cost of Richard's diving equipment. Susan, on the other hand, appeared impressed and kept questioning him on his scuba diving. How many pupils? Does he have an assistant?

Do people in the entertainment industry take his class? She was spending a good forty minutes listening to Richard describe his classes on scuba diving.

I wanted to tell her, "Just take the damn scuba course yourself, and get on with the purpose of this deposition." And that was: Why was he asking to terminate my support of six hundred twenty-five dollars per month?

As Susan began to ask questions about Richard's health, I knew another half hour would be wasted as he talked about his cardiologist, plus many other doctors due to an arm injury, and last year's double hernia operation. In fact, just recently his last doctor informed Richard that he was suffering from exhaustion. He asked his writers on *Santa Barbara* to reduce his work load.

"Last week you did three episodes," Susan said.

"That's correct."

"According to my understanding, you do more than three per work. Maybe four or five per week?"

"Yes, very often, also more text per show."

"You mean more words spoken by you?"

"Yes."

"Do you mean you get paid by—"

"No, I don't get paid by the word."

"You get paid the same income per episode whether you speak for fifteen minutes or half an hour?"

This prompted Richard to give a lecture on how a heavy storyline either makes or breaks an actor. Another twenty minutes shot to hell.

Susan picked up the thread of this to ask, "Do you get paid extra for being an underwater consultant on *Santa Barbara*?" She was smiling coyly at him as if they were chums sharing coffee at Starbucks.

I gripped my hands so hard the knuckles turned white. Previously, I had been ordered by her not to react in anyway. Don't laugh, don't make a sound, no faces. Otherwise I might have leapt across the desk, smeared her makeup, then shoved her head into a legal file.

She could not stop interrogating Richard about his boat. What did he pay to dock it? What were his typical expenses for running the boat? She spent another twenty minutes listening to him explain the general maintenance, hauling, body painting, and even went so far as to give the biography of the boat carpenter who was responsible for the entire rebuilding of the ship's galley. He also removed the ship's rot.

Jesus, Mary and Joseph! Richard is an actor. His tub is a hobby, his avocation. Doesn't she get that he deducts all the boat's expenses from his corporate taxes?

Susan appeared smitten as Richard described epoxy preparation of the hull, a grinding, a plywood skin, as he called it. She has not one idea what he is talking about but then she is just as clueless about an actor's life as well.

Twenty minutes later, she finally got to the heart of this deposition. "Is it your position that you can't presently afford to pay Candace the $625 per month that you've been paying?"

"Objection!" Attorney Stitz fired back. "I'm not so sure what your position means. Can you be a little more precise on that question?"

"Yes, I can be more precise. Can you afford to pay Candace $625 per month?"

Richard paused as though weighing the complexity of the question. "I think that's a legal question so I'm deferring to my attorney." He nodded at Stitz as though the answer was written on his lawyer's blank face.

Susan quickly countered by saying, "Rather than make a fuss, I'll rephrase it later."

Needless to say, she never did. She was swept away by Richard's various expenses for our daughters, his wife's meager job at the library, the care of his dog and his charge on a credit card for an armoire that cost him $1,354. Despite his precarious health, he had no plans to terminate his acting career.

Out of nowhere, she asked, "Do you have a scuba room at your house?"

Richard, of course, responded, "That's my guest house."

The woman was like a dog with a bone. She would not give up on the friggin' scuba stuff.

Finally, the deposition was over and the two men left. Susan turned to me and said, "I can't believe how honest he was."

"You don't understand him, Susan. Look at how he never answered your questions directly. He is his own corporation from which he pays himself a salary. In his declaration of expenses, he gave his corporate deductions against his personal income. This reduces his monthly net. He wants to look poor as possible in court. Why didn't you ask to see his corporate taxes?"

"Well, I just didn't. That's all," she said haughtily, digging her pen into the desk.

Her Beverly Hills address, her cockiness, her know-it-all attitude were a sham. She didn't know what the hell to do with an actor who scuba dives or me a former actress.

A week later it was my turn to be deposed. Stitz hammered away at my résumé as an actress. What was my income when I met Richard? What was my salary in this stock company or that one? It was so long in past history, I couldn't possibly remember twenty years ago. I wanted to point out that Richard can't recall what monies he made one year ago. Stitz raised his voice, "You never had a viable career as an actress. You're chasing a rainbow, for twenty-one years a pie in the sky." I had no idea he had that much poetry in his dry, boring soul. As I stared at him, I wondered what pitiful wife had to kiss that pinched and lifeless face every night, a face that belonged on a second-rate mortician.

It was like old home week as Susan and I met with Richard and Stitz in Department Two of Family Court. The lawyers who inhabit this esoteric world became a blur of black suits, all carrying the same black briefcases. There was a short buzz of conversation as they seemed to know one another. "Hello, hi there, how are ya, good to see ya."

From Department Two, we were assigned to Judge Meldes's courtroom. Richard as Petitioner always went first on the stand. From my viewpoint, Judge Meldes seemed to be Hispanic. Susan doesn't seem to know much about him as she had never litigated before this judge.

After a couple of hours, the judge asked Susan and Stitz to come to his chamber. I paced the hallway worried at this strange turn of events. At last Susan came to me and said, "We're declared a mistrial."

"What happened to cause a mistrial?"

"I underestimated the time for our hearing."

"What do you mean?"

"How in hell would I know that Richard can't stop talking when he testifies? He rambles on and on." I gave her a reproachful look. After deposing Richard, she should have learned what it's like to have an actor testify in court.

She said in a low tone, "Maybe in a way we're lucky. Judge Meldes informed me that you'd have to be a hell of an actress to convince him that you're worth more than $625 a month."

"You mean this judge made his decision before he even heard my testimony? I don't understand that. But what I don't understand is you, Susan. Why you didn't tell him that this is not a case of an actress on trial? But a woman who was a wife and mother for a twenty-year marriage--who put aside a viable career to support her husband's."

It was the first time I saw her at a loss for words.

"Tell me what the problem is, Susan. Did I not have enough children? Was I not married long enough?"

She found her voice. "Well, what exactly do you want here?"

"I want my youth back!" I bit my lip to keep from screaming at her. The infinite pain and despair made me run from the courthouse. What to do now that I was locked into yet another lawyer who didn't understand an actor's complicated life? The scenario was worse than any corny storyline of one of Richard's soap operas. Tune into tomorrow. Like Scarlett, I would think about it then.

Meanwhile, back at the ranch, the Women's Legal Clinic informed me they had written a letter to Leibovitz to return the seven hundred fifty dollars to me. The Clinic never heard from him. Nevertheless, they had suspended him from their staff of attorneys.

Hurrah! Somewhere Lady Justice triumphed in spite of her slow wheels.

"All the world's a stage,
And all the men and women merely players:
They have their exits and entrances
And one man in his time plays many parts."

– William Shakespeare

Chapter Ten

Scuba diving made a big splash upon Richard's life. Who would have guessed? We had been married for about twelve years when we could afford to take our first trip as a family. We chose one of those five-night, six-day trips in Bermuda.

Our daughters were then ages six and eight. Used to playing on the sidewalks of Manhattan, they thought they had found paradise in Bermuda. They raced through the sugar-white beaches until they plunged into the bathtub-warm, blue waves. Here at Cambridge Beaches Richard signed up for his first scuba lesson, which turned into a lifelong passion.

His diving instructor took Richard on a dive that explored a sunken ship from the Civil War. Bermuda is surrounded by more than 300 sunken ships that crashed upon the coral reefs. The ships have long ago been stripped of any treasure, but the instructor told his dive students they could keep anything they found. Some discovered broken crockery. Diving forty feet, Richard brought up dozens of medicine bottles. Outside the door of our cottage he dumped his net sack and said, "Pack these in your suitcase."

I examined his loot and saw thousands of ants crawling through the sand-filled bottles. I took this treasure and threw it into the garbage.

Once we were back home in New York, Richard registered at the YMCA for *3 Steps to Becoming a Certified Scuba Diver.* Before I realized it, Richard had logged in almost 50 dive trips within two years. He said to me, "Since I'm now a certified scuba diver, I want to become a certified NAUI instructor."

"What does that mean?

"National Association of Underwater Instructors. I have to go away to a training camp for a couple of weeks."

"Well, I guess that's not so long."

"I'm also going to become a PADI instructor."

"What for?"

"So I can teach at the YMCA. They also require the PADI Certification."

"Do you have to go to sleep-away camp for that, too?"

"Of course. By meeting the standards of both these agencies, I can teach and train anywhere in the world."

"Somehow it sounds precarious. Like being an actor."

"Hell, you don't scuba dive to make money. It's the thrill of the sport. The discovery of another world undersea. The peace is unbelievable. No phones ringing. No subway crowds. No traffic. No Hollywood agents. You should try it."

"I don't like deep water."

Richard was getting annoyed. "If you were a certified student, guess what we could be doing this weekend in Long Island?"

"I don't have the foggiest idea. What's waiting for us in Long Island?"

"We would dive to find sharks. Study them."

"How do you do that?"

"There's a school of sharks that swim near a cove by the Hamptons. The divers are lowered in a shark cage from my friend's dive boat."

"How do the sharks know that you're waiting in a cage?"

"The crew on deck top throws raw fish and bloody meat on top of the cage."

"Oh, my god, so the sharks can attack the cage!"

"That's the point. How else can we get close enough to observe them for science?"

"Listen, Richard, even if you paid me a million dollars, I wouldn't get into a shark cage."

"If you're not willing to do this, what will we have to talk about in our old age? I'm trying to think of things we can do together."

I didn't want to argue. I thought we shared a lot as a couple: our children, the theater, acting in the same plays, traveling. I even taught Richard how to tap dance for the musical "Seesaw." Michael Bennett's choreographer taught me the routines so I could teach Richard in his free time from his soap opera schedule.

Nonetheless, I tried to be a good sport so I went with Richard to the YMCA swimming pool. He wanted to see if I could pass the swimming test to become a student scuba diver. There was something about the Y pool that reeks of sweaty men, like a gym with no ventilation. The tile was as slippery as if painted with slime. I lowered myself slowly down the ladder into cold water. It was a lie that the temperature is kept at 82 degrees. I looked across the Olympic-size pool where Richard was waiting. The distance seemed as long as a football field with Richard yelling words of encouragement: "Just swim the length two times. That's all."

Slowly I did my version of a crawl. I barely made it to the end, where I turned to start back. My arms felt like dead weights as my achy leg muscles are begging me to stop.

"Keep going!" Richard shouted. "Do the back stroke! Do the side stroke! The breast stroke! Float on your back if you have to!"

I rolled over on my back. Richard trailed alongside the edge of the pool. He leaned over, waving his arms at me. “Don’t sink! C’mon now! Don’t sink! Float! Float! ”

My muscles are knuckling up with fatigue. I reached about midway of the pool. “Can’t do it," I gagged on a mouthful of water. Forcing myself, I dog paddled to the pool ladder.

“Don’t give up! You can swim it. Damn it! Try harder. You’re almost there!”

My arms and legs are so weak with burning pain that I can’t climb the ladder. I clinged to it, resting my chin on a step. I lifted one hand toward Richard and mouthed the word, “Help.” My eyes were stinging from the chlorine. I could barely blink, it hurt so much.

Richard walked away. His shoulders slumped in disappointment. “Oh for god’s sake, get out of the water. I have a class in ten minutes.”

Having grown up in sunny and warm California, Richard doesn’t understand what life was like for me in South Dakota. We have two seasons, winter and Fourth of July. We were part of the Dust Bowl for a good reason. There’s no water for swimming in Huron, South Dakota. There’s no skiing because there’s no hills. Just flat prairies. No ice skating because at 35 degrees below zero you can’t stay outside long enough to learn how.

When Richard asked what life was like for a youngster in Huron, I would describe summertime. On a lazy evening after dinner while there was still light outside, my grandfather liked to say, “Let’s go watch the sunset." Seven of us, family and neighbors, piled into grandfather’s Studebaker, the Royal Model, which could seat us comfortably. Within ten minutes we were on a country road. Grandfather parked the car so we faced the West and the giant yellow fiery ball on the edge of the horizon. “Look at that, will ya?" he said. As far as the human eye could see, there was not one tree, a house or animal to interfere with the flatness of the plains and the sunset. In a few minutes the yellow of the sun turned into shades of blood-red orange. The sight of this spectacle brought forth sighs.

“Isn’t that the most beautiful sight in the world?” Grandfather asked.

"This must be like what it’d be standing on the moon," someone said.

“But not as beautiful as our sunset.”

“Yeah, nothing’s as beautiful as this.”

Slowly as the sun dipped below the horizon, the car grew silent with reverence, like sitting in a church.

*****

Usually we don’t see the sunsets in Manhattan. Richard would just shake his head at my dull life in South Dakota. Not as exciting as New York, to be sure. Being married to an actor-scuba diver, excitement meant that I had eighteen scuba tanks lined up in our living room for six months out of the year. Then for the rest of the year, Richard stored them at the YMCA. He said, “I have to meet the safety standards. All instructors have to provide the diving equipment for students.”

The diving gear also included for each tank: regulators, mouth pieces, masks, buoyancy compensators, life vests, and weight belts. Scuba diving was taking up too much of Richard's time as it was taking up too much of our living room.

My breaking point came when I pulled back the shower curtain to step into the tub and, before I could say "Psycho," a black arm smacked me in the face. Hanging from the shower rod was not one wetsuit but three wetsuits. Richard claimed that one body suit was for regular diving, the second one was for cold water and the third one was for swimming under ice when a diver was in the Arctic waters.

"When will you be diving in the Arctic?" I said through gritted teeth.

"I didn't say I'd go to the Arctic. There are times when there's ice on the Hudson River. If police need rescue work, I'm able to volunteer—to dive below the ice cakes."

"I don't want them hanging in the shower."

"What's wrong with that? They're made to get wet."

"I don't want to sit in the tub with six rubber legs in my lap."

We reached a compromise. Richard tore out the pantry closet in our kitchen to make room for his wetsuits.

A few weeks later Richard came home from the YMCA. He was breathless as he told me, "I was in the midst of teaching my class, when the guy from the front desk comes to me. He says, 'A Miz-O-ni-sis wants to speak to you.' I said to the guy, 'Tell the person I'll call back later.' Well, a half hour later the guy returns and says again, 'Miz-O-ni-sis wants to talk to you now.' So I repeat, 'Tell this person that I'm not through with my class. When I'm finished teaching, I will return the call.' "

"Well, who was it? Don't keep me waiting!"

Richard laughed. "After class I went to the guy's desk, and he handed me the note, which spelled out Mrs. Onassis. I just knew a friend of mine was playing a joke on me. I called the number and a man with a strong Chinese accent answered the phone. I bet some friend was putting on an act with that accent. Then she picked up the phone and said, "Hello, Mr. Forest. This is Jacqueline Onassis."

"Oh, my god, does she want scuba lessons?"

"No, she wants her son John to take scuba lessons. He's planning a trip to the South Pacific and, unless he's a certified diver, he can't go on this boating expedition."

"What are you going to do? Your course is almost over at the Y."

"She said that she preferred John to be in a class but if that's not possible, could I teach him privately."

"But Richard, you don't give private scuba lessons."

"Well, I'm going to make an exception. It's not every day that I can teach a son of a former American president."

"Of course, Richard. And it's not every day that you get to meet one of the most famous women in the world. Who happens to be a very beautiful, rich widow. I don't believe you'd be as enthusiastic if this was Bess Truman or Eleanor Roosevelt."

For his first interview Richard in his NAUI sports clothes drove our ten-year old Lincoln to Jacqueline's address on Fifth Avenue. He asked the doorman what he should do about his double-parked car (there's never a spot free on the Avenue). He didn't want to get a parking ticket. The doorman said, "Don't worry. You won't get a ticket." He then waved toward the two plainclothesmen sitting in the lobby. The men stared at Richard as he was escorted into a private elevator.

When the elevator man opened the door, Richard was on Jacqueline's floor, and she was waiting for him. Even though he won't admit it, I know he was in awe of her. She was taller than he expected, thin like a fashion model. She was all in black, from her blouse to her slacks and shoes as she was in mourning for a husband she didn't love, Ari Onassis. In one hand she held a burning cigarette and the other one she held out to Richard. "Hello, Mr. Forest. Come inside and meet John."

A gangly teenager with a dark mop of hair and big feet came forward. Richard met fifteen-year-old John, who explained he wanted to join a scuba diving trip in the South Pacific. Unless he was NAUI certified, he could not be part of a team diving for sunken ships.

Jacqueline brought Richard into her library. Every shelf, wall-to-wall, ceiling-to-floor, was filled with black leather-bound books about the Kennedys. Richard noticed on an end table a small framed photo of a seven-year old Jackie in her equestrian clothes with her father. This picture stood out as it was the only one of hers in Jacqueline's entire apartment. However, in John's bedroom were ceiling-to-floor pictures of his father. There was the famous photo of three-year-old John saluting the president's casket. He told Richard that he did not remember that moment. In fact he only has a couple of vague memories of those White House years and nothing of his father's assassination.

Richard was amazed at the bright colors of Jacqueline's decor. Some of her furniture was well worn from two teenagers and two small yapping dogs that ran freely around. There was a telescope in the living room. Jacqueline demonstrated how she liked to use it to view people in Central Park or passers-by on the Avenue.

Richard explained to John and Jacqueline that the age requirement for taking a scuba course was usually eighteen. But if John could pass the written as well as the open water tests, he could be certified. Richard said that he needed medical documentation for John that he was approved for diving. John would need certifications in CPR and First Aid. He would have to study books on Scuba Gas Laws. Be able to understand Dive Tables, know how to calculate dive times and decompression stops, know the risks of scuba diving, understand decompression sickness.

By the time Richard would be through teaching John, he would know about mask clearing. He would be comfortable enough to completely remove and replace his mask underwater while breathing. He would learn how to hover and to regulate his buoyancy compensator underwater, how to orally inflate this compensator in case the inflator was not functioning properly. He was required to understand all the methods of safe descending and ascending.

Then Richard opened his NAUI tote bag for the textbooks. He spread them out on the dining room table.

Obviously, Jacqueline was impressed with Richard enough to trust her son, (the only living heir to an assassinated American president) as his private student. The fact that Richard didn't come home until 2 a.m. was a clue. I calculated he had spent eight hours for their first get-acquainted meeting.

Richard said that when he went to his parked car to leave, he saw that the glove compartment's door was hanging open. For the last four years that we owned that car, we couldn't open the glove compartment. It was jammed. We just forgot about it.

Richard laughed. "The Secret Service men searched through the car. I can't believe they searched the damn glove compartment. Since I'll be driving John to scuba dives, these guys wanted to see if I had hidden anything dangerous. Maybe I carried a gun or somethin'. They actually had to break the glove compartment to open it. Then they couldn't get it back in place. Guess what they found? Rotting Mac Donald French fries, a half-eaten hamburger and a rotten apple."

I had to laugh, too. "My, my, for a first interview with Jacqueline, you seemed to be gone so long. What happened?"

"Well, after I explained the diving course, she asked me to stay for dinner."

"You couldn't say no to a dinner invitation?"

"I'm sorry I didn't get a chance to call to let you know. Time just flew by. After dinner, she just started talking about life and how her son loves the ocean the way that Jack did."

"She talked about Jack–to you?"

"I can tell you that she never once mentioned Ari Onassis. When she said 'my husband,' it was always Jack. She's still in love with him. Every time she said his name, the most poignant, distant look came into those big brown eyes. She was pouring herself a couple of drinks. Scotch, I think. I'm not sure. She was smoking and sipping her drinks in a way that I knew she didn't want me to leave."

"Huh, I never knew Jacqueline smoked. Well, that's no concern of ours. Did you tell her what the tuition is for a scuba diving course?"

"I didn't know what to tell her. I've never taught a private student before. She really wanted him to take my class. Be with other students. But I explained that my course at the YMCA just ended. The problem is that John has to be certified before this July."

Richard told me that he would need about 12 weeks to train John. Then Richard changed the subject. Jacqueline didn't recognize him from TV or Broadway, but when he mentioned he was starring with Roscoe Lee Browne at the American Place Theatre in the only play written by Robert Lowell, *Benito*

Cereno, she said she'd come to see it. He was a good friend of hers and Jack's. Not only has she read his poems, she'd read his translation of 'Phaedre'.

"Robert Lowell is considered to be one of the greatest poets in the first half of the twentieth century," I offered.

"No kiddin'." Richard said. "God damn it, sometimes you're so smart."

Richard wouldn't know that Phaedra was the wife of Theseus who fell in love with her stepson Hippolytus or that Lowell won the Pulitizer Prize for poetry because Richard was the product of a California high school. Worse than that, he was thrown out of tenth grade as his juvenile delinquency adventures got in the way. Like most actors he only knows what his character expresses on stage. His brilliance, his knowledge, his eloquence totally belongs to the erudite gifts of his playwright's words. He is truly a rhinestone cowboy, a perfect fit for Hollywood where, as Oscar Levant said, strip away the phony tinsel and you can find the real tinsel underneath.

The days flew by with Richard gone most of the time between performing at night and teaching John during the days. Late one afternoon I looked out our third floor bedroom window on 110th Street and Broadway. Below were two very tall, burly men leaning against the wall of our building. They were wearing flashy Hawaiian shirts with white pants. No one who lives on 110th Street dresses like that. We're part of a Columbia University neighborhood. Students and professors are not into this very Floridian or summer Mafia look. I called Richard to the window. "Who do you think they are? What kind of fashion statement is that?"

Richard said, "They look like private dicks. Wonder what they're lookin' for? Maybe someone here's in trouble."

"Not in our building. Not with all the elderly Jews who live here."

We lived across the street from a synagogue. The Jewish families, who were the main tenants in our building, had been survivors from World War II, and many of them had survived the concentration camps. They elected me to head the building's fight with the landlord over rent control issues. I knew everybody.

"But Richard why do they stay beneath our window? They've been there a long time."

"I'll go outside. Get a closer look. Then I'll go around the corner to the Golden Rail Bar. Have a drink. When I'm done, I'll come back and see if they're still here."

Richard ran off. He went into the bar. The bartender asked, "Are you being followed?" The bartender then pointed out two men in the doorway glancing in Richard's direction. Richard recognized the same guys in the Hawaiian shirts. He said to the bartender, "I'll leave now. If they leave, too, then we'll know for sure."

By the time Richard was back in our apartment, we saw the private dicks or (whatever they are called these days) leaning below our window again. "Richard, you're being followed because of John Kennedy."

"I hope there are several more guys. Let them follow me. Maybe I could lead them to the American Place Theater. Buy tickets. See me in my play."

The next few days, I noticed that every time I was on the phone, clicking started. My girlfriend who called me noticed it. "Is something wrong with the phone? What's that weird clicking sound?"

"Linda, it happens with all our calls. Not just with you. I think the Secret Service is listening in."

Linda said, "How boring to have to listen to us."

I said, "Hi guys, your clicking is really irritating. Don't make it so obvious. But do tell Jacqueline what fans we are. We adore her. Report that back, if you please."

Linda started to laugh. "The clicking stopped."

"And so it has," I said. "About time."

Jacqueline made arrangements to see Richard in the play at the American Place Theater. She was bringing John. Richard tried to play down his nervous excitement. He called the maitre d' at Joe Allen's Restaurant, made an after-theater reservation and asked if Jacqueline and John could be seated without being obvious. The maitre d' assured him of privacy for his celebrities.

Somehow, I was not informed which night Jacqueline was attending the play. It wasn't until Richard came home at his bewitching hour of 2 a.m. that he said he had been with her and John at Joe Allen's. "Why didn't you tell me? I would have loved to come."

"Just because I'm a married man doesn't mean I can't have a hamburger with a lady."

"Idiot! Jacqueline is not just some lady! I don't care about ladies! Just this lady! Why wouldn't I want to meet the most famous woman in my lifetime? Why wouldn't you want to share that experience with me? Why do you want to keep me away from her? Keep her all to yourself! You selfish pig!"

I would have slammed the bedroom door in his face except in our small-rent controlled apartment, my sleeping children would have awakened. The next morning I sat at the kitchen table. I had just plunked down a basket of my newly washed laundry. The phone on the kitchen wall rang. I reached for it.

"Hello, is Mr. Forest there?"

There was no mistaking the familiar voice. I said, "He's not in. May I take a message?"

"Is this Mrs. Forest?"

"Yes."

"Am I disturbing your lunch?"

"Not at all."

"Tell me, Mrs. Forest, what is it like being married to a matinee idol?"

You could have knocked me over with a clean washcloth. The family dog was ripping the laundry basket apart. He shook the clothes in the air, then dragged the basket so that everything spilled out. But I didn't care. I was talking to an idol herself. How do I answer her question? I wanted to say, "I will tell you what it is like to be married to a matinee idol if you will tell me what it was...?" I didn't have the nerve or courage. I said something mundane and thanked her for coming to see Richard in the play. She thought Richard was outstanding as Captain Delano in *Benito Cereno.*

Often I looked out the apartment window at our parked Lincoln on the street while Richard ran inside to collect scuba gear. I could see John Kennedy waiting in the car. Richard said John passed the tests in the YMCA's swimming pool. "We're ready to dive in open water. The first test is a quarry in New Jersey. If he passes that, and I am sure he will, tomorrow we'll go to Long Island and do the wading in, shore entry." Richard added, "Oh, don't wait up, I'll probably be late with John. He needs tutoring on how to read the dive tables."

As the Lincoln sped off with husband and student, the Secret Service cars raced behind it like a scene in the movie "The French Connection." A few times after dives with John, Richard stayed for dinner with him and Jacqueline. Richard confided to me that Jacqueline mentioned that she might like to take scuba lessons, too. She wanted to wait until John was certified. She did not want to distract him or seem to be in his way.

"I can't believe that you'd dunk Jacqueline in that putrid pool at the Y. The place smells like dirty, wet sweat socks. Are you going to put her into a class with other New York peons?"

"Of course not. I ran into Gwen Verdon the other day, she's interested in scuba diving."

"Are we talking about Bob Fosse's Gwen?"

"Yup. Wouldn't it be great? Jackie and Gwen in a class together!"

As all good things must end, John was ready to graduate from the scuba diving course. Richard said that John passed the math for scuba gas laws, Charles's Law, Henry's Law and Boyle's law.

A small graduation ceremony took place shortly after midnight in Jacqueline's apartment. Jackie, Richard and John were in blue jeans. Richard said that Jackie wore jeans quite often as she jogged around the pond in Central Park every day. No one recognized her as she covered her head and wore those huge sunglasses.

Richard handed John a card (showing his certification) to keep in his wallet. By showing the card at any dive shop in the world, he was eligible to use their scuba diving equipment. Richard also mentioned that on the same card, his name was printed and signed below John's. Everyone reading that card would know who trained John Kennedy, Jr.

A week later there was a letter from Jacqueline in our mail. It was a pale blue notepaper envelope addressed in her Miss Porter's School penmanship. Richard opened the letter and a check fluttered out. "Oh, my god! Look, what the fuck she's done! I can't accept this."

I took the check in hand and saw that it was for one thousand five hundred dollars. "Why can't you accept this?"

"It's not ethical. My YMCA students pay me eighty dollars for my course."

"Idiot. She's making up the difference. Your classes are around eighteen to twenty people. Isn't that so?"

"I don't feel right. I can't accept this amount."

"Accept it! Or I can frame the check and just let it hang on the wall. If we don't cash it, you won't feel unethical."

Richard snatched the check from my hand. "You can't frame this." Then he read her note. He choked. His eyes were teary.

"Well goodness, what did she write?" I took the note from him. I was taken aback at her words. She wrote that Richard had given her the greatest gift she had ever received: For the first time, John achieved something on his very own. There were no real male figures in his life to emulate, but Richard was a person whom John could look up to; she hoped their friendship would go on, that they would all do many things together.

Needless to say, we deposited the check and John went on to his summer vacation diving in the South Pacific. I assumed that was the end of Jacqueline O. I was unprepared when Richard said, "Ah, remember I said that when the American Place Theatre ends the run of *Benito Cereno*. I have a break of about three weeks before I return to a daytime TV? The producers might want to do the play in Paris as part of an exchange program."

"That sounds wonderful. Can you take your family?"

"Don't know yet. But for one of those weeks off, Jacqueline invited us to stay with her in Hyannisport."

"Terrific!" How thrilling it would be to meet her at last.

"But I explained to her we couldn't go. I promised the girls we'd go to California so they could meet their cousins."

"You turned her down?! For California cousins! I don't believe you're so stupid!"

"I made a promise to the girls that this year we could go to Los Angeles."

By this time Tina and Jennifer were skipping around and yelling, "California! We want to meet our cousins–our cousins in California!"

"Richard, they have the rest of their lives to meet your relatives. This is their only chance and mine to meet Jacqueline Kennedy. She's part of our history! What a great opportunity for us! Are you stark raving mad?"

"I gave my word to Tina and Jennifer. My word is my bond. By example they will learn that when a promise is made, you keep it. We're going to meet their cousins."

Richard doesn't fool me with his promise speech. I intuited that if Jacqueline were to meet me with two kiddies in tow, we might spoil his fantasy. Might deflate Jackie's friendship with him. We made the trip to California. Richard spent the vacation time with Gregory Peck filming *MacArthur* while I babysat with the girls and their California cousins.

*****

Years passed then one day I was in Kenneth's hair salon on the East Side in Manhattan. I was in the gift boutique when Jacqueline strolled in. What would she have said if I went up to her, and reminded her that when we last spoke, she asked what it was like to be married to a matinee idol. John Kennedy, now at Brown University, was still in contact with Richard. Recently, John wanted to review scuba gas laws. Richard arranged for him to come backstage at his Broadway show. Between scenes, Richard met with John in the actor's green room.

That day in Kenneth's I observed her without her noticing. She appeared much older than in recent photos. I still thought she was beautiful. There's no denying her charisma. She had no press agent, no public relation firms to keep her in the news, yet magazines had clamored to put her on their covers. I wanted to just stare but was afraid she might look over and catch me admiring her. Even that might be considered an invasion of her privacy. I never introduced myself to her. I didn't want to intrude upon her. I still had her phone number in my address book. Richard once said I was never to call him there unless our apartment house burned down or one of the girls was in a hospital dying.

A girlfriend asked me what I would have said if Richard had a mad affair with Jackie O. What could I say but, "I regret that I only have one husband to give to my country."

After our daughters grew up, I mentioned the Hyannisport invitation we turned down with Jacqueline. They were furious with me. I should have known they were too young to know the difference between a visit with California cousins and Jacqueline Onassis. Of course, they would rather have gone to Hyannisport. They asked me why I didn't insist? Parents never win. Not when you have an actor as a father.

Jacqueline did come to see Richard in another play. She brought Caroline along. Richard claimed that even though he spoke to John on occasion, he never spoke to Jacqueline again. She had a new escort in her life. There really was no room for a scuba diver-actor. Another very wealthy man, Maurice Templesman, a diamond merchant, was accompanying her to Hyannisport. He bought her a yacht. Something that a co-starring Broadway actor could never afford.

> "Actors are like cross word puzzles in which there are no words to fit the clues. Their personality is made up of the parts that they play and the basis of it is something amorphous."
>
> – Somerset Maugham

Chapter Eleven

After our family trip to California, Richard announced that in celebration of the American Bicentennial, the producers of the American Place Theater invited the cast of *Benito Cereno* to appear in Paris. This was an exchange program with the Theatre Oblique, whose company would come to America. To make up for his low salary ($150 weekly), the producers offered plane tickets for his entire family. We would spend a week in Amsterdam then three weeks in Paris.

The idea of seeing Paris and Amsterdam for the first time with my husband and children seemed like an impossible dream. My disappointment over losing out on a trip to Hyannisport with Jacqueline O was shelved somewhere in my brain along with some other of Richard's unpleasantries.

Now that our daughters had met their California cousins, they no longer had cared about them and were quite bored. They were thrilled at another trip, a new adventure. Richard hugged them enthusiastically. "You girls are now old enough at thirteen and eleven to come see me in *Benito Cereno*."

"What's it about?" Jennifer asked.

"Well, an American sailing vessel comes upon a Spanish slave ship in trouble. I play Captain Delano, who wants to be of help to the ship. All the officers have died. Apparently of the plague. As captain I'm rather tolerant of slavery but scornful about the ineptitude of the Spanish as sailors. On the slave ship, things aren't what they seem. The leader of the slaves is Babu. That's Roscoe Lee Browne's part. He and the other slaves have taken over the Spanish ship. But none of the slaves read or write and, of course, do not know how to sail a ship!"

"Do they kill you?" Tina asked.

"No, because they need me to sail their ship back home to Africa."

"Do you end up in Africa?" Jennifer asked.

"Oh, I don't want to ruin the suspense for you. I'll give you a hint. It ends in an uproar of gunplay and slaughter. It's a true story."

"How many girls are in your show?" Tina asked.

"None."

Tina asked, "Lots of pretty costumes?"

"I wear knee breeches, a wig. The African slaves are in rags."

"Any music in this play?" Jennifer asked hopefully.

"This is a drama not a musical comedy."

"I don't want to hurt your feelings, Dad. Can we go to the movies instead?" Jennifer exchanged looks with Tina, whose nose was crinkling as if a bad smell passed by. Richard smiled without amusement. "We are not going to Paris and Amsterdam to see movies. We're going for culture. When you grow up, you'll be able to tell your husbands that the first time you saw Paris was with your father when he starred in *Benito Cereno.*"

I interrupted, "What clothes should we take?"

"Bring your cocktail dresses. As Americans performing on stage, we'll probably be invited to official parties. Jackie O wants me to call Pierre Salinger as soon as we arrive in Paris. Now make sure to include down jackets for the girls and some heavy sweaters for us."

"Why would we bring winter clothes for July and August in Europe?"

"It could get cold and rainy like New York. And I'm not fucking going to end up buying sweaters and jackets." He turned away, absorbed in himself, as he checked his scuba equipment spread about the living room. There was a longing on his face as if he wanted to finagle some way to bring a scuba tank to Paris, too.

*****

Amsterdam was warm and sunny. The forecast predicted that a heat wave was headed for Europe. Having brought from bathing suits to wool jackets, we were hindered by dragging heavy suitcases up and down staircases. Experienced travelers were carrying light backpacks as they raced past us. How I yearned to be like them with just a backpack while biking along the street.

Richard refused to join the girls and me on any tours. "Sweetheart, I can't wear myself out riding a tour bus when I have to be rested for my performance at night. I'm too busy. Plus the director, Austin Pendleton, wants me to help him cast the smaller parts with local actors. After that, I have to run scenes with the new actors."

Every day, Tina, Jennifer and I took tours of tulip fields and museums, which bored them. We ventured inside windmills, then tried on wooden shoes, which they loved. We climbed through the hidden attic at the Anne Frank house where I began to sob. The girls, horrified at my reaction, raced ahead of the line so the tourists wouldn't guess they were related to a mother who was having an emotional meltdown.

I kept asking Richard if one day, he couldn't join us for at least one tour. He begged off, saying the weather was too hot. He preferred to stay in an air conditioned hotel room. He needed a nap every day to restore his energy for the play.

The night before we left Amsterdam, Richard had invited another couple to join us for dinner. I was so curious. "How did you meet them? Are they Dutch actors?"

"They're not actors. I met them on a nude beach."

"A nude beach! Where?"

"Around here. Nude beaches are quite common. Europeans approve of them. Everyone here loves to sun themselves on a nude beach. It's quite relaxing."

At dinner time I was introduced to a very tan couple. In fact they were a deep shade of Coppertone Bronze. He was a banker, and she was his girlfriend, Brigitte. She was petite but curvaceous. Her bovine eyes were fixated on Richard with that look of awe fans get when meeting an actor. As I was chewing my food, I tried to picture them naked on the beach together. A lurid picture came into my imagination of being naked on a beach towel and having this couple standing over me. How can you make conversation when confronted with body parts swinging overhead? A red flag went up in my mind. A nudist named Brigitte spelled trouble. I reminded myself that I should be glad that Brigitte had a boyfriend, and that this was the last night Richard and I were in Amsterdam. Tomorrow we would be safe in Paris, rid of this couple and their hedonistic lifestyle.

*****

No one in Paris, it seemed, was prepared for the worst heat wave since the 1600s. Below the Eiffel Tower people dropped over dead on the pavement. Cows were dying in the countryside. Richard, the children and I were squeezed in a sweltering taxi that brought us from the airport to the Richard Lenoir Hotel. Previously Richard made sure the Theatre Oblique was within walking distance of our hotel. This was an Actors Equity union rule.

The four of us stood on the narrow sidewalk in front of a tavern. Richard went inside for a moment. When he returned, he had a key. "The hotel is above the tavern." Thus began the four-story climb dragging suitcase after suitcase behind us. Those we couldn't carry we left downstairs. Richard fell face first on a bed as I ran back to retrieve the rest of the luggage. I unpacked our clothes and hung them in closets and placed other stuff in dressers.

There was a roar of engines just outside the windows. In a plaintive cry, Richard said, "What's that noise?" I looked out the window. Right below, trucks were driving along the Richard Lenoir Boulevard. If I jumped from the window I would land directly on the hood of one. "It seems," I said, "that this street is a truck route."

Richard rolled over on the bed, his eyes still closed. "I can't stay here. Not with that noise all day. I have to be able to sleep. Or I can't perform at night."

I sat on the bed beside him. "Actors Equity put us here, close to Theatre Oblique–within walking distance. Remember?"

"Fuck Equity, we're getting out. Pack up!"

I jumped from the bed and called to Tina and Jennifer to come immediately, we were moving. We shoved all of our possessions as fast as we could into seven suitcases. At the top of the stairs on the landing, we pushed our baggage so that it tumbled down the staircase to the next landing. We repeated this act four more times until we made it to street level.

Three hours later we were still trekking along the Right Bank. Not one hotel had accommodations left. The innkeepers chastised us for not having reservations in the height of tourist season. Once we covered the Right Bank on foot, we went over to the Left Bank. The hotels there were also booked for the rest of the summer. The girls began to cry out how much they hated Paris.

At every other street corner, we stopped to catch our breath in the sweltering 105° temperature. The heavy luggage was becoming too much to carry. The average Parisian was rude to us each time we asked for directions. Richard said, "The next fuckin' Frenchman that pretends he doesn't speak English, I'm going to remind him that if it weren't for the Americans, the Nazis would have cooked his goose a long time ago."

"Richard, we have to eat. Let's find a place."

We were on a corner with a street sign, ST-GERMAIN-DES-PRES. The street was filled with soigné boutiques, 18th century apartment buildings and cozy-looking bistros. We leaned our suitcases near a door of one and I said, "Oh, Richard, let's sit outside." Of the four of us, Jennifer was the only one who spoke French. We were forced to have her translate for us. She placed our food order by rattling off something in her schoolgirl's French to the waiter as she pointed to her choice in a menu. Ten minutes later the waiter served four banana splits dripping with hot fudge. "Jennifer, it's dinnertime. Why didn't you order real food?" I no longer had the energy to argue.

"Cause they stopped serving dinner an hour ago. Sundaes are served all day long here." She and Tina were so happy to slurp up cold ice cream.

Again on the Boulevard, our tired journey took us to the square in front of Notre Dame. "Look everybody! Look at the Cathedral. It's centuries old. This is where Joan of Arc had her trial. Maybe we can tour it." But no one paid any attention to me. No one cared about this masterpiece of French Gothic architecture. The girls were whining, "How much longer before we find a place to stay?" Then they started hitting each other. I didn't care. I wanted to stop a minute to drink in the scene of Notre Dame, the true heart of Paris. Richard shouted, "Hurry up! For God's sake, what're you doing?" I didn't pay any attention. I wanted my chance to look back on the beautiful past, to imagine my footsteps tracing those of Napoleon who was crowned here.

A few minutes later we found Hotel Esmeralda. We entered the foyer with fake art and tapestries strewn about. It was straight out of Flaubert's' "Madame Bovary." The clerk at the desk spoke English. That was encouraging. Behind him was a vertiginous spiral staircase. Most of these picturesque hotels were built before the invention of the elevator. I was about to ask Richard how could we ever climb the staircase with the luggage, when he ventured, "The concierge guy says we're in luck. There's no room here, but they're leasing out an apartment a block away. Let's go."

We strolled along a very quaint street. The address was across from an old church and above a tavern. "Don't worry. No trucks on this street. We're on the third floor," Richard said.

The children, Richard and I climbed up a narrow stairwell. Richard unlocked the apartment door to a huge hallway. A closet on one side contained a filthy hot plate and sink. The main room had two wooden platforms that held mattresses with another one on the floor. The large front windows had panes of colored plastic to cover the missing glass, as if to prevent the ominous flies and moths. He and the girls ran for the makeshift beds and collapsed. No one wanted to help me unpack so I just sat on a stool and stared out a broken window. Though it was past ten in the evening, the sun still shone. There was a warm balm that settled around us. I could hear the lazy chatter of people coming from the distant cafes. Richard had settled into a slight snore that meant he was in a deep sleep.

Simultaneously two male voices lifted in a harmonious song. I went to the French window and, pulling it aside, saw a couple of men sitting below on the curb. They were in that state of inebriation where there is no pain. From the apartment above, a voice broke out in French curses. Within a second a flood of water ran past me and splashed on the men below. Thus the duet stopped and so the romance of the night ended.

The next day, as Richard went off to rehearse his play, the girls and I pored over "Michelin's Guide Book" on how to see Paris for twenty dollars a day. We boarded tour buses bursting at the seams with irritable tourists. Passengers were griping at the lack of air conditioning. The tired guide assured everyone that once the bus began moving, the air would feel cooler whipping through open windows.

We ran around the dead gardens that once bloomed in better days at Chateau De Chantilly. We viewed all the rows of superb paintings in the Grand Salon there. At the end we could not remember one face of a duke, of a king, or a monk's; they began to blur together in a collage of homely royals that graced so many French museums.

In the afternoon we decided to visit Château de Malmaison, Josephine Bonaparte's home. Researching our guidebook we took first a metro then a city bus. Once we left the bus, we walked a short distance. There was a boulangerie. Jennifer and Tina ran inside for an ice cream cone. "Buy some water for me," I cried out to them. Seconds later the girls returned, licking their ice cream cones. "Where's the water." I said.

"Mom, you can buy water at Josephine's house." Jennifer said as she and Tina skipped ahead of me.

By the time we found the entrance for the tour of Josephine's maison, I was parched from the heat. "Look! There's a man selling from his cart. Ask him, Jennifer, for water." She said, "Don't want to, he has a mean face."

I screeched, "Ask for water or I will strangle you!"

Hesitantly, Jennifer murmured in French to the vendor, then glanced over her shoulder at me: "He doesn't sell water, just popsicles." She and Tina ran the rest the way to the main house. I saw a guard and asked him if knew where I could find water. I gestured in a way that got my message across. He pointed to a spigot for garden hoses in the sunburnt lawn. I fell to my knees, then crawled through the dirt of what once was a flower bed until I was able to turn on this faucet. I heard my daughters hollering, "What're you doing? You're embarrassing us!" I caught the water in my hands. I threw it into my mouth, wetting my entire shirt front and hair. No desert camel driver ever suffered such thirst as I did that day.

By the time we made it home to our shabby, chic but filthy apartment, Richard was waiting for us. "Hi, everyone. Having a good time?" Tina complained, "Too many museums in Paris." She and Jennifer fell upon their mattresses as they were worn out.

"I did the laundry for you," he said with a bit of hesitation.

"Thanks. You found a laundromat?"

"I tried. I stuffed the dirty laundry in my duffel bag. I walked for blocks stopping people for directions to a laundromat. They answered in French, gesturing this way and that. I was lost. So I gave up. Came back with some soap and threw everything into the tub. I hand-washed the laundry."

"What an awful task to do alone, my darling."

"I'm afraid I made a big mistake. I threw Tina's red playsuit in the tub. After letting the clothes soak for a half hour, I went to wring out the things. Then I saw that all the white T-shirts and socks are bright pink."

"Oh, dear, dear. How are we going to dry our stuff?"

"I found a dive shop. The guy spoke English. He sold me fishing line. Look." Richard led me into our living area. There strung out high across the middle of the room was the fishing line draped with our pink clothes. Water dripped everywhere but in this heat wave, a wet floor no long mattered.

*****

Benito Cereno opened to great reviews. The headlines read: "Gripping Lowell work by visiting U.S. group." Both Richard and Roscoe Lee Browne were praised as outstanding and superb actors.

Smash hit reviews in New York guarantee that a play will be a hit, sold out for the entire run. However, Parisians didn't care. Very few wanted to sit in a theater without air conditioning. Some nights there were only eight to ten people in the audience. Usually there were more actors on stage than audience members. Richard said he thought one night he might faint on stage. The hot lights on the stage added to the actors' misery. The perspiration ran so heavily down his face, he was almost blinded. He said, "Here I am stuck in my wool costumes. How do I keep performing in this fuckin' heat? I don't know how I manage to do it!"

The next morning he gave me the news that Pierre Salinger had called. Because of Jackie Onassis, we were invited to his apartment on the Rue de Rivoli. "Sweetheart, wear one of those cocktail dresses you brought." Then he said, "I can't go because I have to be at the theater early. We're having a photo session for a French magazine."

"Does this mean I have to take Jennifer and Tina alone?"

"Sorry, it can't be helped."

Early in the evening, the girls and I sat in the spacious living room of Pierre Salinger and his current French wife.

We said, "Hello."

They said, "Hello."

We smiled.

They smiled.

Mrs. Salinger brought us each a lemonade. There was a round of thanks from us and more smiles. We sipped politely. The Salingers didn't bother to indulge in lemonade drinks.

I mentioned *Benito Cereno* as a great opportunity to see American actors at their best. My suggestion was met with an awkward silence.

Salinger didn't exhibit any interest in the visiting American theater. In fact he turned away to make a business call, speaking in French. He stared at us the entire time as though we were aliens that had crept into his home. Finally after an hour, I made our excuses and thanked them.

They thanked us for coming.

We smiled and waved goodbye.

They smiled and waved goodbye.

We ran out of their building anxious to remove our fancy and uncomfortable duds. I tore off my high heels and tread the cobblestone streets barefoot. So much for Jacqueline's recommendation of President Kennedy's PR man.

After the night's performance, we waited for Richard by the stage door. The first thing he said, "Does Salinger want to see the play?"

"Sorry, he never said a word about your play."

"You mean he never said anything? Jackie recommends the play and—"

"Forget it, Richard. He probably knows the theater's not air conditioned. It's too hot to go to a theater in Paris."

"I guess you're right. I was so hot on stage tonight, I thought I might pass out. See Paris and die–in this heat wave."

Early in the morning Richard woke me up. "Sweetheart, I have a surprise for you. I went to a travel agent. I've arranged for you to take a trip, get a break from the heat and hassle."

"Oh, honey, what have you done? We can't afford to be extravagant."

"Doesn't matter, when it concerns your well-being." He held up a pamphlet with a picture of Mont Saint-Michel. "Look at the beauty of this place. An isle surrounded by beaches. Take your beach towel and bathing suit. Lie out and relax on the beach."

I studied the photo, which resembled a Disneyland castle. "Oh, it's beautiful."

"This is a 264-foot mound of rock topped by an abbey. Look at the timeless majesty. In the Middle Ages, pilgrims considered Mont Saint-Michel an image of paradise on earth. That's where you're going for four nights and five days—paradise!"

"Sometimes, Richard, you're so thoughtful. When do I go?"

"This afternoon, I'll put you on the train."

"But, but, it doesn't seem fair to leave you alone to entertain the girls."

"Don't worry. There is a public swimming pool built out over the Seine. We can sit in the water all day and keep cool. They're tired of touring museums anyhow."

Richard and the girls accompanied me to the train station. "Richard, are you sure the hotel and Mont Saint-Michel has an English staff?" I felt hesitant. This seemed a little fast. I like to prepare for my adventures.

Richard said, "The hotel is multilingual. Don't worry."

"How long is my train ride?"

"About three hours and forty-five minutes."

"That's long!"

"Well, you're going to the coast of Normandy, that's why. You'll be able to see the English Channel. Here's a packet of your reservations and prepaid train tickets." He shoved the papers into the beach bag I brought with me. "After the train, there's an itty-bitty ride on a bus."

He opened the compartment of the train with four private seats. I was traveling first class. We kissed goodbye. After he left, two Frenchwomen entered. They motioned to me that I was in the wrong seat. I stood puzzled then stepped out into the aisle of the train. From nowhere, Richard appeared again. "Hon, I thought I'd better check on you. Just in case."

I showed him the ticket. "What did I do wrong?"

"Oh, my darling, all the seats have numbers. Like getting a reserved theater seat. Not like American trains." He pushed me back in the compartment, apologizing to the French ladies. He matched my number to the correct seat. I gazed at him fondly. "Oh, dear sweetheart, I feel like a stupid tourist." He said, "You're not," with a kiss and a wave of goodbye again.

After a couple of hours the train stopped at Rouen. I disembarked with the rest of the passengers. My instructions were to take a bus, which was located in front of the train station. I wanted to stay and to look around Rouen. It was here that Joan of Arc gave an agonized cry of "O Rouen, art thou then to be my final abode!" The English dragged her out to be burned alive. The exact spot of the pyre was marked by a cross in front of the Eglise Jeanne-d' Arc, a modern church. Unfortunately, I was handicapped as I don't speak enough French to inquire if there were time enough for me to explore Rouen.

Outside the train station, I saw twelve buses lined up. Which was the one for Mont Saint-Michel? I asked the station master but he didn't understand English. He directed me to another man at a desk, who didn't understand me either. Then for some reason, I said, "Parlez vous Espanol?" "Si, si," he said. For the first time in my life I was able to use my high school Spanish. "Donde esta Mont-St. Michel? Qual autobus?"

He held up three fingers: "Tres."

I assumed he meant the number three bus. I picked out a bus, then climbed inside to find both a driver and a man who seemed to be in charge of making change. I said with a thick French accent as though it would help, "Mont Saint-Michel, s'il vous plait." The men stared at me in silence. I opened my hand with what I hoped was the right change. The change maker picked out the correct amount. I proceeded to the back of the bus. Soon we were on our way. The bus seemed also to be a city bus. It kept stopping at neighborhood bus stops. People got off. More people got on. A half an hour later the passengers were gone. Then, about twenty schoolgirls in uniforms boarded. The bus now became some kind of school bus. One by one the girls eventually left.

The bus traveled through city streets then into the countryside. We were now just a lonely threesome. The bus made a turn onto a bumpy road. We seemed to be entering a thick, dark forest that looked like Sherwood Forest, only this wasn't England. I had no idea where we were. The bus slowed, then parked by an old tavern. The driver and his change-maker exited. I watched them enter the tavern. I saw them sitting at a table. A waiter soon brought them mugs of beer. I wanted to join my comrades. But what if they took off and drove away without me? I was afraid to leave the bus. After an hour, the men came back to the bus. Once again we were on the move. They kept looking over their shoulders at me. Their expressions were not friendly. I had a feeling that if they weren't stuck with me as a passenger, they could go home.

The bus rolled into a tiny village, Ponternon. Pulling up to another bus stop, the driver slammed on the brakes. The two men stared at me again without so much as a word or nod. I got off anyway and entered the one-room bus station. The female clerk, speaking English, told me that it is a ninety-minute wait for the next bus to the Mont. I began to cry. It was impossible for me to wait so long. This station didn't even have one chair for a weary passenger. She saw me sniffling then offered, "If you want to pay a taxi, it's a fifteen minute ride."

I dashed across the street to the only taxi parked next to a train station. Another stroke of luck, the driver spoke English. He motioned me inside and smiled when I said my destination was Mont Saint-Michel. "Aha," he said, "Did you know that after the Eiffel Tower and the Louvre, Mont Saint-Michel is the most important historic place in France?" I shook my head no. He chuckled. "I bet you didn't know that in the Middle Ages this spiritual destination was as important as Rome and Jerusalem were to the French Pilgrims." "Really?" I answered, hungry to hear my mother tongue spoken to me for a change. "Tell me more."

"Did you know," he continued, enjoying his spiel as much as I was, "England tried to capture this Mont during the Hundred Years' War. When the French Revolution came, they drove the Benedictine monks out. Later Napoleon used it for seven hundred political prisoners. Tortured every last one of 'em."

By the time he finished with the history lesson, the taxi was within sight of the famous abbey, this wonder of the Western World. The minute I noticed it, I understood what historians meant that to gaze upon the abbey was to see an unforgettable view. It inspired visions of medieval grandeur; intoxicated you with its beauty.

We turned onto a causeway that linked the land to the Mont. Finally we parked at the entrance. The driver carried my overnight case up three steep flights of stairs to La Mere Poulard, a legendary hotel. I thanked him profusely for the fabulous history lesson and gave him an extra big tip. He left smiling as I went to the concierge. No one here spoke English. The night manager did, but he was not here at the moment. However, the staff understood me as I presented my passport. A porter took me up a couple more flights of stairs to my room. It was breathtaking, too. I hurried to open the huge French windows. There was a small balcony with a view of what seemed to be the entire world, the faraway sea, the villages and the magnificent beaches spread about the mount.

There was no time to waste. The sun was still bright enough for me to go to the beach. I slipped into my swimming suit, put a beach dress over it. Pulled on a hat and tucked a beach towel into my tote bag. I raced down the stairs and out to the narrow steps. I spied another staircase that appeared to lead to the beaches. I climbed down them. There were some huge rocks. I managed to slide over them, too.

Ah, the beach, it was quite breathtaking. So restful. I proceeded downward looking for the best spot for my beach towel. The warm sand was chalky white, but there also seemed to be a great deal of marshland in the way. Looking about, I realized that I'm the only one on the beach. Maybe it was too late in the day for hotel guests or tourists? Frankly, I loved the privacy and continued strolling. Suddenly I heard a bull horn blowing, just like in a prison movie. A voice from a loudspeaker boomed out, "Garde-a-vous! Garde-a-vous!" From one of the turrets of the abbey I saw a guard waving frantically. The loudspeaker squawked again, "Va-t-en! Allez-vous-en!" I don't know what that meant.

Throwing down my beach towel, I prepared to sit. A sharp whistle pierced the air. A Jeep with two uniformed guards headed in my direction. If they're not careful, they were going to drive over me. The Jeep skidded within a foot, making the tires spit sand across my towel and into my face. One of the guards stood in the Jeep. He shouted, "Garde-a-vous! Va-t-en! Allez-vous-en!" He threw out his arms as if to push me back.

There was no language barrier any more. It was very clear that for some reason I'm not allowed on the beach. I scrambled back up the rocks, swinging my beach bag. I ran up the steep stairs to my hotel. Once inside I noticed from the manager's face that he knew what was up with the French watchdogs. I began sputtering, "What's wrong with the beach." I tried to catch my breath.

"Madame Forest, no one is allowed on the beach. It is quicksand."

"Quick—quicksand?" I repeat in shock.

"Yes, we are completely surrounded by it. Some people come here to commit suicide. Of course, we rescue them."

Before I could stop my sense of humor, I said in a tiny, mild voice, "Oh Mont Saint-Michel, art thou then to be my final abode?" The manager raised his eyebrows. Discomfited, he replied, "I don't find that amusing."

I forgot the French don't have any real sense of humor, especially about Joan of Arc who said that line.

He lectured on as though he were talking to a naughty child. "That's why we have the guards to patrol and watch the beach areas. If you kept going eventually, you'd sink and—" he snapped his fingers—, "disappear like that."

I realized that I had to leave this place immediately. How was I going to last five days and four nights? A feeling of abandonment came over me. "I—I need to make a phone call to Paris. Can you help me?"

"Madame, we have no phone service with the mainland this late."

How in the hell am I going to tell Richard there's no way I can stay in this fortress for the rest of the week? Did he know about the quicksand? He seemed to know everything else. Maybe the travel agent forgot that little detail. I was stuck, and there was nothing left to do but make the best of it. I was suddenly too tired to understand or to care.

The hotel's location, right by the main gateway, was most convenient to investigate the small restaurants and shops, which sold tacky souvenirs at tourist-inflated prices. I attempted to order a dish of ice cream in one of the cafes. I held up two fingers to emphasis two scoops of vanilla. The perplexed waiter brought me nine saucers with a scoop of ice cream on each one. Since I couldn't order in French, I smiled at him and pretended to enjoy all nine scoops of ice cream of which I left three to melt.

In the early evening I dined at the hotel's restaurant. A large elegant menu boasts of Norman food as the best in France. Since my waiter doesn't speak English, I put my finger on a drawing of a lobster and nodded. The waiter bowed with a smile and disappeared. He returned carrying a small basket. Leaning over me, he whipped off a checkered napkin. A large lobster waved a taped claw at me. His feelers wiggled. The crustacean struggled to crawl out. I knew this was to show me how fresh the lobster cuisine was, but I couldn't bring myself to eat anything that had eyes staring at me. In fact, I had just lost my appetite.

Bored, I retired to my room. There was no television or radio, not even a magazine, a book or a Gideon's Bible. The only reading material I had with me was my 'Michelin's Guide: How to See Paris on $20 a day.' I'll read that again and see if I missed something to tour with my daughters.

I threw open my French windows and let the magic of the night enter, as the song goes. Switching on a lamp light, I crawled into bed with the guide book.

A few minutes later, I felt a plop on my blanket. Did I imagine this? The second plop came. At the foot of my bed are two large black, feathery creatures that resembled vampire-bats with their beaks and long legs. I glanced up at the ceiling, which was coated with hundreds of these critters. They are now raining upon me. I leaped out of bed, clicked off the light, then opened the door to the hallway. Jumping back on the bed, I took my pillows and swatted at these creatures from the quicksand lagoons, hoping to drive them toward the light in the hall. There are too many. I was outnumbered. My retreat was a chair in the hall where I spent the rest of the night until daybreak. Soon the dawn's early light culled the black creatures back to the sandy marshlands.

At eight o'clock in the morning there was a tour of the abbey, which was given in English. I asked the female guide from London what the sign near the first gate meant? She said, "It's a warning. The tides here are the largest in Europe. When the moon, earth and sun are aligned, the water can rush over the causeway and beach like a galloping horse at fifty miles per hour."

"How often does this happen?"

"Twice a month," she said. "Wasn't a schedule given to you at the tourist office in Paris?"

I shook my head no. She continued, "If you're stranded here, just enjoy the lovely hotel and the omelettes of La Mere Poulard."

All I needed now was to be stranded on this Mont. I accompanied her and the English tourists. She explained there are some steps to climb, in fact ninety steps for us to reach the entrance of the abbey, but who's counting? But now she made us ascend the famous Grand Degre, a wider flight of steps to the Saut Gautier Terrace. All the stone figures on the columns have had their faces or heads hacked off. I asked her why these magnificent statues here and everywhere on the Mont are missing their heads or faces. She said, "During the French Revolution, the peasants destroyed them."

Without her, all of us would be lost entering the maze of vaulted halls. She led us through the refectory where monks took their meals in silence as the life stories of saints were read. Soon we were in the dungeon where Napoleon threw his prisoners in small windowless rooms where the men couldn't stand and eventually became crippled and blind. Then onto the ossuary once filled with the bones of monks, which housed a giant wheel where two to four men like giant gerbils walked inside and by doing this pulled supplies up the side of the wall. She explained the prisoners were anxious to be picked for this task as it was the only form of exercise they received here.

Then she led us to Excalier de Dentelle. Set atop one of the "flying buttresses" of the main church, this is the famous perforated "Lace Staircase" that leads to a parapet adored with stone gargoyles, 390 feet above the sea. I murmured to myself, "Oh my, oh my, not this staircase, too." But, our guide soldiered on and no one protested the steep climb. The guide pointed out the golden statue of Saint Michael placed upon the steeple for it was he who appeared in a dream to the bishop of Avranches in 709 and ordered him to build this edifice. She turned to us. "The French believe that it was Saint Michael who protected the abbey during World War II."

An Englishman whispered to me, "It was really General Dwight Eisenhower who saved the Mont. The Mont was filled with Nazis who wanted to shoot down the Brits by flying over the Channel. Some of the allies wanted to bomb the place, but Eisenhower wouldn't allow it. The bloody French have a way of forgetting that along with D-Day!"

Even though my legs felt like wobbly rubber bands, I made it back to my hotel where I collapsed upon a couch in the lobby. Nearby was a middle-aged couple who sounded as if they were speaking in English. I called to them, "Excuse me. Can you tell me how one leaves this place? I don't speak French, and the employees here don't understand enough English. My prepaid ticket says a bus will pick me up in three days for the train. I can't wait that long."

The husband said, "We're leaving tomorrow in the morning at six. There's a bus that goes straight to the train station."

His wife explained that being Canadian, they were bilingual (French and English). "My dear, bring your suitcase to the entrance of the causeway. We'll exchange your train ticket, too." I thanked them saying, "I have always depended upon the kindness of strangers." They looked at me blankly. From their expressions, they still didn't understand so I excused myself and hurried to my room.

My hands were trembling as I packed my pink shirts and underwear in my overnight case. I was escaping from the tides that might come if the moon or something else was aligned with it. I was left wearing one pink cotton blouse. Even though Richard carelessly put our daughter's red suit in the wash, I must remember to give him an A for the effort.

In the morning the Canadian couple and I rode the bus to the railroad station in Ponteronon where I could connect with the train to Paris. This time I won't have to manage a bus transfer. The husband showed my prepaid ticket to a man in a booth. There was a long conversation in French about exchanging this ticket for a new one. The husband's voice rose impatiently. I tried not to panic

At last the Canadian couple returned to me. The husband gave me the new ticket and said not to worry, I am on my way to Paris in just a few minutes.

After arriving in Paris in the middle of the afternoon, I was quite proud that I found the right metro to the Left Bank. I knew how to say, "Ou est"—then give the name of the hotel and follow the direction people gestured. Upon reaching the neighborhood of the Hotel Esmeralda, I ran the block to our flat. I unlocked the door of our rooms. What a surprise to see Tina and Jennifer lying on their beds looking rather bored. I was dismayed to find them alone.

"Hi, Mom, did you have a nice trip?" Tina said.

Jennifer said, "Are you more relaxed, more rested from us?"

My heart seemed to race. "Where's your father? Why're you alone?"

"Oh, he said he would be gone for just awhile. Don't worry, we're safe." Tina wanted to be reassuring.

"Where did he go?"

"He had to walk Brigitte to her room. He 'll be back in an hour?"

"Do you mean Brigitte from Amsterdam? The girl he met at the nude beach?"

"Yeah, that's the one," Jennifer said. "Brigitte was so sorry her boyfriend couldn't come to Paris with her."

"How long has Brigitte been here?"

"The day you left on the train. We waited at the station, and soon Brigitte's train arrived. Dad was able to get her room at the hotel, too."

"Why do you look upset, Mom?" Tina asked. "Brigitte just hung out with us every day at the swimming pool. We didn't really do much else."

"Kiddies, I have to go on an errand. I'll be right back." I ran from them, bolted down the stairs two at a time. I raced along the street passing the Tunisian and Moroccan restaurants with the naked carcasses of beef and chicken swinging in the windows. At this hour in the day, the street was empty. I tried not to sound breathless as I entered the lobby of the hotel. The bored manager barely looked up when I asked if he could ring the room of my dear friend Brigitte, the very pretty Dutch girl who came about four days ago. He didn't need any more explanation. He seemed to know her quite well. How often had Richard been escorting Brigitte to her room? Did the manager know that my husband was using a room for his clandestine affair with his amour from Amsterdam? I was perspiring, and it was not from the heat. The manager dialed the house phone. It rang and rang. The suspense was growing. At last the manager hung up. "Sorry, no answer."

Slowly, I left. Standing against a wall, I felt I couldn't breathe. Paris, which seemed so beautiful, had lost its luster; the sidewalks were an ugly gray, the wafting of greasy bistro smells sickened me.

In the distance, Richard was coming toward me but he hadn't noticed yet. I studied him. He wore his pink shirt and pink matching athletic socks. He looked as if he were airing his dyed laundry in public. Then he saw me and smiled. He seemed untouched by any hint of sin or emotional larceny.

As he crossed the street, I had to choose between confronting him in a bloodless but unruly scene or react as if nothing had changed in our lives. He called in a casual way, "Hi sweetheart, did you have a good time?" He approached. His arms lovingly outstretched.

"I had a great time."

“Oh, I’m so glad. You deserved a break from us.” He squeezed my arm as we sauntered toward our flat. He didn’t even appear surprised at my early arrival. I reminded myself that in four days we would be on a plane home to New York. Brigitte would return to sunbathing nude in Amsterdam, out of harm’s way.

Richard appeared happy and cheerful. “Are you hungry? Wanna eat?”

“Not right now. Maybe later.”

“Sure, sweetheart.” He stopped at a newsstand.

*****

How can he carry on as though he had not left behind some Dutch girl in our hotel? What vague promises did he leave on her lips? Does he not realize the misery his unfaithfulness causes me? The July heat crushes down upon me. The tears will be secret. I have two daughters to shield from his abominable behavior. They plead with me to keep the family together. They don’t care that the experts claim children of divorce are happier living apart from parents, our daughters want us together forever.

And this infidelity, too, shall pass.

"Some of the greatest love affairs I have known have involved one actor – Unassisted”

– Wilson Mizner

Chapter Twelve

Twelve Years Earlier – 1962

Roy Scheider and I sit together during a rehearsal break at Arena Stage in Washington D.C. This fall the opening play of the season is the screwball comedy "Once in a Lifetime" by Moss Hart and George S. Kaufman. It's the same old story of starry-eyed kids who want to come to Hollywood to be in the movies. Even though the satire is set in the twenties, the characters are stereotypical. We're reviving this play, which hasn't been done since 1930. We're trying to come up with ideas to infuse into a play that is not the best of Hart and Kaufman. Our artistic director, Zelda Fichandler, who has chosen to direct this play, has no sense of humor. Her forte is raising money such as the one million dollars Ford Foundation contributed to her theater. She should stay in her office and do what she does best. She is of no real help to either Roy or me.

I'm in awe of Roy. He is the first young actor I've met who has been married, a stepfather, divorced and now married a second time, and owns a pet monkey. Where I come from, pets are dogs or cats. No one has a monkey swinging through his house. How sophisticated of Roy, how *je ne sais quoi.*

This past summer I spent at the Olney Playhouse in Maryland where I played opposite Sam Wanamaker and Dana Elcar in Ionesco's "Rhinoceros." It was the biggest success of the Playhouse in ten years. As I tell Roy, there is no high like rave reviews and an audience's applause and cheers. Forget snorting cocaine, the high I receive from an audience's affirmation of love is what sends me flying across the ceiling. Sam Wanamaker and I flew back to New York City together. He arranged for me to meet author Irwin Shaw (The Young Lions) as he has written a play for Broadway that Sam will direct. I auditioned but didn't get the part. So I returned to Arena Stage for my second season. Recently discharged from the Air Force, Roy has no real theater credits yet.

"Roy, I have something you can do that would be fun," I said as I pulled him to his feet. "As you exit, do a tap step 'Shuffle off to Buffalo.' It's a standard time-step done by vaudevillians. Here I'll show you how." I demonstrate. Roy moves behind me as I do the step again. He tries but can't coordinate his footwork.

"Look, Roy, the left foot shuffles down as you hop on it, raising the right leg. Then hop back on the right, crossing the left foot over the right ankle. Then repeat."

He confuses his right leg with his left, as his arms bounce awkwardly about him.

"Roy, for now just do left foot, slap down, then hop on it."

But he can't get that combination together either. I suggest, "Hop on one foot."

He loses his balance hopping. He has no sense of balance, no rhythm, no coordination. This is shocking in a young actor. He must have been some prom date's nightmare. "I have a better idea, Roy. When you exit with the other actress, hang onto her arm as you hop on one leg. Then give a big smile and a big wave to the audience, and they will be so distracted that no one will catch on to the fact that you can't dance."

Years later, Roy was nominated for an Oscar in "All That Jazz," portraying one of the greatest dancers and choreographers in the Broadway theater, Bob Fosse. I couldn't wait to see the movie. What did Fosse do when he discovered that Roy has two left feet? Well, Fosse learned what I experienced. Roy, in the movie, stood still and puffed on a cigarette as the dancers leaped over him, did arabesques around him, threw kicks before his tense face. He strutted through a throng of dancers as though ministering to each one. In one scene, he ran and slid on his knees as if dancing. The chorus line jumped over his head in splits as others twirled before him. It is an achievement to Fosse's direction that the audiences never noticed that Roy didn't dance a step in a movie about dancers.

"Once in a Lifetime" was not particularly a good show at the arena. The costumes were quite beautiful, making it a dressed-up "turkey" of a play. As I said to Roy, "Don't worry, the next play is "Volpone," directed by Nina Vance from the Alley Theater in Texas. She's already done the play there. It was a big success for her. We'll be okay."

Reflecting on life, I noted that now in the first two years of our marriage, Richard and I have been separated almost ten months. While I have been working in Washington D.C., Richard made the rounds in New York. We lost our first apartment as the building was torn down by developers. We're now back subletting the same actor's apartment on Tenth Avenue in Hell's Kitchen. The décor was still the same with its "early reign of terror" look. What was really beautiful were four gorgeous mirrors hanging in the railroad flat.

Richard explained that the 6' x 6' mirrors came from the Vanderbilt mansion on the East Side. His actor friends learned that the mansion was being torn down so the night before the bulldozers came, ten out-of-work actors scavenged the place. They removed telephones, marble counter tops, 19th century light fixtures plus the mirrors. They used a slab of marble to carry their loot out the door. They were met by New York City's finest, who faced them with guns drawn. The police cars' headlights went on to illuminate and to identify this ring of thieves. The actors put their hands up and hollered, "Don't shoot, we're actors!" That caused the cops to pause long enough for the actors to pull their Actors Equity cards from their wallets. They cried out in unison, "See, we *are* actors! Here's the proof!" This was a first for the police, who told them to take the stuff, get out of there, and never come back to the East Side. As Richard said, "Who cares about the East Side? Broadway is on the West Side anyway."

That spring I'm finally back from Arena Stage and in New York with Richard, my true love. He is in the process of auditioning for the Tyrone Guthrie Theater in Minneapolis. The opening of this new theater is considered one of the most exciting theatrical events in this century. Guthrie is the greatest stage director in the world. He will direct 'Hamlet' with George Grizzard as the first play. Guthrie has directed this many times before with Alec Guinness and Sir Laurence Olivier. Every actor I ran into was brushing up his Shakespeare for an audition. Night and day I hear Richard mumbling a soliloquy.

On the other hand, I am not feeling well. One day I ran for a litter basket on the street corner, where I threw up. At the doctor's office, I learn in shock that I am with child.

I go home with the news. "Richard, guess what the doctor said was wrong?" He is watching himself in the mirror as he practices his audition. "Well, tell me. Are you okay?"

"I'm pregnant."

"Oh, my god, how did that happen?"

"Your guess is as good as mine."

"I feel sick." Richard lowers himself into a chair, then holds his head.

I bring Richard a glass of water. His face is drained of color. He really looks ill. His voice cracks as he says, "You're not going to go through with this, are you? What about your career? What if I get accepted at the Guthrie Theater? Do you want to be pregnant in Minneapolis?"

"How can you be so sure you're going to Minneapolis?"

"I have a final callback. It's for Laertes."

"Congratulations. That's great."

"If you weren't pregnant, you could audition for Ophelia." There is an awkward pause. "Get an abortion."

Then I take a long pause, a pregnant pause so to speak. In the movies of the '50s when a husband discovers he is about to be a new father, he joyfully swings his wife into the air with hugs and kisses. "Richard, I married you to have a family someday. Well, that day has come. I'm keeping this baby."

Five minutes later, he speaks again. "My future is unknown. I'm not ready to be a father. I'm too young."

"You're almost thirty years old, Richard. Almost middle-age."

"You'll be sorry, so sorry," he says, his voice shaky.

A couple of days later, Richard learns that he has been cast as Laertes. What should have been a celebration only made us sadder. I try to cheer him up. "It's still possible for me to work. It'll be months before I even look like I'm expecting. Next week I have a part on 'Naked City'. I play Sanford Meisner's wife. It'll be so great to meet him. I sent him letters once asking to study at the Neighborhood Playhouse. Never heard back. Now I'll have a chance to ask him again."

"What difference does it make now?" Richard says disconsolately.

"Don't forget I have three weeks of work in a movie. I'll be able to pay for maternity clothes—a layette."

"You're making the biggest mistake of our lives. I've agreed to be part of the Guthrie Company in Minneapolis. I leave next week." He speaks sadly, in a tone as if he were going off to fight in a distant war. "When you're through making your movie, if you want to come and spend your pregnancy watching other actors act, then join me in Minnesota." He turns away then takes a step toward the door. I try to stay him with my hand, but he brushes me aside. The door slams behind him. I hear his footsteps as he runs down the stairs.

Soon Richard was really gone—gone to Minneapolis. Trying to keep busy, I was strolling along Fifty-Seventh Street when I ran into Roy Scheider. We grabbed each other, trading war stories as actors love to do. Then he said, "Cynthia is going to have a baby this July. And I don't have a job. What's worse, we're having to move in a month. Where're we going with no money?"

"Wait a sec, the director of the movie I'm filming next week hasn't cast the villain's part yet. The pay is five hundred a week for three weeks."

"Oh, my god, that would be great, if you could suggest me."

"Roy, you have a natural evil look. Like a bad George C. Scott. I bet you'll get the part."

"What's the movie about?"

"It's a horror film, 'Curse of the Living Corpse,' and it's an awful script. Everyone dies a terrible death except me and the villain. I'm the ingénue in a Mary Pickford wig."

"I don't care." He wrote his phone number on a slip of paper then gave it to me.

"Coincidentally, Roy, I'm pregnant."

He clutched my hand and held it up in a gesture of sympathy. We needed no more words to express our mutual finance predicaments.

The best part of being in 'Curse of the Living Corpse' was that we filmed it in Stamford in an estate that belonged to the director's wife. This meant that we could commute back and forth to New York City. The director loved Roy's look and cast him in the villain's role. The director thought that Roy would never have a real movie career as he was not that tall and too much a lookalike for George C. Scott.

Needless to say, the director kept noticing my waistline. Each week he thought I was growing wider, which was not looking right for an ingénue. He said, "If we keep padding your breasts out, your waist will look smaller."

I protested, "Isn't that just going to make my head appear smaller?"

The climactic scene of the movie was between Roy and me. The setting is in a dense forest with a muddied pond of make-believe quicksand. After murdering everyone else, Roy, in a swirling black cape and hat with a sword in hand, was to poke me, forcing me to back up and fall into the pond. I was to be the last to die an untimely and terrible death. The director said my task was to fall in the water and to gasp as I drowned. However, this must be done without getting my Mary Pickford wig wet. It cost fifty dollars. The budget didn't allow for a replacement. I can't take a chance and ruin the wig today as my character still has more scenes to shoot. Roy is staggering in an attempt to balance the heavy sword as he swings it toward me. He keeps stopping himself as he feels the slippery mud giving away beneath him. The director is frustrated. So what if Roy starts to fall? The director will cut around him. Why worry, Roy? The pond is only two feet deep. I have to sink on my knees as I scream for help. I keep arching my neck as high as I can so the water won't splash on the wig.

The last week of filming, Roy's wife came to visit. Six months pregnant, Cynthia is huge like a beach ball, which seems to swallow her small frame. She and Roy are in a panic as they have to move in two weeks. They can't find a low rent apartment in Manhattan. "How would you like to sublet my sublet for seventy five dollars a month? I'm going to Minneapolis."

"We'll take it," they chorused.

"I have to tell you, this apartment is in a tenement in Hell's Kitchen, on the fourth floor. Be aware there is no fire escape. There are the original 19th century gas light spigots in the ceilings. When the first tenant realized there was gas leaking in the apartment, he taped up the spigots."

"That's fine with us," Roy said.

"I'll leave the house keys with our neighbors underneath us. That's Seraphim and Cherubim. They're a husband-and-wife team that performs Elizabethan and Medieval songs. You'll hear them strumming their lutes. Seraphim wears striped tights with a tunic and felt slippers. As he drives away on his motorcycle, the Puerto Rican kids run after him, shouting 'Robin Hood! Robin Hood! You're Robin Hood, aren't you?' Seraphim hollers back, 'I'm not Robin Hood. I'm Seraphim!' "

"Do you mind if we bring our pet monkey?" Cynthia said.

"Go ahead. Bring your primate."

Roy, Cynthia and I agreed on the date for them to move in and that would be after I left for Minneapolis. In the meantime, I got a long distance call from Richard, who sounded miserable. "I'm in trouble. Guthrie says in my costume, a trench coat, that I act like a leaping Errol Flynn in a 'B' movie."

"Oh, no, my darling. Does he say anything positive about you?"

"He says I have a good voice but a nervous tic. No one's ever told me I had a tic."

"What kind of direction do you get as Laertes?"

"In Ophelia's grave scene, he wants me to say my lines quickly. Guthrie says there is no realistic way of playing this scene. It's too late in the evening for pauses and psychologizing. My speech must be sacrificed to the shape of the evening."

"Well, Richard, you have to remember you're doing a four-hour uncut version of *Hamlet*."

"But, it gets worse. When I return to avenge Polonius's death, Guthrie has me entering the King's chamber and threatening Claudius with a revolver, which he takes away from me. I asked Guthrie why would a guy looking for vengeance give up his gun so easily? Guthrie said because it says so in the script."

"It sounds as if Guthrie is not familiar with actors who've studied with Strasberg or Meisner."

"Yeah, imagine what Strasberg would say when he asks, 'What did you work on for your scene?' And I answer, 'I'm pausing for breath, cushioning the "R" sound in the middle of words—following a vowel as in "buried." Or elongating the vowel sounds as in, "disappointed." That I use a lower tone of voice because it suggests darkness — I'd probably be thrown out of class."

After we hung up, I was worried. I understand what he means. There is a sickening panic that happens to an actor when the director stops the actor after every scene, pulling him aside as the other actors wait in silence. This frequently happens with the less gifted or less experienced actors, and the director must coach him where to move or to stand still, and worse still, give him line readings.

A couple weeks passed, and it was May first. Only six more days and it would be the long-awaited opening night of the Tyrone Guthrie Theater. Richard called me again. "I'm afraid Guthrie's going to replace me."

"How can he do that? It's too late. The play opens in a week."

"There are a lot of apprentices or journeymen around."

"Oh, Richard, I can't believe this."

"Well, believe it. That's why I don't want you to wait any longer to see *Hamlet*. I need your help. Come tomorrow. You'll be in time for dress rehearsals and the opening."

I spent the night packing for the noon flight to Minneapolis. I thought my heart would break at Richard's cry for help. Watch out, world! Watch out, Guthrie! I'm coming to Minnesota! The melancholy Dane doesn't stand a chance when I get there!

It was a gorgeous spring day. Warm enough to walk around New York without a coat. Seraphim offered to drive me to the airport. We got there in plenty of time to make the Northwestern flight at noon. We checked my baggage. "Seraphim, we still have forty minutes before my plane leaves, let's look around." We strolled through the gift shops and newsstands. Then deciding it was time, we went to the gate for Northwestern Airlines. There were no passengers waiting. That was quite peculiar. I was becoming worried as I said, "Seraphim, I have at least fifteen minutes before take-off." Checking his watch, he said, "You're right."

We walked out the gate in time to see a workman pushing an aluminum staircase. I called to him, "Sir, where's the Northwestern airplane?"

"You just missed it," the workman said.

"But it's not supposed to leave yet. I'm 15 minutes early."

"Sometimes they leave early if everyone's on board."

"No! No! Impossible! I have to be in Minneapolis! Tonight's the dress rehearsal!"

The workman nonchalantly pointed his finger. "See that plane taxiing down the runway? It makes the turn at the end, then heads in this direction for take-off."

I gave my makeup case to Seraphim. "Carry this for me. It's too heavy for me to run fast. Follow!"

Whatever came over me, I will never quite understand the courage. I ran out onto the tarmac. The airplane was just making the turn. I ran faster, faster! The plane was starting toward me. If I timed it right, I would be directly in its path before take-off. I waved my arms frantically. How could the pilots miss me? I was the only human being mad enough to run into the nose of a jet. Closer and closer the plane came. I could see faces in the cockpit. Jumping up and down, I screamed, "Stop! Stop!"

Miracles of miracles, the jet's brakes went down, screeching to a stop. The passenger door flew opened with a waiting stewardess. As if on cue, the workman turned the aluminum ladder around, rolling it as fast as possible across the tarmac until he lined it up with the stewardess in the door. Seraphim, out of breath, tossed my makeup case to me as I climbed the steps. As I entered the plane, passengers' heads were riveted in my direction. Some people stood to see who or what caused a plane to stop at lift-off. I held my two fingers up in a victory sign. "Contact!" Contact, as the pilots say.

My reunion with Richard was so joyful. His green eyes were gleaming, and he never appeared more handsome. This was one of those times so radiant with expectation, we felt immortal as if there were centuries and centuries to come, and we would never give in to old age.

I sit in the 1,437-seat theater waiting for the dress rehearsal to begin. I have now been introduced to Tyrone Guthrie, Zoe Caldwell, Jessica Tandy and Hume Cronyn. George Grizzard, who is Hamlet, I met a couple of years ago. The stage is pentagonal. All the auditorium seats are a festive range of colors: red, orange, purple, gold, beige, blue, green and yellow. Tanya Moiseiwitsch, the theater's designer and Guthrie's long-time collaborator, has done the play in modern dress, which is to be the period before World War I. There will be a European look, with men in ceremonial uniforms and the women in long gowns and full-length gloves.

I am the only civilian sitting in the audience with Guthrie. There is a star charisma about him, a power and a charm, too. He gives the actors the illusion of freedom, but make no mistake, he is the master of this show. I prepare myself for four hours of *Hamlet*. Richard says that after his first exit, when Laertes goes to France, he has an hour and a half off stage before he returns in time to find his sister, Ophelia, stark raving mad.

I have never seen a stage production of *Hamlet.* Will audiences accept Grizzard and Guthrie's non-traditional modern-dress approach? Grizzard is the first American actor Guthrie has directed in the title role. They both are taking an artistic risk.

Five hours later, Richard and I return to the small hotel and a suite he has rented. "What do you think?" he asks tentatively.

"Richard, we have a great deal of work ahead."

I spread out from his script all of Laertes's scenes on the floor. One by one, line by line, I try to interpret Guthrie's direction in terms for an actor whose training has been the Actors Studio method. As I said to Richard, "This is why you've never seen scenes from Shakespeare done in Strasberg's class. Lee doesn't like plays in verse."

Eight hours later with dawn's early light spilling through the windows, Richard and I have finally reached his last scene, a duel between Laertes and Hamlet. I coach him, saying, "Your problem here is that you entered on stage as though intimidated by the duel. Laertes is not hesitant for he is known to win every fencing match in Denmark. He is confident. It is Hamlet who should feel threatened. I read, Hamlet says:

> "I'll be your foil, Laertes, in mine ignorance
> Your skill shall like a star in the darkest night
> Stick fiery off indeed."

"Then Laertes answers, 'You mock me sir.' He would almost laugh if he weren't so angry." I was quite exhausted and said in a sigh, "Oh, Richard, do you realize it's time for breakfast?"

Richard sank back on a couch, enfolded in the pillows. "I'm too tired to eat. Too tired to move. Just give me five minutes, just five—" He fell into a deep sleep. I wanted to overlook the fact that not once since I arrived, had Richard asked about my pregnancy. I felt a tear wander down my cheek. I am appalled at my self-pity in the face of what Richard might be going through: losing his pride as an actor, almost losing his Laertes role, and losing his reputation among his peers.

The preview performance was before a mainly invited audience composed of construction workers who built the theater, cab drivers, hospital personnel, staff members and secretaries. I wondered if Minnesotans realized that appearing in this new theater were legendary Broadway actors with Sir Tyrone Guthrie, considered to be the greatest stage director in the twentieth century.

Minneapolis was the largest city in the four-state area. That's why Guthrie chose it. When I grew up in South Dakota, newlyweds either honeymooned in a log cabin at the Black Hills or went to Minneapolis to see what a real nightclub was like. It was glamorous to shop at Dayton's there, the biggest department store in the four-state area, too. From now on the Midwesterners will have a reason to come to Minneapolis besides honeymoons and buying prom or wedding dresses at Dayton's.

I sat behind Guthrie for this performance. Maybe I can feel his vibrations during Richard's scenes. Oh, powers that be I pray I steered Richard's Laertes in the right direction.

This is part of Guthrie's comments to the actors on tragedy:

> The performance of tragedy must aim higher than at an audience's susceptibility to pathos. An audience will cry readily; the death of little Willie or a pretty girl singing the sorriest rubbish will melt to tender tears the hardest-bitten men and the hardest-bitten women. The emotion aroused by even a half-decent performance of great tragedy cannot be measured in terms of chewed hankies and misted specs. The full impact of great tragedy is not immediate; it takes effect slowly. It lies in wait on the fringe of dreams. It wakes one with a start in the small hours. It can shake the confident and strengthen the weak, stop the clock, roll back the seas. It can give a new meaning to life, and old meaning to death.

After the preview performance, I waited for Richard in our suite at the hotel. The first sign he was arriving was his footsteps. I knew from the sound, he was excited. He threw open the door, I held my breath. He flung out his arms to me: "Sweetheart! You did it! Christ, you saved my ass! Guthrie came backstage. He said 'Young man, you've got it now. This is the Laertes I wanted. Good job.' "

Richard and I embraced dancing and shrieking with joy. Oh, life can be so fabulous at times.

Excitement permeated the air on opening night. Life magazine photographers were snapping pictures everywhere: the stage, back stage and outside the theater. Florists were filling the Green Room with flowers sent from theater companies all over the world. Hundreds of telegrams were pinned to the call board.

The sound of trumpets heralded the start of Act One. The audience seemed to enjoy the play. They applauded after many scenes and exits. At the end, they gave the actors a standing ovation.

A week later *Life* came out with their story on *Hamlet.* The introduction for the Guthrie Theatre was a full-page picture of Richard as Laertes kneeling at Ophelia's side as she prayed at the grave of their father. Flipping the page over, there was a small picture of George Grizzard as Hamlet. Richard was so taken aback at his prominent photo that driving home on a motorcycle, he spun out and crashed it on a curb. Hanging onto the magazine, he arrived home with his clothes ripped, with black and blue marks on his arms and legs. One arm was bleeding slightly. He did not feel any pain. "Look at my photo!"

At last the hysteria of an opening night settled down into a run. I never had the time to unpack my luggage. A week later I hung up my clothes in the closet in our hotel suite. There was an extra bureau in our bedroom, one that I could use. Richard's stuff was in another dresser.

I pulled out the top drawer of the bureau. It was empty except for one letter torn in half. The writing was feminine. At first I thought, 'Why would Richard tear up one of my letters?' I carried the letter over to the light from a window. I put the two halves of papers together like a puzzle. The words were crystal clear. A figure skater in the chorus line of Ice Capades wrote how much she loved Richard. As soon as her tour ended, she planned to return to Minneapolis so they could be together. She swore her undying love for him.

An arrow just went through my heart. I couldn't breathe. The shock was so great I worried that I might lose the baby. The phone was ringing. Like a robot, I moved to answer it. The first words I heard were, "Hi, how are you? It's Nina, Nina Vance."

Another surprise as I hadn't spoken to her since we last did "Volpone" at Arena Stage. She said the purpose of her call was to invite me to spend the new season with her repertory company at the Alley Theatre. I would get to play Masha in "The Three Sisters." This is the kind of part an actress of my age should do in order to develop her talents. After playing in so many comedies like "Bus Stop" and "The Seven Year Itch," I needed the chance to do a great classic like Chekov's "Three Sisters."

"Nina, I'm pregnant. My baby is expected in September."

"Come to Houston. Have your baby here. We'll take care of you."

I knew that if I weren't pregnant I would jump at this opportunity. I'd leave Richard, run back to New York to share my apartment with Roy, Cynthia and their pet monkey until the date to start rehearsals in Houston. The thought of going to Houston to have a baby and to rehearse at the same time seemed a bit overwhelming. I didn't know the doctors, didn't know what life was like after a baby is born. This is the time when a decision can change one's life forever.

"I'm sorry, Nina. I just can't go. I adored working with you. How I wish we could do it again. Thank you so much for inviting me."

Long after we hung up the phone, I just sat staring at the nothingness. I'm in hell. Hell in oneself is where the pain is so deep, I am orphaned by it. There is no escape. The world goes out of focus. There are no illusions left. The loss of innocence vanishes like shattered glass, never to mend, never to return again.

Richard is stunned when I show him the letter. The look of shame on his face is the same as a little boy whose hand is caught in the cookie jar. He fumbles for the words to exonerate himself. Actors are so good at lying. The thrust of his mendacity (as Tennessee Williams liked to describe it) was an accidental meeting with a chorus girl in the Ice Capades. The Guthrie gang were invited to a performance of the show when it played Minneapolis. This skating tootsie recognized him from a TV show.

"She mistook my intentions for a friendship. You know how some fans are like stalkers?"

Never once in this half-hearted confession does Richard apologize. He puts the blame on some girl who's willing to jump out of her skates to jump into his bed. It's all her fault. I shelve Richard's excuse in my brain along with his others. My obstetrician warns me about stress. I'm to concentrate on being as happy as possible for the sake of a new baby. Maybe Richard will change his juvenile ways once he sees his newborn child.

> "One of my chief regrets during my years in the theater is that I couldn't sit in the audience and watch me."
>
> – John Barrymore

Chapter Thirteen

By the middle of summer, Minneapolis was hot and humid. It was considerably cooler to spend my evenings backstage at the Guthrie Theater waiting in the Green Room where I became acquainted with the other actors. I used to think that the leading man and leading lady were the actors who had the biggest parts. But Hume Cronyn and Jessica Tandy set the bar for leading actors with their professionalism: They always knew their lines; they were never late; they were generous and thoughtful of their fellow actors; they never exhibited "star" behavior; they made themselves available to all actors no matter how small the part.

Then there was George Grizzard, one of the sweetest actors I have ever met. Like me, he was an only child. Like me, his career began at the Arena Stage in Washington D.C. Since Guthrie had added "The Miser" and "Death of a Salesman" in repertory, George had some free time from "Hamlet." We decided to hang out together one day. I drove a ten-year-old Buick, which Richard bought for me for fifty dollars. Its main drawback was that it couldn't go faster than thirty miles an hour. I picked up George and we cruised around the streets of Minneapolis. There are about seventeen lakes within the city limits. The city is quite lovely in the summertime despite the heat.

I told George that one of the first plays I ever saw on Broadway was "The Disenchanted" with him and Jason Robards and, of course, I had just seen him this past year in "Who's Afraid of Virginia Woolf" with Uta Hagen and Arthur Hill. I asked George if he had ever tasted a Midwest milkshake. The kind where it was so thick, the straw stands straight up in the glass.

George and I went to the local ice cream store where I promised him he would have one of the great ice cream experiences in his life. When we had our chocolate milkshakes, I said, "Right now, we're in a Norman Rockwell painting."

He said, "You're the first person I've met from South Dakota. What was it like growing up there?"

"Well, it was in Huron where I found out what the world's biggest kiss was."

"Don't leave me in suspense. I have to know this one."

"Okay, Hamlet. I found out what the biggest kiss was the summer I had just turned twelve. That fall I'd be entering the seventh grade. My mother said, 'Now that you're starting junior high, why don't you put on a little lipstick?'

'Oh, ick, no,' I protested.

'But you're so pale. You could cheat a little with a tangerine lipstick. It's really a natural shade with a hint of orange.'

'I don't want to, Mother.'

'Why don't we make an appointment at the beauty shop for a permanent?'

'I don't wanna do that either.'

'Your hair is so straight, dear. How about a home perm like Which Twin has the Bobbi?'

'I like straight hair.'

'Don't you want to look pretty for junior high? Next year your braces come off. Lipstick will compliment your straightened teeth and complexion, too.'

I just shook my head.

'Most of the girls in seventh grade have wavy or curly hair. I know you'll want to look as pretty as they do.'

'Let me think about it Mom. I'm meeting my friend Barbara to go to the fair.'

That afternoon Barbara and I hiked several blocks to the state fairgrounds on the edge of town. The state fair was a big deal for Huron (population 13,000). Every year we waited for it to come. Barb and I decided not to pay the entrance fee of seventy-five cents but find a way to sneak inside as we could get at least three rides apiece at the Midway Carnival with that amount. Last year at the carnival I saw for the first time a professional stripper, and a tent filled with formaldehyde-soaked babies and fetuses in jars. During the afternoon, there were stock car races at the grandstand and at night a musical show that always ended when a husband and wife were shot out of a cannon. It was a setting right out of Vincente Minnelli's "Meet Me in St. Louis" ("Meet Me at the Fair" as sung by Judy Garland).

We ran along a country road. At the end we climbed a wood fence and sneaked into the fairgrounds. We came upon a barn. We strolled inside as though we belonged to a farm family. This barn had no animals but was set up with a display of electric milking machines on three tiers that surrounded the interior. There was a slight hum coming from the shiny steel machines. A banner hung on the wall: *The Milking Machine Is the Most Important Piece of Equipment on the Dairy Farm.*

A couple of bored farmers were leaning in the doorway. A tall, lanky one with red hair called to me in a casual tone. "Hey, blondie! Ever been kissed by a milking machine?"

"Nope. Why?"

"Come here. I'll show you what it feels like."

I turned to him as he reached for a pulsating teat cup shell from what appeared to be an octopus arrangement of hoses hanging from a machine. He plopped this apparatus with its rubber mouth on my cheek. There came a twisting and suction of my cheek that produced a pain that was so intense and severe that I thought my face was being ripped off my head. I screamed! I tugged at this thing but the pulsating suction produced by the vacuum pump was not going to let go of me. The farmers, in a state of panic, bent over me, but no one could get the teat cup to stop sucking my face. Barbara yelled, "Help her! Stop it! Someone stop it!"

I fell to my knees as the constant sound of suction muffled my tearful pleas. Only my feeble screams escaped as I realized I was yoked to a monster. For a fleeting moment I felt sympathy for any cow whose udder went through this torture every day.

My duet of screams with Barbara's brought the attention of the spectators who were exiting the grandstand show. A crowd formed in the entrance of the barn. People yelled, "What's going on? My god! What's happened? Look at that poor child! Turn off the machine!"

"How do we turn it off?" The farmers could not locate the switch for the milking machine as all the machines were connected to one outlet. "Where's that?" cried a stranger. "Find the circuit breaker!" Another man offered, "God damnit! Turn off the electricity for the damn midway, if you have to."

Another man yelled, "That's 150 volts runnin' that pulsator! Shut the electricity off for the whole goddamn fairgrounds, right now!"

I was drenched in tears as what I can only call indescribable pain. Unless you have ever been kissed by a milking machine, you can never imagine what this nonstop, pulsating, sucking pain feels like. I could tell from the shouting in the background and the look of horror and alarm on people's faces that I was in critical condition. Finally, someone found the main circuit breaker. The lights went out in the carnival on the midway. People were stranded on the Ferris wheel, and other rides along with black-outs in several barns and the food and game concession stands.

I didn't know what happened, only that the monster released my cheek. Someone picked me up, then held me until I regained my balance. The crowd parted as Barbara and I left this scene as quickly as possible.

I had no idea of what I looked like. I found out when I came home and saw mother. She gave a small cry, her hands crossed her heart as though in shock. "What happened to your face?"

"I was kissed by a milking machine." Then I peered into a mirror on the wall to see what upset her. Half of my face was swollen, a purple blob as if I were disfigured from a huge, unkind birthmark.

She said in a very quiet but deadly tone, "Tell me exactly what happened."

My mother's anger made her grow quieter like the Marlon Brando character in "The Godfather" except she was on the right side of the law. When she spoke or made a call, people listened to her. Half of the police force had been her high school students when she taught English and history. The Red Cross hired her to investigate Indian rights for Indians who were still forced to live in tents. She was chairman of the Republican Party for our state. No Republican governor campaigned without her at his side. Even the public library listened to her: If she said a book was not fit for young eyes, the book was pulled.

That's why I felt confident as she said, "I'm going to call Mr. Hafner and report this to him immediately." She picked up the phone.

I knew that he was the president of the state fairgrounds. I listened as she explained about what happened to my face.

She turned to me, "Mr. Hafner wants to know the exact location of the barn with the milking machine."

"It's the only barn next to the grandstand."

She repeated the information then asked me, "How many farmers were involved? And which one of them did this?"

I described the men as best as I could recollect. When she hung up the phone, I asked, "What did Mr. Hafner say?"

She smiled and again, as quietly as before, said, "He's taking a couple of his men over there tonight to look for this kissin' machine. Don't worry, dear. This terrible accident will never happen to any young girl again. Mr. Hafner gave me his word."

That evening my father came home. I could tell from Mother's whispers he was to control himself when he saw my purple face. Still his face reddened as he asked, "Who did this?"

"A farmer wanted to show me what it was like to be kissed by a milking machine."

My father chewed furiously on his cigar. Soon my grandmother arrived. She, too, had been warned not to say anything about my face.

The next night, my family gathered for what was like a powwow as they say in Huron. From my upstairs bedroom I could tell from their soft voices that I wasn't supposed to hear. Leaning over the banister, I caught a few words such as, "Maybe we should take her to a plastic surgeon. That means a trip to Minneapolis. Probably the closest city with a plastic surgeon." Father chimed in with, "Let's sue the sons of bitches! I want to sue 'em!" There were some "Shh! Shhs!" His voice went silent.

I enrolled in seventh grade showing off my purple face. Some of my friends said it looked like the biggest hickey they'd ever seen. I asked, "What's that?" They whispered to me it's what happens when a boy chews on your neck so passionately, he leaves a purple mark that won't go away for days. You have to wear neck scarves to hide this vampire-like love mark.

I learned that my dark purple blob was a hematoma condition, and no doctor seemed to know when it might disappear. We were told by the doctors at Huron's Clinic to wait to see how long this disfigurement would last. Mother thought the prognosis was hopeful because of the healing properties in a child as young as I. I wasn't too concerned because as long as my cheek was purple, blue and with a new touch of yellow now, mother stopped nagging me about wearing tangerine lipstick or getting a permanent.

By Christmas my face recovered its former pale, anemic look that I was happy with until mother said one day, "What about a tiny dash of rouge?"

George stared at me. He appeared quite mesmerized by my life in South Dakota. Our soda glasses were empty. He said to me, "Let's have another chocolate milkshake."

"Let's do. After all, I'm eating for two."

Almost forty years later, George won a Tony for his Broadway performance in the revival of Albee's "A Delicate Balance." When my oldest daughter went backstage to meet him, the first thing he said to her was, "Did your Mother ever tell you that story of how she was kissed by a milking machine?"

*****

September came, and the heat wave was still making Minneapolis a miserable place. I was eight months pregnant with severe back pains and a few pre-labor pains. Roy Scheider called from New York to ask a favor. If he didn't pay me the seventy-five dollars for the sublet, he would be able to put a deposit on an apartment for him, Cynthia, and the new baby. "By the way," he said, "the baby is still in the hospital. She couldn't digest her prenatal food. She survived an operation, but she's still sick—not out of the woods yet."

Of course I would never keep an actor from finding a home for his family. It gave me an idea: I could return to Manhattan immediately. Be there while I waited for the baby.

Richard complained, "You'd rather be alone in New York because you like your doctor there better than the one here?"

"The Minneapolis doctor tells me that the only pain medication he approves of is a shot of Demerol. There's no epidural given any more in the state of Minnesota. He says he won't put me to sleep either that I have to stay awake."

"Well, what does your New York obstetrician say he'll do?"

"He's going to give me what is known as the Jewish delivery at Mount Sinai and that is twilight sleep. I told him I want to get everything that has been invented for the last 100 years to keep women from suffering childbirth."

"Ah, he just said that so you wouldn't be scared. If it were possible, then this guy here could do the same thing."

"Dr. Kaplan promised me. I believe him."

Manhattan's heat wave was as bad as Minneapolis's. The kind of heat that made me breathless as I climbed the four flights of stairs to our apartment. I thought that somehow I must find a new apartment before this baby is born. If I didn't, the baby's birth certificate would state that her legal residence was 850

Tenth Avenue (Hell's Kitchen) and that label would follow her the rest of her lifetime like a curse. People would assume she came from a Puerto Rican gang rather than a child of actors.

I entered our railroad flat, and everything seemed to be the same as when I turned it over to Roy. Until I opened a drawer in the kitchen and saw that the silverware was missing. From the bathroom linen closet, the towels had disappeared. I opened my closet. All my clothes were gone, too. Had there been a robbery since Roy and Cynthia left?

I went to Seraphim's apartment just below mine. I knocked frantically on his door until he opened it. I asked him about a robbery.

"There's been no robbery. But I can tell you that Roy and his wife argued a lot. I could hear things banging against the wall. Bet that was your silverware."

When Richard phoned me from Minneapolis, he warned me not to be too hard on Roy and Cynthia. "They got a baby in the hospital. They're too worried. They can't think straight."

I called them anyway. Cynthia said they had to give away the monkey now that she had a baby. After I expressed my sympathy, I asked tentatively, "Do you know where my silverware is?"

Cynthia said, "It's there. Just look around."

"Do you know where the towels are?"

"They're there, too. You'll find them."

"Cynthia, I noticed that my clothes aren't in the closet."

"Oh, I took those. I knew you couldn't use the dresses being pregnant. So I'm wearing them now."

"Well, that's okay," I said weakly. "Call me when your baby comes home from the hospital. I'd love to see her."

Hunting through the apartment, I found silverware behind chairs along with a used towel or two. Gradually, I recovered most items. I climbed up the ladder to the loft bed and, to my horror, this was the place Roy and Cynthia kept their monkey, who turned the mattress into a king-size litter box.

Never again will I entrust property or rent to any soul who owns a primate.

*****

Richard had been home a week from Minneapolis when we learned through a friend that there was an available apartment on Broadway and 110th Street, which was also known as Cathedral Parkway. "Thank heavens, Richard. This means I can fill out the baby's address on the birth certificate as 535 Cathedral Parkway." We signed the lease. We could move within the week.

The next morning, I went into labor. "Is this it—-the real thing?" Richard asked. "Is the pain worse than it was the last time?"

"I don't know. I can't tell the difference."

He was referring to the night before last when I sat up in bed with severe cramps. At the time he immediately put on his blazer and tie, then washed his socks out in the sink as he didn't want to spend the day in a hospital wearing dirty socks. By dawn the pain ended, and I fell asleep again with Richard still sitting and waiting in his best and only blazer.

"When the fuck are you goin' to have this kid?"

I was already three weeks late. I phoned my obstetrician and described my symptoms. "According to my baby book, I'm supposed to be able to time the labor pains. But, doctor, I'm just in constant pain. There's nothing to time. It doesn't start or stop." I hung up the phone then turned to Richard. "He said to come right away to the hospital."

Richard grabbed my overnight case. We climbed down the five flights of stairs as fast as I could make it. "Richard, I'll wait in the doorway while you flag a taxi. I've been warned that if a driver sees you're pregnant, he won't stop to pick you up."

Richard hurried onto the street where he let out a loud whistle in the direction of a cab. Just then, our landlord from his shop on the first floor spied Richard carrying a suitcase. The landlord ran outside. "Mr. Forest! Vere do you tink you're gonna go vithout paying the rent?" He said, tugging at Richard's arm.

As a cab came to a stop, I waddled from the doorway. Richard said to the landlord, "We're going to the hospital, sir. My wife is having a baby. Right now!"

The landlord said sheepishly, "Sorry. Very sorry." He crept back into his store in shame.

The cab driver was quite kind. He kept assuring me that if I didn't feel I could make it to the hospital, he knew how to deliver babies. He drove slowly so the pot holes in the city streets wouldn't injure me, but I said, "Please don't slow down. Go as fast as you can!"

Twenty-seven minutes after we arrived at the hospital, baby Jennifer was born. Richard was not there. Previously, the doctor suggested that Richard have some lunch as the labor for first babies is usually a few hours. Since I was under the influence of twilight sleep, I never woke up until five o'clock in the afternoon. The nurses informed me that Richard had been back and forth waiting to give me the news. At last when he showed up, he said that our baby girl was beautiful. I couldn't be more surprised when the nurse put her in my arms for the first time. The baby's eyes were swollen, and she looked like James Cagney after a fistfight. One side of her head was black and blue. There was a cut over one eyebrow. I learned that was due to the forceps as she weighed almost nine pounds. Ouch! Thank goodness for the doctor who put me to sleep! The nurses said they had no trouble identifying her as she was the only baby in the nursery without hair.

By the time the baby was a month old, Jessica Tandy and Hume Cronyn paid us a visit. We still didn't have any living room furniture in our new 110th Street apartment, so I received Jessica and Hume in the bedroom. Jessica gave me a bottle of perfume and a baby's sterling silver spoon. She laid across the king-size bed on her back, then demonstrated the exercises that she used to do after a baby's birth. Hume said,

"I'll show you how to get your figure back." At the foot of the bed he did a series of sit-ups then proceeded to do more complicated exercises. "Every morning, whether I'm hung over, sick, no matter what, I work out for thirty minutes." He went on to explain that in his youth he had been a boxer. As he was always a small kid, he was picked on my bigger boys. Once he learned to box, he defended himself. The bullies left him alone after that.

Hume was in great shape. I never knew how muscular he was. A couple of days later, Jessica offered to baby-sit if I dropped Jennifer off at their apartment. I did, so thrilled to have a break, which meant I could go to a beauty shop.

Richard wanted to give a party for Christmas Eve. "But Richard, we only have two pieces of furniture in the living room."

"I can borrow some card tables and folding chairs," he said, refusing to let me discourage him. "We'll invite Hume and Jessica too."

"Why would they want to come to our place on Christmas Eve? With all the producers and Broadway stars they know, they couldn't possibly be interested in an invitation to the West Side, 110th Street, for our party."

"I'm gonna ask them anyway."

Not only did they come to celebrate Christmas Eve with us, but George Grizzard brought his parents and Zoe Caldwell came with the Guthrie stage manager Ed Call. Richard and I worked like professionals for two days baking hams, turkeys, pies and cakes. Twenty people squeezed themselves into our living room. We plied them with enough liquor so that no one felt the pain of a crowd. Guests seemed to be everywhere, on the floor, sitting at card tables as though we were "Studio 54." It was one of those parties where the chemistry of the guests was so right, I felt ecstatic with happiness not only for the guests but for my young husband and new baby. If only I were a writer, I would put to paper this inexpressible but glamourous time that for the coming years would last forever when memories faded.

My baby was about six months old when my agent called me. "How'd you like to reprise your role of Stella in "A Streetcar Named Desire" – with Elaine Stritch? The producers saw you do that part when you were with Vivian Blaine."

"I don't think I can travel with a new baby."

"Please work it out with Richard. The producers agree that if you do this tour, you can then play the queen in 'Becket' at Princeton."

After a great deal of thought, I gave my final no to the agent. I knew from his voice how annoyed he was. There were too many available actresses who weren't pregnant or saddled with young children. Richard was now doing a soap opera, "The Secret Storm," at CBS. It seemed every night he had pages and pages of lines to memorize. We were so happy that he was cast in a storyline that the fans loved. He played a married college professor who was having an affair with one of his students. This meant the writers kept adding episodes for him every week. Yet we still didn't have the kind of money to hire a nanny to tour with me.

Almost a year later, one afternoon, I ran into Jessica Tandy on Fifth Avenue. The sky was sunless, and there was a cold mist of snow in the air. She looked fabulous in a shadow-gray mink coat. Side by side we made it across the street. She was on her way to Bergdorf Goodman's. She seemed in a hurry. I didn't want to detain her with nonchalant conversation. The last thing she said to me was, "Don't stay away from the stage too long. If you do, the next time on stage your knees are apt to shake, your hands will tremble from stage fright."

> "I know a woman's portion when she loves
> It's hers to give, my darling not to take.
> It isn't lockets dear, nor pairs of gloves.
> It isn't marriage bells nor wedding cake.
> It's up and cook, although the belly ache."
>
> – John Masefield

Chapter Fourteen

Back to Divorce Court & Beverly Hills – 1980s

Since Susan Goldstein was my last attorney of record, she unexpectedly received an OSC (lawyer's lingo for Order to Show Cause) from Richard and his attorney, David Stitz. On the phone I ask, "What does this mean?"

"Your ex wants to terminate spousal support. He claims his health has deteriorated since he had to undergo a cardiac angioplasty."

"But that was three years ago!"

"Well, Candace, he states in his Declaration he now has a heart condition that eventually will make him quit the stress of TV acting. He'll have to pursue a low-paying career as a boat captain."

"Do you remember when you deposed him? He admitted he spent $85,000 to decorate his boat. The slip at the marina costs $2,000 a month. That's expensive for a sea captain. No wonder he feels he can't pay $625 monthly for my support." I waited for her to speak.

She was silent for a few moments. "Well, now," she said as if protecting his interests, "did you know that recently he was seriously injured in an auto accident? Damaged his left hand. Sustained brain injury."

"Does that mean he can't memorize his lines anymore? Gosh, Susan, that's the worst news yet."

She ignored my comments. "I have to prepare a counter OSC for Modification of Support."

"This time, Susan, can we ask the judge for a ruling on my community property interests in his residuals?"

"He's already spent that money!"

"So what? I mean, what if I were the IRS? They wouldn't accept that as an excuse if he owed taxes."

Instead of an answer, she said, "For a thousand dollars I'll go to court with you."

"Susan, let me think about it."

The last time we were in court together we went before Judge Jill Robbins, a bleached blonde with a dark tan like a surfer dude. The Honorable Robbins didn't see that in the last two and a half years since I was in court, there was any change in my expenses. Susan didn't clarify that my rent increases forced me to rent out a bedroom, that I now had car payments and car insurance and couldn't afford health insurance–not on alimony of a monthly $625. She didn't bring up how much an increase Richard's income was compared to the first time when he appeared in court as an out-of-work actor. This year he was making around $300,000 from his TV appearances plus another $65,000-85,000 yearly in residuals.

I couldn't trust Susan. She was too smitten with Richard. From his deposition to our appearance in court, she constantly let him off the hook. Someone recommended another family lawyer, Ronald Litz. Out of desperation, I made an appointment for a consultation, which is always free. His office was on Westwood and Wilshire Boulevard. On the door of his firm was *Antin, Stern, Litz & Grebow.* Unless money is no object, never ever retain a lawyer who's in partnership with three other attorneys. Actually, there should be a sign under their names: '*Can You Afford Justice?*' and under that '*Can You Afford Us?*'

As I cross the threshold I do not realize that I have entered Finance Hell 101. I'm in a large waiting room, and as nervous as if I were here for an audition. I worry as to how chauvinistic this new lawyer might be. Or how will he represent me against Richard's lawyer who said to the last judge, "The Respondent has never worked as an actress before, during or after her marriage. She's chasing a rainbow in the sky. She has commenced no vocational Rehabilitation. Instead, she found time to write 3,000 pages of an unsold novel. Her refusal to find employment has created a serious emotional and economic drain on Petitioner and his family. He cannot afford to have a child because of her shenanigans."

*****

Ronald Litz's secretary opens a door then beckons me to follow her (like a lamb to the slaughter) through a long corridor. She says to me as an aside, "You finally got yourself a great lawyer. Ron's a real tiger in court. Do excuse him he has laryngitis today."

Another door opens and a girlish face pokes out. "Hi, I'm Judy, Ron's paralegal. You'll really like him. He's a tiger in court."

Two feminine votes for the tiger! Yeah! This reassures me. The secretary ushers me into a swanky corner office. Through the windows is a magnificent view of Los Angeles's skyline. A quick glance around the office, I notice there are no family photos. Usually attorneys sprinkle their offices with family photos to comfort them while away from home for so many long hours. I spot only one framed photo. That's of the attorney with Mary Hart of TV's *Entertainment Tonight* and Shirley MacLaine. A warning bell goes off in my head, but I pay no attention to the idea that Ronald Litz might be divorced and resentful, too. There is also one of MacLaine's silly books on reincarnation on his desk. The warning bell rings louder in my head, but I don't listen as I gaze into the eyes of Ronald Litz. He looks as if he stepped out of Central Casting as he's probably the most handsome lawyer I have seen so far in my journey. He is forty-five, tall, with lean muscles, like someone who skies at Aspen. (Later I learned I was right about that.) He has the honey-color tan of someone who visits Tahiti or Bora Bora. (I must be psychic as I find out I am right about that, too.)

I plunk my current files upon his desk. Without a word to me, he searches through them, pulling out certain papers, which he hands to his secretary, "Shirley, copy these for me." He looks at me and, in a husky voice, whispers, "Don't worry, when I get to court I'm a tiger."

I am thrilled to know that I might have a tiger on my side. His retainer fee is $1,250. Three of my friends loan me the money. Is that payment for my new lawsuit, they ask? I tell them, "No, this is like a big card game in the sky in which the retainer is paid out first like a stack of poker chips on the table before the cards are dealt. A card player can't predict how much he or she will end up winning or losing."

Two weeks later I meet with Ron, who has now found his voice with a hint of a New Jersey accent. "Your husband makes around $40,000 a month. Your alimony should be about $8,000 a month. What did you do to turn off judges? To give you such a low award? After twenty years of marriage!"

"I didn't do anything."

"It was suggested that you have vocational testing. Did you do that?"

"No, on my $635 a month alimony, I can't afford testing like that. Is there a test for homemakers? During my marriage, I put aside my career, became the tender of the hearth, the custodian of religious customs, the guardian of our children's welfare, while my husband, an actor and sometime scuba diver, pursued his nomadic obsession for stardom. I won't bring up his need for conquests of younger women." I manage to say this on one breath.

Ron stares indifferently at me. He is humorless. "You were given two years to rehabilitate yourself."

There was that word again, "rehabilitate." Why do judges equate wives with the same word used when sentencing drug addicts and alcohol offenders? I hand Ron a diary I made. In it were the names of twenty employment agencies. To register at each agency I spent a day, taking typing tests, computer tests, English and spelling tests.

Ron studies my pieces of paper. "Your Claim for spousal support falls on deaf ears in California courts. They assume you're as capable as any man to support yourself after divorce. Your husband states that you purposely take low-paying jobs."

"Why would I want to do that? I didn't set the going hourly rate, which is five dollars and fifty cents. Doesn't the court know that middle-aged women are the last to be hired and the first to be fired?"

"The court doesn't care. Let me tell you about California judges. They are political appointees with primary experience in criminal courts. They have no interest or experience in family law. Some judges don't bother to read briefs or case law precedents."

"Maybe they should be retrained. Like mandatory judicial education."

"It's your retraining that concerns me. What're you going to do about it?"

"Well, a California survey of the job market for employment suggests that the top two positions for the best opportunities are: cable installer or paralegal. I can't see myself climbing telephone poles to check wires. That leaves paralegal. I guess I'll look into paralegal schools."

"Fine. Investigate paralegal schools. Give me the list and the school you choose. I'll use it as an exhibit. The court is interested in your diligent search to be retrained."

"Whatever happened to my standard of life being the same as when I married? After all, it was Richard who signed the lease on the apartment that I can't afford any more."

"Judges here don't care. If you return to court and testify that you're still trying to write or to appear as an actress again, your spousal support will be terminated."

"But–but Richard's career assets were our family's main asset. What about the intangible property that comes from investing in careers and human capital? Since I contributed to his earning power, then under the equal division rule, I should have been awarded an equal share of this property."

He answered without sympathy, "California judges do not consider a husband's career as a community or a partnership asset."

Soon after I hired Ron Litz, Richard called me. He received from Litz the Respondent Interrogatories. He went berserk like a character in an old melodrama. I pictured him swinging a black cape and twirling a mustache. His voice projected so loudly through the earpiece that I had to hold it away from my ear: "If you ask for any community property, I'll bankrupt you with legal bills! What monies or inheritance you ever get, your barracuda lawyer's bill will put you in the street!"

Richard filed an OSC, too. Again he repeated his precarious health concerns and his injuries: brain damage and joint damage in left hand. His TV career was over. Evidently he didn't think I would notice that in the Hollywood trade papers he has been nominated for a Daytime Emmy for Lead Actor, Drama Series for *Santa Barbara*. Or the story in the current *TV Guide* in which he brags that he didn't need a double when his character went scuba diving for lost treasure. His scuba students include *Santa Barbara* cast members and some NBC executives.

Like an old record Richard and I are back on track for another trial in Superior Court on Hill Street, where we report to Department Two. I'm with Ron, my fifth attorney, and Richard is accompanied by David Stitz, his third. That's eight attorneys between the two of us; that means eight retainers plus other fees and costs for each one. As soon as my meager support payments arrive, the money goes right into a lawyer's account. If my life didn't depend on this, I would feel as if I were playing with Monopoly money.

In the Petitioner's (Richard) Declaration he respectfully asks the court to terminate Respondent's (me) spousal support effective immediately. His attorney Stitz cites the precedent of the 1983 Sheridan case.

Judges love it when there is a precedent as it relieves them of making a decision on their own. Mrs. Sheridan's support was terminated based upon the fact after five years of alimony, she failed to become self-supporting. As a mother of two small children, she studied at a real estate school but had no success selling real estate. She had a polyester silk flower and plant business but that didn't last either. She attempted to sell business equipment on a commission basis but did not make enough money to cover her expenses.

Mrs. Sheridan appealed to California's appellate court. The judges there agreed that the former husband, a doctor, had the ability to pay $1,200 a month. However, after five years spent working at a job that paid zero money, and going to school for enjoyment (flower-making), she involved herself in creative endeavors that cost her more than she was making. She had done too little to seek gainful employment.

Her petition for a hearing by the Supreme Court was denied. In my pleadings, Ron fought back. He pointed out that Mrs. Sheridan was married for only thirteen years compared to my marriage of twenty years. He argued that Mrs. Sheridan had received $102,000 in cash as her share of community property. I never received any monies, and any I obtained were used to pay outstanding legal fees. I was also some years older than Mrs. Sheridan.

Stitz and Litz, Stitz and Litz at the Ritz, it's the pits. When relaying what is happening, these names sound like an old vaudevillian act or one of those obscure cartoons in *The New Yorker* that nobody really understands.

I catch sight of Ron in the hallway of the courthouse. He is on crutches, his leg in a cast, and he is limping. I groan. He tries to reassure me. "Don't worry. I just broke my leg skiing in Aspen. I'm fine." (I was right about his athletic pursuits.) Judy, his paralegal, has come along. Mentally, I can hear the ka-ching of the cash register ringing up her bills, which run $175 an hour.

Ron tells me, "The court has changed some of the rules. We are required to meet first with a mediator. You and Richard will not be with David Stitz and me. We present our cases alone to the mediator, who is supposed to give us an impartial decision. Also, this mediator will give an opinion about the strengths and weaknesses of our case. If we don't like the decision, we can veto it."

Ron limps away with Judy as I walk behind. Stitz and Richard are already at the assigned room waiting.

Richard and I sit on benches in the hallway as our attorneys and Judy disappear into the room. Barely a couple of minutes have passed when Ron exits the room as fast as his crutches permit. "Oh, my god, you won't believe this. What a coincidence. But Susan Goldstein is the mediator."

"What–what happens now?" The idea of seeing her again gives me a painful knot in my side.

"We have to be assigned another mediator." He crutches back toward the main courtroom to request a new mediator. Judy, Richard, Stitz and I troop along after him.

The Court reassigns us, and the whole process begins again. Back along the hallway we go to another room. Again Ron, Stitz and the paralegal disappear behind closed doors. After a few minutes I peek into the small glass windows of the doors and see that the legal eagles are busy arguing. At the end of the hall, Richard paces nervously, making sure not to cross my path.

After forty-five minutes the doors open. Stitz rushes out first. He grabs Richard by the arm as he whispers into his ear. Ron and Judy come over to my side of the hallway. He says with hope, "The mediator advised us that you, the Respondent, deserved an award of $8,000 a month for spousal support, because the Petitioner's career has been burgeoning. He is more a marketable star than he ever was. Particularly now that he is starring in *Sheriff Lobo.* The petitioner is to pay my attorney's fees-the sum of $3,500."

For an instant I wanted to scream *hooray for our side.* At last a mediator who believes a woman has earned the right to alimony, which is an essential part of the marriage contract, both implied and expressed, that a husband should share his income with her.

We pause and glance over at Richard and Stitz. There is an agonized expression on Richard's face, which turns gray again. Stitz's pallor never changes. He maintains that pasty look of a mortician who spends too many hours indoors with the dead rather than outside with the living. His narrow brown eyes dart back and forth as he attempts to advise Richard, who seems to be spitting slightly at the decision.

Finally Stitz nods to Ron. The two lawyers come together like coaches in a game while the rest of us sit in suspense on the wood benches. I feel my throat filling with emotion. Richard keeps his back to me. How cowardly, how like a snake crawling away on his belly.

Ron returns to me. "Richard refuses to accept the mediator's decision. In fact, he is quite upset by it."

"Oh, no, no. What happens now?"

"Since the parties can't agree, we report back to Department Two. Then we'll be assigned a judge. It's too late for today. After I check my calendar, I'll notify you of the next trial date." He lapses into silence as he limps toward an elevator, his paralegal carrying his briefcase with my life inside it.

My tiger seems vaguely wearied. Maybe his broken leg hurts more than he admits. Richard with a sneer of righteous indignation heads for the escalator. After a safe time I ride the escalator to the ground floor. Tonight I register at the University of West Los Angeles School of Paralegal Studies. It is two years of night school, but when I am done I will have two certifications, litigation and corporations, plus a Bachelor of Science Degree. What the hell will I do with any of that at my age?

Ron wrote a letter warning me, "I implore you to carefully review the Court's Order. If the next time you come to Court and give the judge excuses why you did not comply with the order that you make a diligent search of job training courses, you will lose. Never admit or hint that you might be writing again. Remember Mrs. Sheridan."

> "To be a woman and a writer
> Is double the mischief for
> the world will slight her
> who slights the 'servile house,'
> and who would rather
> make odes than beds."
>
> – Dilys Laing

Chapter Fifteen

I speak to Judy on the phone with as much civility as I can summon. "In my monthly bill from Ron I see that you charged me for calling paralegal schools. That's something I can do. I don't need legal help to call registrar offices."

"Sorry, but Ron asked me to do it."

"Well, I've already enrolled in the University of West Los Angeles School of Paralegal Studies. It's two years at night school. Tell him I'm following court orders. Also, Judy, please don't bill me for this phone call."

"I was about to call you anyway. Your husband's attorney wants to take your deposition next week on Wednesday. Be here at twelve so that Ron can prepare you for the deposition at one o'clock."

"What! I was deposed just a year ago with Susan Goldstein."

"You're to bring all records of employment, bookkeeping papers, check, contracts—"

"I know what to do, Judy."

"Please mark your calendar accordingly. They will be focusing on your job attempts and your financial needs. I'll send you a letter of confirmation. See you then. Good luck."

*****

On the day of my deposition, I enter my attorney's office and stand before him awkwardly. He is seated at his desk. I recognize the anger in his face. Ron never wanted to do a deposition of Richard as he said it is too costly for me in my burgeoning bill with him. We didn't know how the other shoe would drop. Now we're compelled to spend the afternoon in a conference room with Richard and David Stitz anyway. There goes a quick thousand dollars. Ka-ching. Ka-ching.

Ron is wearing wire-rimmed glasses which magnify his irritation with me. He speaks in a quiet, controlled tone: "Did you review the memo Judy sent you where she sets forth three major paralegal schools in L.A. And the pertinent entrance requirements for each?"

"Yes, ah yes, yes, I d-did." I'm almost stuttering. I feel as if I'm in grade school again being reprimanded by the principal as I was ten and still did not know how to tell time. I broke the record for tardiness in the entire school district.

"Did you note that UCLA and Cal State require only 64 and 58 units of college credit? You've probably already completed that at the University of Iowa. Correct?"

"Probably."

"From what I gather from your conversation with Judy, you are entertaining thoughts of going to the University of West LA Paralegal School."

"Because it offers an undergraduate degree upon completion of its two-year program."

"That's twice as long as the other schools."

"The admissions office informed me that to find employment, a paralegal must have a college degree as well as a certification from an A.B.A.-approved paralegal school. That's why I chose U.W.L.A."

"I am concerned that any prolongation of your training will be fatal to you. If you attempt to obtain an extension of support at the next hearing, do you know what could happen?" His voice begins to rise as he emphasizes his words precisely: "You must show a judge that you're making an undiluted and forceful effort to enter the job market at the earliest possibility. The judge does not care that you're attempting to work full time to support yourself in night school! Or that you're trying to obtain an undergraduate degree! He *will* concern himself with the date by which you will have a marketable skill. Or the date by which he feels you should have a marketable skill! Do not try to second-guess the judge by thinking he'll be lenient and grant you additional support to get you through a two-year program! Not when there are programs for which you're eligible that can place you on the job market in less than half that time."

The most important question, which I dare not ask is, what if I obtain my marketable skill and an employer won't hire me because of my age? I've been told by employment agencies that it costs an employer twice as much to pay for my healthcare than a person twenty years old. During this time in history I've just read that one of Grace Kelly's former bridesmaids lives in a homeless shelter in Los Angeles. This was a result of her divorce. I met another woman in her fifties who lives out of her car and spends the days in the library. At an appointed time each week, a maid at the Beverly Hills Hotel lets the woman inside an empty bungalow to take a shower. She tells me that at certain shopping malls there are days when the markets give away free food samples. Her lifestyle was the result of a no-fault divorce from a wealthy man who hid his assets from the court.

We live in a disposable society. Everything is made to throw away, even ex-wives now. Ron knows very well that there is no evidence that the California courts in the 1990s are aware of the economic turmoil that has been created for older women. Stitz mimics them when he states in Richard's motion before the judges that it is healthier for me to go out and get a job rather than live off the lap of alimony. Why is alimony an insult to me, who has nurtured a family for twenty years, who at my age is without a career, a job, pension or health insurance? I earned the right to alimony. It is the share of family income that a wife is promised for her contributions to the marital partnership. What about the intangible property that comes from investing in his career? I was brought up to believe that women whose marriage was as long as mine earned the right to alimony. Because of what Richard has done to me, not just emotionally but financially, it is he who has not earned the right to a divorce.

Ron interrupts my thoughts with, "It is a waste of your energies to double-check with various agencies about the value of U.W.L.A. Paralegal School. Concentrate your energies on being accepted into the vocational program, which will make you employable at the earliest possible date. It will not do either of us any good for me to represent you at the next hearing unless you do so."

Judy opens the door and announces, "Mr. Stitz is here with Mr. Forest. They're waiting in the conference room."

Ron stands. "Let's go. This way." I notice that he is no longer on crutches. Perhaps he'll be in a better mood now that he has recovered from his skiing accident.

We walk solemnly to the conference room. I feel like those royal women in historical novels who were marched off to meet their executioner. I see mine, Stitz, as he waits in the doorway. Behind him is Richard. Then there is the court reporter with her machine propped upon the end of a conference table. There is no exchange of pleasantries as Ron and I sit at the table opposite Stitz and Richard, who sit the same time we do like a rehearsed chorus line. The court reporter tells us her name, Muriel. She looks like a Muriel, dowdy, plain, with an impassive face. As she is also a notary public, she asks me to give my name and to swear to tell the whole truth as if I were in court.

Stitz begins his examination. He reminds me that I took an oath and that I have been sworn to tell the truth under the penalty of perjury. He asks me to listen very carefully to his question and to wait until he's done asking before I respond. I'm told not to nod my head as the reporter can't record nods of the head. He goes on to say that everything I testify today will be typed up in a little booklet known as a deposition booklet. If I make any testimony changes to my "*little*" booklet that I should be advised that might prove to be embarrassing to me in court. Do I understand thus far?

I can't help nodding my head, but I also say aloud, "Yes."

"Is there any reason you can't be deposed today? Have you had any alcohol, any medication or any kind of drugs that might interfere with your testimony?"

I shake my head. "No." (Oh, what I would give for a crushed mint frappé.)

Stitz cocks his head as he leans over the table, the better to hear with his good ear. He bats his hairless eyelids. His pupils have dilated to the color of black marbles. Already the beads of perspiration gather on his forehead outlining his receding hairline.

Richard stares at nothing under the table as if it were something. In all of our court appearances, the coward has never been able to look at me straight in the eye. I can feel the tension from my attorney. He is so annoyed with me. Probably as much as he seems to be annoyed by Richard. I'm a nervous wreck. Ron's veiled threat to leave me without representation sickens me. My life is running on empty. In my wildest nightmares I could never imagine that I would end up in a windowless chamber with three men who can't stand to be in my presence.

Unlike the IRS who will audit tax returns for the past seven years, Stitz wants me to go back as far as the age of nineteen. His interrogation drags us through the time in my life that has no bearing on Richard's marriage with me. He asks what I majored in, in college. My answer of course was," I majored in Dramatic Arts."

Did I ever have a job that wasn't acting? I answer, "Yes as a dancer." Where was that, he asks? "As one of the world, famous Copa girls, I danced at the Copacabana in New York." He wants to know what my salary was and how long did I dance there. I remember that when I testified to this for the first judge, he wasn't a bit interested in my salary but wanted to know if I met any gangsters. I told him Frank Costello-on a Sunday night, which was family night for the gangsters. That judge loved my gangster stories as he had been a law student at Columbia University when the Copacabana had more sheer star power than any other nightclub. It was considered New York's headquarters for great stars. Obviously, Stitz has never been to the Copa.

I explain to Stitz that I can't recall what I was paid at the Copa or for every summer stock job as we're talking more than thirty years ago. I know his ploy. He wants to see if my testimony is different from the last deposition he took. If I had previously said that in-such and-such play I received sixty dollars a week, but now might say instead seventy dollars a week, that would be one of his "aha" moments. He would ask me in court, "Which statement was true? Were you lying the first time or lying the second time?"

Stitz wants to know why I never got a job at Saks Fifth Avenue. Maybe Neiman Marcus? Why didn't I wait tables at the Charthouse in Burbank? I thought that was peculiar but then I realize that since Stitz lives in the Valley (North Hollywood) he's most likely eaten at the Charthouse. To become his waitress would be a fate worse than Richard's threats to make me homeless. Stitz is relentless. What was the total money I ever made from acting in my life? Since I can't answer that, he wants to break it down by years:1965,1966,1967, then the '70s, then the '80s.

I give Ron a look begging him to put a stop to this questioning as it is ancient history. Doesn't he realize I'm suffering? Get this picador off my neck. Ron refuses to acknowledge me. The prolonged minutes seem interminable.

Finally, Muriel, the court reporter, asks permission to stop. She explains she had no idea this deposition would take so long. She has to pick her mother up from the hospital. Muriel suggests she come back tomorrow. Stitz and Litz both rise in panic. Neither of them wants to continue deposing me another day. Stitz decides he has had enough and agrees to stop.

Stitz is frustrated as he has not finished with my summer or winter stock credits. He has yet to cover my writing credits or the two years of private classes with Sanford Meisner and the writing workshops I have attended that are listed in Richard's Declaration on how I wasted his money. Richard claims that he had to subsidize my chasing rainbows plus my dreams of being a movie star or famous writer. The economic drain on him prevents him from having a baby with a new wife. He has also to pay the government $50,000 in taxes by next April. How can he keep a roof over his family's heads and food in their stomachs?

The last sentence is so trite I know that Richard did not write or say it. He probably never bothered to read any of his declarations. As a stage actor he's basically more literate than cornball Stitz.

All my attorneys of record have argued before a judge that each time we go to court, Richard argues he has another big IRS tax bill. If he's always an out-of-work actor, how in the hell did he accumulate so much debt in taxes?

I thank my lucky stars that Muriel has to tend to a sick mother. This has taken the steam out of Stitz's inquisition. We have been sitting for three hours dissecting my life. I can tell the arthritis in Richard's neck and spine is making him uncomfortable by the way he's twitching and stretching out his shoulders. Rivulets of perspiration run down the sides of his neck. On the other hand, I have grown colder with fear. Ron is so perturbed he doesn't care to look at me but throws one of those "See ya laters" over his shoulder as we exit the conference room.

Has Ron forgotten that he is supposed to be my tiger? Despite his negative feelings toward me and my case, he went after Richard and Stitz, with every gun blazing from the jurisprudence arsenal of family law. Then Ron received from Stitz Richard's Answers to Interrogatories. Ron found them inadequate. In his letter to Stitz he sets forth deficiencies in the nature of 'Meet and Confer' so that he will be entitled to sanctions and attorney's fees should Stitz not be responsive and we have to file our motion to compel.

Stitz submitted the wrong records to Litz.

Litz objected over the amount of Richard's gross income.

Litz demanded to know the amount of money paid into retirement funds.

Stitz didn't answer that either.

Litz pointed out that there were TV residuals in which I have an interest.

Stitz again didn't respond.

Litz complains to Stitz that Richard is using the wrong date for separation.

Stitz doesn't respond to that either.

In the same letter Litz tells Stitz that he has never seen such shabby interrogatory responses in his twenty years of practice. Litz reminds Stitz that his client has an obligation to give a full and complete answer. A good faith and specific answer is required.

No response from Stitz.

Litz believes Stitz is taking advantage of the Rules of Discovery. Litz says that if he is not served with supplemental responses which fulfill the requirements set forth in this letter, we will make an ex parte motion for further responses and will request at the Trial Court that Stitz not be entitled to submit or produce evidence in connection with the topics which he has failed to answer.

My tiger attorney sent out subpoenas to Richard's managers for Notice of Taking Deposition. The exhibits he requested went on for four pages. He sent subpoenas to the accountants for Actors Equity Association, Screen Actors Guild and the American Federation of Television and Radio Artists. The heavy paperwork flew about, several phone calls between him and Stitz, his meetings with the paralegal, his review of files, his file preparations for the next OSC hearing.

In three months my legal bill has escalated to $15,000. This is more than I ever received in a year of alimony, in fact twice as much as last year's alimony. Ouch!

"God is the author, men are only the players.
"These grand pieces which are played upon the earth have been composed in heaven."

– Honoré de Balzac

Chapter Sixteen

University of West Los Angeles Paralegal School was in Culver City. The classrooms were in eight modest bungalows framing a parking lot. The school's name was painted on a large piece of canvas strung across the front of the buildings. This place is to be my night life for the next two and a half years. How can I afford the tuition? Easy, they say at the registrar office. I only have to apply for a student loan backed by Fannie Mae. What's another ten thousand dollars of debt for tuition? Is it going to change my life in any way? There seems to be another fortune in books as I am required to take: Legal Theory, Torts, Civil Procedure, Legal Research, Real Property, Accounting, Contracts, Family Law, Legal Writing, Litigation Specialization, Corporations. I choose not to sign up for Wills and Trusts or Criminal Law.

Our professors were lawyers themselves and, as I soon learn, many are not talented as teachers. My torts professor is an angry black woman who brags that seventy-five percent of her students flunk. She is convinced that this testifies to her strength as a teacher rather than her weakness at communicating law to her pupils.

There was a great diversity among the students. Some worked at dreary day jobs that held no future. They complain about their dull positions at the post office or being clerks for doctors or hospitals. Many were legal secretaries tired of typing lengthy briefs. As I learned, the word "brief" does not mean short in length when it is done for a lawyer. The students believe the TV advertisements that the future for paralegals meant starting salaries of $50,000-$80,000 a year plus the annual bonuses. The students also believed that getting a paralegal job was as easy as shooting a fish in a barrel.

I am the oldest one in my classes as the majority of the students are in their twenties or thirties. No one in the registrar's office ever gives a hint that a new graduate in her or his forties without past legal experience would be considered too old for lawyers who hire only young paralegals for *entry-level* jobs. These were the days when it was illegal to fire or not to hire someone because of age discrimination. How are you going to prove this? Want to start a lawsuit? Got $5,000 for a lawyer's retainer? Got two other employees willing to lose their jobs if they testify on your behalf?

In my first class the professor explains that our courses are the same as for aspiring lawyers in the law school. The tests administered are also the same as for a law student. The only difference is that what the paralegals take a semester to learn, the law school students were given the same subject to learn in one year. In other words, he said, "You paralegals have to be brighter, quicker to learn everything in half the time."

This means lengthy assignments and weekends spent in the law library. Legal Research was the most valuable subject because I learned how to use the law library. Unlike the public library, there is no Dewey Decimal System in this library. There is no way a lay person off the street will understand or have the tools to provide access to the mass of chronologically published decisions and statutes. He or she will not understand case-finding or how to use Shepard's Citations, which verifies the current status of each case in order to establish whether it is still effective law or has been reversed, overruled or its authority diminished. But soon I know my way around the library. As a client, this ability does not endear me to lawyers. "A little learning is a dangerous thing," so said Pope. My spark became a flame.

One of the most important things that I learn at school is that all people are not created equal. There is the real truth of a case, and the truth decided by the judge's decision, and they are not necessarily the same. Paralegals are taught to think like lawyers in that they will have to learn and identify with rules that they don't agree with and to understand that judges can't be persuaded by emotional declarations of faith.

This semester our main assignments are reading and briefing cases of which most are decisions of appellate courts, designed higher courts. Here's where lawyers carry their objections about some point of law ruled on by the trial judge. Then it dawns on me: We are studying cases of the very rich who can afford the huge legal fees of prosecuting an appeal. Divorcées like me or the peasantry of California or anywhere else are never going to be subjects of courtroom battles likely to be published in casebooks. Any sense of social injustice or society's wrongs will be cut off from our basic idea of what is fair. Lawyers and judges will never admit to the violations of law or the disproportionate impact on the poverty-stricken.

Ron asked me to write out everything that happened or went wrong since day one with Judge Shafer, the first judge. I listed all the monies that Richard hid from me, such as he borrowed thousands of dollars against the cash surrender of his life insurance policy and closed out the employee benefit plan from our corporation. My first lawyer and I believed he used this money for a down payment on a house in California for Meredith, the librarian, and himself.

Richard likes to bring up the fact that in our tenth year of marriage we separated for a while. He mentions this in order to make the court believe that we weren't together as long as twenty years, but never tells what really happened. Of course I related the whole story to Ron.

It all started with the purchase of a puppy. Jennifer and Tina were now ages seven and four. They were in mourning for two baby turtles that died under our care. Richard held a mock burial at sea by flushing the turtles in the toilet. To make up for this loss, the girls suggested gerbils as pets. The nuns at their school, St. Hilda's and St. Hughes, wanted to find homes for some gerbils. Jennifer pleaded, "Couldn't we just take two of them?"

I can't stand the thought of rodents, even in a cage. So a couple of days later, I did what friends warned me never to do: I went to a pet shop. Previously, I had gone to Gimbels for something else and only out of curiosity strolled into their pet shop. The manager swore that the puppies were not from the infamous puppy mills in the Midwest or anywhere else.

Then I see a four-month old wire-hair terrier. He notices me, too. He jumps at the plexiglass window to get my attention. Naturally, I come to him. He performs by running in circles, then rolling over a couple of times. The manager said, "Would you like to hold him?" I nod. The manager brings out the puppy then places him at my feet. The terrier jumps and jumps. He wiggles his tail at me. The manager said, "Look how healthy he is. What pep." I pick up the puppy and receive several licks on my hand and face in gratitude. The manager encourages me with, "Wire-hair terriers are wonderful around children."

Twenty minutes later I am carrying a special pet box under my arm. I ride the subway balancing the box steady on my lap so as not to frighten my little darling. I decide to name him Whiskey, in memory of my childhood dog Soda.

Opening the door to our apartment, I summon my daughters. "Guess what I have?" They squeal when they see the box and the furry nose poking through a hole. I put the box on the floor. The puppy takes one step, gasps, then falls on his side with his tongue hanging out. "What's wrong with him?" The girls try to get the puppy as if to encourage him to play.

Richard appears from the bedroom. He looks down at the puppy. "You went and bought us a sick dog! What the fuck is wrong with him?" The puppy begins coughing weakly between gasping for breaths. I cradle him in my arms. He is limp and barely can keep his eyes open. I realize that all the pep and vigor he displayed in the pet store was just an act so I would take him home and, in doing so, save his life.

The next afternoon my children and I stand at the side of an examination table with Whiskey lying motionless as Dr. Meador, the veterinarian, counsels me in a dispassionate tone. "This puppy is very, very sick."

"Isn't his cough the usual kennel cough that most dogs catch in a pet store?"

"His is worse because he has a heart defect."

"Oh, no, what does that mean?"

"He has a malformed heart valve. Get rid of him."

The girls yell, "Get rid of *you*. How'd you like that? You go away."

Dr. Meador speaks over their protests. "Take him back to Gimbels before it's too late. He's going to die. If not soon, then by the time he reaches his full body weight at the age of one year. He will die."

"Please, doctor, understand it is already too late. We've spent one night with this puppy." I scoop up Whiskey in my arms. "If I return him to Gimbels, what would they do about him?"

The doctor peers over his glasses with a grim look. "That's not your concern. Get your money back. Find a healthy dog through a private breeder."

"We're keeping this puppy. Just give me a prescription for his pneumonia."

He scribbles on a prescription pad then hands me the papers. "Good luck. Maybe I'll see you in a year."

Once the girls and I carrying Whiskey were on the street, we ran as fast as we could to find a taxi as if to escape the doom and gloom of the veterinarian's office. I promise them that Whiskey will live longer than a year. We'll show the doctor because we'll take such good care of Whiskey he will live a long life with us.

That night in our small kitchen I close the door. I tuck towels in the crack of the door. The humidifier on the counter produces hot steam. I nestle Whiskey in a towel in my arms, rocking him back and forth. I give him an antibiotic pill. Everyone has gone to bed. Richard calls out sleepily from the bedroom, "Make sure the pup's face is near the steam. That's gonna help his congestion." An hour later, Richard in a muffled voice warns again, "Keep holding him up if you want him to live. Don't put the pup down. Make sure he faces the steam."

Morning light creeps into the kitchen. The window is smeared in a cloud of steam, and the front of my hair is damp. The puppy gazes at me with huge brown eyes. He licks my hand, a response to assure me he is going to recover.

A week later Whiskey is playing with the children. We are thrilled to watch him chase a ball, then give it to one of us to throw. This Sunday is Mother's Day. Richard and the girls give me a special present. Tina and Jennifer can't wait for me to open the shiny box from Saks Fifth Avenue. It is a peignoir made in France. I am so surprised. What an extravagant gift.

Maybe it was about a half hour later, but out of nowhere came the sudden and horrific words from Richard: "I'm leaving you. I met someone else. I've fallen in love with her." A lump of shock sticks in my throat. Tina bites the back of her hand to keep from crying. Jennifer lets out a wail that doesn't stop until she runs out of breath. The three of us cling together in disbelief. My eyes swim in pools of tears. I can't focus. Richard slams the front door behind him. His footsteps echo down the hallway, then die in the sound of the elevator. The tears keep coming and melt onto the heads of my daughters, who weep, "Where's he going? Why? Why? Doesn't he love us anymore?"

What a feeble mockery Richard has made of Mother's Day. He approves the purchase of a new puppy, gives me an expensive gift, but wraps it up with the announcement he is in love with someone else.

I gather the peignoir in my hands. It is quite lovely with the pink and blue floral design. I fold it into a square of tissue paper then put it into the bottom drawer of my bureau. I will never ever wear the peignoir in this lifetime.

The "other" woman is a twenty-four-year-old airline stewardess from Texas. Richard had recently met DeeDee Divine on a flight from Texas to New York. She served him coffee. He invited her to dinner. She wears bright green eye shadow at high noon and chews Bazooka bubble gum. Jennifer describes this to me. She went on to say, "Dad took Tina and me to their new apartment. DeeDee keeps a large jar filled with Bazooka bubble gum, her favorite. She wears fake ponytails that feel just like Barbie's hair."

I phone Richard to explain I don't want our daughters meeting his sex life over the breakfast table. They are too young. This is confusing to them. Richard takes umbrage at my words. How dare I insinuate there is something wrong with his daughters being part of his happiness with DeeDee Divine?

I talk on top of him. I won't permit Tina and Jennifer to visit him. Soon there is much cursing then a bang. I know that Richard has thrown the phone. It is impossible for him to react civilly when he doesn't get his way.

During the trauma of this separation, I began losing weight unintentionally. When Richard comes once a week to see the girls, he notices my skeletal look. He advises, "Why don't you become a nun?"

"Huh?" I am truly baffled. The last time I heard this line, it belonged to Hamlet.

"As a nun you can still contribute to life. Be useful, too."

"Well, I'll take your idea under consideration." I know he is influenced by the Episcopal nuns who teach our children. I repeat Richard's "Get thee to a nunnery" speech to a girlfriend who shrieks with laughter. Because she knows Richard, the actor, she believes me. Only a man as bizarre as Richard would order his wife to a nunnery.

"Dah-ling, he's crazy! Cra-zy!"

Through friends I find a lawyer who advises me that I am correct. The New York state law does not allow a father to share custody of children if other women are involved. Nevertheless, Richard does not believe this. He says we're not in the Victorian ages any more. He hires his lawyer who is actually an entertainment attorney but is willing to accompany Richard at our hearing before a judge.

The judge reads my complaint. His face pinches in anger like his gnarled fist. He grabs his gavel and whacks it so loud on his desk that Richard and his lawyer flinch in unison. The judge stretches out his arm and shakes the gavel in Richard's face. "No more women! Understand? No women! If you ever bring women around these young girls, you will lose all rights to custody!"

My attorney whispers to me. "See, I told you we'd win. No more women. Or he loses his children."

*****

In the evenings my children and I recline in the living room to look at television as it provides a distraction for us in our loneliness. Tonight we watch CBS, and Walter Cronkite who announces the news. The commercial break comes. The voice says, "My wife is incredible. I think I'll keep her."

We look up startled. There on the TV screen are Richard and I. Our faces are pressed cheek to cheek. Jennifer jumped to her feet. "Isn't that your old Geritol commercial?"

It sure was. About a year and a half earlier, Richard and I were cast in the new Geritol advertising campaign. The sponsors wanted to break away from the image that Geritol pills were for old people but, instead, young women and men should take them, too. Since Geritol was a pill, Richard and I had to assure the advertising agency that we were what the commercial said, married with two children and a dog. Truth in advertising made this a legal issue. The Geritol commercial ran for a couple of months then was taken off the air. Richard believed it was because of the line, "My wife takes Geritol. My wife is incredible. I think I'll keep her." Women's groups were furious. On the street, women yelled at him, "Maybe she'll keep you! Maybe she won't. Who do you think you are, you disgusting idiot!"

In the commercial Richard and I wear fashionable night clothes; his is a cashmere bathrobe; mine is a Christian Dior negligee. I say nothing as we sit on the side of a bed, but I gaze adoringly at Richard as he proclaims, "Look at my wife. The way she takes care of the kids, the house, a job and me—it's incredible. She looks better than any of her friends. And they're all about the same age. Aren't those nice words for a woman to hear? But to be able to get all those compliments, you have to take care of yourself. Eat right, get plenty of rest, exercise. And to make sure you get enough iron and vitamins, take Geritol every morning. Geritol has more than twice the iron of ordinary supplements. Plus seven vitamins. My wife takes Geritol. I think I'll keep her." (Mary Chase Carpenter, the folk singer, was so inspired by this commercial that years later, she won an award for her song "I Think I'll Keep Her.")

It is too much. I switch the TV channel. As we're getting ready for bed, Richard's voice booms forth again: "Look at my wife..." Obviously, the ad agency decided to rerun the Geritol commercial on more than one network. What irony. Richard has moved out, and yet I can't seem to escape him as the Geritol commercial runs throughout the day. The reiteration of that phrase, "I think I'll keep her" is doubly annoying as I pass acquaintances on the street who wave hello. Invariably their next words are, "Take Geritol. Maybe he'll keep you! Keep getting those residuals." I don't show how resentful I am. If they only knew my husband is keeping an airline stewardess, a woman who doesn't need jewels or furs, just Bazooka bubble gum.

Almost a year later, Richard's interest in the stewardess starts to wane. One evening when he is performing in a Broadway play, Miss DeeDee Divine calls me. In her unfortunate Texas drawl, she tells me her side of the story. How she met him on the plane. She thought he was just another nice guy. She had no idea until much later that there was a wife and children in the background. She bursts into anguished sobs. For the next hour I console her. "Please, DeeDee, don't throw your life away on a man old enough to be your father. Frankly, you don't want to put up with an actor–he's never home–he believes he's Don Juan–he's a lousy father–he's more in love with himself than any woman. Believe me, in a couple of years, you'll find the man of your dreams. You'll be so glad you didn't make a bigger fool of yourself over an unstable, pretentious actor."

Richard has broken another heart. She is too naive to understand how lucky she is to be free of him.

*****

Richard agreed to go with me to a family therapist. Previously, the therapist pleaded with me to dump him, that he was a lifetime of heartbreak. I know she is right, but because of my two daughters I don't have a choice. As a stay-at-home mom, I haven't the money to keep them in private school or to afford another apartment in Manhattan. I have no family to back me up, no siblings to offer help. If I were alone, I would have jumped ship or taken the plane with the stewardess to Texas and beyond.

A year later, Miss Divine called me again and, over the phone, expressed how happy she was. She went to a family funeral in New Orleans where she ran into her cousin. It was inexplicable love at first sight. He swept her off her feet as they used to say. She married the cousin soon after the funeral.

Maybe it's not exactly like meeting an old boyfriend at a high school reunion, but in the South a family funeral is like a reunion as it were. Northerners look askance at marriage between cousins. However, all that in-breeding in the South does produce many great writers.

Tina and Jennifer are so happy to have their father at home again. They pretend the past year never happened. Or maybe I'm just a "cock-eyed optimist" as the song goes.

"Love, like Ulysses is a wanderer
For new fields always and new faces yearning.
Put by, O waiting ones, put by your weaving.
Unlike Ulysses, love is unreturning."

– Roselle Mercier Montgomery

Our family photo with Whiskey, our pet.

Chapter Seventeen

Back to Los Angeles and Divorce Court

After Ron Litz read my assigned treatise (forty pages) of previous court trials, he quoted certain examples of Richard's past bad-boy behavior in my Declaration in Support of the OSC for Modification of Spousal Support that was calendered for the next month. Obviously, this set the enemy on their heels for the new battle.

In retaliation, Attorney Stitz filed a Notice of Motion to Strike portions of the Declaration. I never heard of this motion before. Between the legal eagles and paralegal school, my new jurisprudence seems boundless. Stitz claims that support cannot be ordered to punish either party. The award cannot be based upon good versus bad faith conduct.

A psychiatrist used to say past behavior is a good predictor of future behavior. However, that is the medical community, not the legal world. As far as Stitz was concerned, any allegations of misconduct are not admissible such as: monies spent by Richard to support his affairs with an ice skater, an airline stewardess, cashing out community life insurance to buy a house for the librarian, and the fact that his sea captain's ambition was a tax write-off for his boat, and that he spends more on a boat in one year than he has given me in total support.

Stitz even took offense that Litz threw in my Declaration that Richard had suggested I should become a nun. How could that offend a judge? The fact that Richard thinks a life of a nun in a religious order would be the most satisfying and fulfilling place for his ex-wife to spend as the bride of Jesus Christ might impress a judge. Especially if he or she were Hispanic and most likely a devoted Catholic.

Surely the judge would consider that Richard is a devout Christian and only wants a middle-aged wife safe in a convent rather than ending up in a shelter for the homeless. How ethical and thoughtful of him.

Attorney Stitz requests that these statements in my Declaration be stricken, as they are false, improper, irrelevant, immaterial or non-essential matters. As his precedent, he uses California Code of Civil Procedure Section 4509 that says "allegations of specific acts of misconduct are inadmissible in any pleadings or proceedings for dissolution."

Well, that just about covers the ball game, as they say back home in South Dakota. Ron informs me that he will not go to the expense of filing an opposition to Stitz's motion since we will have achieved as much mileage by having inserted Richard's misconduct into our original documents. This is the same as when a witness testifies at trial, and the jury is ordered to ignore the testimony but, as a lawyer says, once you rang the bell, it's too late. The jury heard it anyway.

Ron goes on to say that Stitz is quite right that these statements are not really relevant or admissible in our present proceeding. Ron admonishes me in a letter for wasting my time checking with various employment agencies or vocational schools and that I have provided him with information regarding Richard which more often than not proved irrelevant or, when inaccurate, detrimental to my cause.

I am bewildered. What does he mean "detrimental?" I have supported my information with evidence of a paper trail that made the ex-husband go ballistic. Richard forgets that during our marriage I was the bookkeeper; I was the one who fought with his theatrical agents over delayed or missing payments; I was the one who prepared the taxes each year for the accountant; I balanced all the checking and savings accounts; I paid the bills.

As a result, when Richard testified that during our marriage he never filmed any TV shows that produced any residuals for my community-property interests, I came forth with a list of forty-five TV shows made during our marriage. I had saved all the statements from his agencies, plus the check stubs and bank deposit slips as proof.

Not only am I baffled by Ron, but I am alarmed by his statement of doubting my integrity. I dare not call his office and ask for an answer because this becomes a conference call, billable to my account, adding most likely another $500 to my proliferating legal fees.

Again we have to report to Department Two in Los Angeles Superior Court. Our appointed time is one o'clock after the lunch hour for the court. I study the lawyers and clients as they file past me into the assembly room. I have been here often enough to recognize the unhappiness, the anger and some of the tragedy written on the faces of the wives and husbands in this room. They split apart with their lawyers and sit on opposite sides as if the separation is a protective barrier. These couples who end up in Department Two have declared war. This is the end of a chance of a peaceful resolution for a divorce now deemed hopeless. Their lives are in turmoil.

There is a buzz of conversation between lawyers, the clicking of briefcases, the flipping of legal papers and the muffled whispers. In this courtroom the nervous tension is like a taut wire about to snap at any moment, which charges the air like a Kafka scene. I see Ron and Judy crossing the faux-marble hallway floor toward me. She is lugging an oversize file folder under one arm while pulling a small black suitcase behind her. Though she is twenty-eight, Judy looks forty-eight. She admitted that the last seven years of being a paralegal have worn her out. Her office is packed floor to ceiling with file folders; they are even on every chair and her entire windowsill. Sometimes she works until eight o'clock in the evening. There is no overtime pay as a paralegal position is considered a titled employee. She attends night school as she plans to become a court reporter. In that job, the day ends at five and, when the court closes for holidays, the reporter is paid anyway. Privately she had asked me, "Are you sure you want to be a paralegal?"

Ron greets me in a condescending way. "I just spoke with your last judge, Jill Robbins. I said you were represented by Susan Goldstein when she heard your case. Of course, she doesn't remember you. I explained this was a twenty-year marriage and that she admonished you with the order that if in two years your efforts to find employment have been no different, a future court may terminate your rights to support. Jill said that was impossible, she would never have done that to a woman who had been married with children for twenty years. I said, 'Well, you did. You ruined this woman's case and her life.' "

He looks at me impatiently. "What did you do in court to annoy her?"

"I didn't do anything. I explained that my attorney, Susan, made some mistakes at trial. She didn't understand residual payments. Or what was corporate income and what was not."

"This is the second judge you have annoyed."

"That's not true. The first judge gave me alimony for life even though it was only $625 a month. And that low award was due to the actors' strike. Richard claimed he was an out-of-work actor. His career was over."

Ron turns from me as though my useless remarks bore him. He enters the courtroom with Judy and me trailing behind. She whispers, "I printed out a copy of the Calhoun Case for you. It's our ammunition against Stitz's use of the Sheridan Case."

Stitz loves the Appellate Court's opinion for Mrs. Sheridan. He claims I'm just like her: go to school for enjoyment not education, a failure at jobs like realtor and salesgirl where the commissions aren't enough to cover expenses. Her defense was that her choice of employment was the result of bad judgment, not bad faith. The court found that even though her doctor-husband had the ability to pay $1,200 a month, he had done his duty for five years. Her support was terminated.

In Ron's Points and Authorities he uses the Calhoun Case where the Court of Appeals denied the husband, a successful ophthalmologist, the motion to terminate support because the supported wife's needs continued to outweigh her ability to support herself. Also she lived below "the style" to which the parties had been accustomed during the marriage.

As I read my copy of the Calhoun Case, I am impressed with the wife's education: a BA in English literature, a master's degree in science and mathematics, another master's degree in theoretical statistics. She just finished a course for her doctoral degree. She works in Stockholm, Sweden, as a systems analyst. Her annual salary is $19,000. Stitz would have gone crazy with this information so unlike me with three years of college and two years at the American Theatre Wing, a drama school. Stitz thinks I'm hiding a degree somewhere in my theatrical education.

Despite the fact that the appeal judges recognized Mrs. Calhoun's significant education and employable skills and was not a typical "displaced homemaker," her needs far outweigh her ability to support herself. The husband wanted a step-down from $900 to $600 per month then an action to terminate spousal support. To put this in a nutshell, the marriage was for twenty-four years, and according to the judges, too lengthy to terminate her support and to deny her request for $900 monthly. Hooray for Mrs. Calhoun. Now the question is, what will our judge decide to do this afternoon when he reads Ron's citation for the Calhoun Case or will the judge read no further than Stitz's use of the Sheridan Case? Tune in tomorrow for the answer.

After the roll call is taken, we are assigned to Herbert Klein, Judge Pro Tem. In his chambers he has supposedly taken a few private minutes to read my request that the spousal order be increased, that jurisdiction be extended and for a contribution toward my attorney's fees and cost of suit. Using Mrs. Calhoun as an example, I state in my declaration that my income is not sufficient to meet my expenses. The judge enters our courtroom wearing his black robe and looking like a choir director as he sits behind his desk on a dais.

While the lawyers and Judy set out their files and exhibits on the witness table, I notice that Judge Klein's eyes are slowly closing. His head falls on his chest. The jerky movement wakes him up. He blinks as if to make sure where he is then stifles a yawn. Maybe he had a martini lunch. We are his first case this afternoon. There's no logical reason for him to act tired. Or already bored! He's not that old as he is in his early fifties. What hair he has left is dull gray. The whole aura about him bespeaks dull and unmemorable. Five minutes after leaving his courtroom, I wouldn't be able to pick him out in a police line-up.

As the Petitioner, Richard always takes the stand first. He begins by playing the sympathy card. Since the dissolution, his health has deteriorated. He had to undergo cardio angioplasty, which left him with a heart condition so that he can no longer survive the hours and stresses of television acting. In addition he was seriously injured in an automobile accident and sustained brain damage and extensive joint damage to his left hand, which was paralyzed for ten months.

"I have been ordered by my doctor to go on a diet of 500 calories a day to reduce my blood pressure."

He inhales deeply so he could say the next sentence without stopping. "Oh, I almost forgot, since we were last in court I underwent a double hernia operation with inverted abdominal wall reinforcement at Cedars Sinai Hospital." He pauses for dramatic effect before he continues with downcast, sorrowful eyes. "I'm going to pursue a less stressful and low-paying career as a boat captain. I have acquired the boat and am a practicing licensed U.S. Coast Guard Operator. As a captain I can implement this plan."

Stitz keeps up the same line of questioning: "Are you now working as a sea captain?"

"I can't include this new career until I have saved enough money to sustain my family and me. This can't take place because of her demands for spousal support." Richard chokes a bit as he is so emotional. If he had been playing this scene on "Young Doctor Malone," there wouldn't be a dry eye left in the audience.

Ron starts his interrogation. "Despite your brain damage, are you able to memorize your lines for *Santa Barbara* and other TV shows?"

"Well, ah—at the moment—"

"This is not an essay question. Yes or no? It's a simple answer."

"Yesss." Richard said almost in a hiss.

"Last year did you make three hundred thousand dollars in TV residuals alone?"

"I wouldn't know. I'm not an accountant," Richard snarled.

"You signed Candace's lease for an apartment in Beverly Hills so that your daughters could benefit from the high school in the district." Ron held up my lease. "Is this your signature?"

"They're not in high school anymore."

"Just answer the question yes or no. Is this your signature?"

"Yes."

"In spite of the paralysis of your left hand, did you continue to drive your motorcycle?"

"I have to save money on gas. So it's more economical for—"

"Answer a simple yes or no."

"Yes."

"According to a recent *TV Guide*, you were the only actor from the *Santa Barbara* TV series to be nominated for a Daytime Emmy—in the category of leading man. Did your bad heart prevent you from going to New York to attend the Emmy's Ceremony?"

"Well, I had to, I mean—it's my job—"

"Answer yes or no."

"Yes, I went. The producers made me."

I thought to myself, if Richard were on his death bed he would rise up like Lazarus if there were a chance he could win an Emmy.

Then Ron stepped on dangerous territory when he opened a file to read, "According to the Ventura Yacht Surveys you own a custom 53-foot vessel, twin screw, diesel-powered, flying bridge cruiser that has a replacement value of $257,000—"

"That's not what the boat would sell for now."

"According to the American Marine Surveyors this vessel is paid in full and has almost $80,000 invested in recommended repairs, new electronic equipment, new deck and safety equipment. This amount is more than the entire alimony you have ever paid Candace. As an out of-work actor, how do you afford the docking?"

Richard was in a fight within himself to control his anger. "I operate a business with this boat. It belongs to my corporation. I use it for scuba instructing and as a public relations tool with my celebrity students. As a captain, I leased the boat for a day to director James Cameron—"

"I don't see any income declared for this boat. How can a brain-damaged captain with a bad heart risk taking people far out on the ocean-cruising to Malibu?"

Richard lost it. He began to shout that he had to gain valuable experience even though he wasn't making any money at the moment. Ron argued that an out-of-work actor as poor as Richard claims to be, wouldn't have this kind of money to buy a boat and to pay huge amounts for repairs.

"I have spent thousands of hours of my own time to rebuild a boat, which is now insured for $85,000!"

"If you can afford the expense of this boat, why can't you pay alimony?"

The argument grew until Richard threatened, "I'll sue you!"

"Do you want to open suit now?" Ron extended his arms out as though ready.

A red flush of embarrassment colored Richard's brow and cheeks. Ron waited motionless. I waited breathless. Stitz waited in shock, his mouth twitching. Would Richard be so stupid as to sue a lawyer in open court?

It was one of the rare moments I have ever seen Richard at a loss for words. After what seemed an eternity of silence, Ron continued with his questions.

All this time, the judge's face was expressionless. There was no clue as to what he was thinking. With his elbow on the desk, he rested his chin in the palm of his hand. It was hard to tell if his red-rimmed eyes were shut in concentration or had he gone to sleep again.

Then it was my turn to be grilled by Stitz. He ran over the same argument: Why did I find temp work that paid five dollars an hour? He claimed that I was like Mrs. Sheridan who only took college courses for fun. Why didn't I see a vocational counselor? The previous court had ordered me to be tested. What made me think I could be a paralegal? What was I doing living in a Beverly Hills apartment?

I answered that after my daughter moved out, I rented the bedroom to strangers in order to reduce my rent. It was cheaper to live there in a rent-controlled apartment than anywhere else. It was then that Stitz got his "aha" moment with the question, "What did your tenant pay you in rent for the bedroom?"

"Three hundred fifty dollars a month."

"Three hundred fifty dollars a month!" He grabs a sheet of paper from one of his files. "Nowhere on your Declaration of Income have you listed this rental!"

"It's not income when my rent has almost doubled over the years."

Stitz ran to the side of the room where there was a huge blackboard. He snatches a piece of chalk, then writes in huge numbers $350 X 12 = $4,200. He turns toward me shaking the chalk in my direction. "When I deposed you, this amount of four thousand two hundred dollars for rental was not mentioned."

"No! I didn't mention it because I was deposed during the summer when my student tenant left—"

Stitz ignores my testimony. He is like a mad dog as he scribbles my meager budget on the blackboard. Every temp job I had, he lists as though each one lasted a year. I try to protest, to explain in hopes the judge would interfere and allow me the chance to speak. But there was not a glimmer of reaction from him. I wasn't sure whether he was sighing or lightly snoring.

Stitz is writing more mathematical figures and multiplying them all by twelve months. He inflates his calculations to reflect an annual income of $40,000. I want a chance to challenge him, to scream that he is misrepresenting the facts. But Ron accuses me of annoying judges, which makes me afraid to contradict Stitz at the moment. Surely my tiger attorney will speak out in my defense, but Ron was silent as though he didn't care to interrupt.

Finally Stitz turns from the blackboard, his eyes squinting. If eyes are the mirror to one's soul, he has an ugly one. Gertrude would say 'cold like a witch's tit'.

"So there." Stitz waves his chalk at me like a semaphore of caution.

Then it was time for the attorneys' summation just like my high school debate class. Only we were never allowed to be dishonest or to present facts not relevant to the debate. We had to be the paragons of virtue.

Ron told the judge, "It is the nature of the entertainment industry that an actor is frequently unemployed. It's the Petitioner's ploy to come into court at contract renewal time claiming that he will either soon be out of work or that his salary will be dramatically reduced. Yet after each court hearing he miraculously lands starring roles with more than lucrative salaries. His so-called disabilities are a smoke screen designed to arouse the pity of this court and to detract attention from his financial resources. Because of his past appearances as a star on nightly TV and other major motion pictures, his income will never fall to zero. He'll receive residuals for many years to come.

"The court should recognize that a husband cannot have it both ways. He can't have his wife remain at home while he provides for his own education or experience in show business. After a twenty-year marriage, it's cruel and inhuman to deprive Candace of the only income she has now, simply because he doesn't want her services."

Ron turned to Richard and Stitz. "I propose that it would be fair to give her twenty percent of his income each year. If he is an actor out-of-work and made no money for that year, than she gets nothing."

"Oh, no, no, no," Richard was shaking his head as Stitz grimaced at the idea.

Ron continued on, ignoring Richard's protests. "What about the intangible property that comes from Respondent investing in Petitioner's career? Under the community property rule, she should be awarded an equal share of this property."

The upshot of Stitz's rebuttal was: I purposely applied for jobs that wouldn't hire me such as a cocktail waitress where I was considered too mature to be hired when they could hire an eighteen-year-old Raquel Welch lookalike; I enrolled in a two-year paralegal program without benefit of vocational guidance testing; this proves I have not acted in good faith compliance with previous court orders; since I studied with the finest theater professors and coaches, I could be an associate professor or a high school drama teacher.

Stitz wrapped up his argument by accusing me of filing the annual barrage of motions and trials that have been emotionally and physically exhausting for the Petitioner. The cost and frequency, too, have begun to seriously affect his relationship with his new wife. The facts cry out! How much longer must Petitioner subsidize the Respondent's twenty-one-year dreams of becoming a famous actress? Or a writer!

At last our hearing ended. Judge Klein perked up a bit with the pronouncement that he would give the court's rulings in ten days.

A few minutes later, Ron and I went to the parking lot on Hill Street. He appeared disconsolate at my prospects. "Better sell that book soon. Or your screenplay. Sell something, anything fast."

We didn't have to wait ten days for Judge Klein's decision. Within four days it arrived. As I read my copy of the "Findings and Orders to Show Cause," I was appalled at Judge Klein's rulings but not surprised. He claims I have not complied with the admonitions of previous judges to prepare for self-supportive status. He cites the Sheridan case even though Ron had pointed out that I was married twice as long as Mrs. Sheridan and was fifteen years older than she and, unlike her, I didn't receive $100,000 in cash for my community property settlement.

Judge Klein accuses me of taking temp jobs at $5 an hour with no medical insurance, no retirement and no indication of chances for monetary advancement as further proof that I have not attempted any serious rehabilitation or training program to develop employment skills. Nowhere does he cite the Calhoun Case, where the Court of Appeals found that due to length of marriage the Court is without authority to reduce the amount of alimony.

Judge Klein ordered that the Petitioner pay me alimony of $1,250 for six months terminating as to one dollar a year (reduced to $1 a year is also a legal precedent). Then to add insult to injury, I'm to make monthly reports on the first of each month starting immediately to notify the Petitioner and his attorney and, thereafter, in my job and school searches until I enroll in a particular job-training course.

In the legal library at the UWLA School of Paralegal Studies, I found in Article I Section I of the Constitution for the State of California: the requirement to report to Petitioner requiring the Respondent to notify him locations and terms of employment is an abuse of discretion and constitutes an invasion of Respondent's right to privacy. This requirement is demeaning, serves no useful purpose and would only cause Respondent to be harassed, embarrassed and inconvenienced. The Petitioner is not about to report to her when his financial states improve.

I guess that Judge Klein forgot about that Article I in the State's Constitution.

When I call Ron's office, Judy answers the phone, "I'm so sorry about the new Order." Then she transfers me to Ron's phone. He picks up immediately. I knew he would be upset as he was awarded only

$1,000 on my new $8,000 legal bill. "I want you to send me monthly reports regarding your training effort. Stitz will argue that you could go to LA City College and for fifty dollars a semester, you'd complete their paralegal program in one year."

"Ron, you know as well as I that the paralegal program there is not ABA-approved. All the law firms I checked with said there's no point in taking a course that's not going to pass the Bar's approval. They won't hire any paralegal without a college degree and a paralegal certification either from UWLA or UCLA."

As soon as Stitz learned that I enrolled in the UWLA's paralegal's program, he contacted the Director of Admissions and the Dean asking for my records of attendance, the subjects of the classes I had enrolled in plus the names of the instructors.

When I last spoke to Ron, I mentioned my upcoming trip to New York for four days. He said, "How can you afford that? That's the question Stitz is going to ask six months from now at our next hearing in Court."

"My trip is paid for because I'm going to be a guest speaker at a film convention."

"What do you mean?"

"Remember the cult-classic movie I made, *Carnival of Souls*?"

"No, I don't remember."

"In my other life as an actress I did a low-budget movie, *Carnival of Souls* in which I now have become an icon in New York."

> "Actors are the only honest hypocrites. Their life is a voluntary dream; and the height of their ambition is to be beside themselves. They wear the livery of other men's fortunes; their very thoughts are not their own."
>
> – William Hazlitt

ACT THREE

Chapter Eighteen

(In the beginning was Carnival of Souls, created in twenty-eight days and nights.)

Early in 1960, on a long drive back home from an assignment in California, Herk Harvey, a young filmmaker from Lawrence, Kansas, reached the outskirts of Salt Lake City at dusk. At the edge of the Great Salt Lake he saw the weirdest-looking place he had ever seen: an abandoned amusement park and Pavilion.

It was like something out of St. Petersburg. He parked the car, then hiked up the three-quarter-mile ramp. He studied the deserted and neglected amusement park, the quiet despair of it all. The pavilion seemed to be something from a psychedelic dream, designed like a Russian tabernacle with Moorish turrets gleaming in the twilight. Inside the pavilion, the caress of a drifting wind blew leftover, tattered crepe streamers back and forth in their haunting dance. A kaleidoscope of silver and gold party hats and torn paper lanterns swirled about the ballroom floor. Herk thought to himself, what a tremendous film location! Completely isolated, the Saltair Pavilion was the largest, open-air dance pavilion in the world. In its heyday, the pavilion could accommodate 3,000 dancing couples.

As Herk gazed around, he saw that the Great Salt Lake, which was once a couple thousand square miles in area and quite deep, had receded. The old slogan "Saltair-Try to Sink" used to attract legions of summer tourists, who enjoyed the most delightful bathing in the world. Nonetheless, when Salt Lake turned into a dead sea, the romance of the place seemed to vanish into the dried up salt beds that killed the resort business for the amusement park.

Inspired by the ghostly white of the deserted salt beds surrounding the pavilion and amusement park, Herk took out his camera and photographed the scene. He guessed that this place had been abandoned for about twenty years or more. Most of the amusement rides were still standing. The only thing torn down was the roller coaster.

In Lawrence, Herk met with John Clifford, a writer who worked with him at Centron Corporation, the film company where John had written and Herk had directed geographical films, commercials, musicals, and documentaries. Herk said, "John, I found a terrific location for us to make our first feature film. The atmosphere is so eerie and spooky. I want you to write a horror screenplay so that it ends with ghouls dancing around inside a pavilion."

"How soon do you want a script?" John asked.

"Can you finish it in three weeks?"

"Done."

"That's great. My vacation starts then." Then Herk advised John, "Remember it's low budget, so not too much dialogue as that costs more." Herk felt confident that he could rely on the facilities at Centron. He had at his disposal: a sound stage, cameras, sound gear, editing rooms, mixing equipment and a projection room. He decided to shoot in black-and-white and give the film a patina of a far more costly film by shooting it in 35 mm. Thirteen local business men and friends of his each gave him $1000 as their initial investment in the movie. With a total of $13,000, he was ready to start his production.

His cinematographer, Maurice Prather, had worked with director Robert Altman in Kansas City before he came to Centron. Maurice and Herk both agreed that the movie should have a sinister quality. To achieve a sense of strangeness, a sense of something not right, Maurice would use deliberately contrasting film textures—a flat rainy look for day-lit exteriors, and muted, shadowy effect for interiors, and the final confrontation with the spirits of the dead. He wanted this sequence in which the dead rise from the lake and pursue the leading girl to combine beauty yet to be menacing just like the best moments of a Val Lewton movie. He also said to Herk, "By shooting in black-and-white rather than color, we can achieve an Ingmar Bergman look, too, with its definite contrasts."

When Herk read John's final script, he saw that the most important role was that of the girl who was in every scene of the movie now titled *Carnival of Souls*. As a former professor at Kansas University, Herk auditioned some of the actresses in the theater department. None of them could portray a girl who was passive before a near-death accident gives her the motivation to really want to live. When faced with death she refused it and came back as a lost soul trying to escape her watery grave. Not one of the collegiate actresses could scream loud enough or believably enough to convince Herk to cast any of them in the part of the girl.

Sidney Berger, a theater major and a grad student at KU, had acted in some of Herk's shows. Herk had him audition with the local actresses for *Carnival of Souls*. Sidney was going back to New York for a visit with his parents. Herk said to him, "We've got to have a lead for this show in a hurry. Could you find me a good actress from New York?"

It just so happened that Sidney's best friend was a New York agent who represented actors. Sidney and one of Herk's assistants auditioned actresses for three days in the New York agent's office. That's how I came to audition for Sidney. I read from the script with the assistant as Sidney listened. Both men looked rather young to have the responsibility to cast an actress for a director who was far away in Kansas. It seemed a bit odd to me. By the next afternoon, the agent called me with the good news. The part was mine.

My agent Marty and I were quite happy as we sat in his office. Another film company had just offered me a leading role in *Black Autumn*, a movie to be shot in Stamford, Connecticut. He said, "It's incredible. This week you got two movie offers. Aren't you excited about that?

"Of course, I am. It's just that my new husband and I will be apart for the first time."

"He'll recover. It's your career we need to discuss now."

"What's your advice?"

"*Black Autumn* is being filmed in Stamford. It's an easy commute. You leave Manhattan in the morning; then you're back at night in your own bed. The movie has a good cast—-Shepperd Strudwick and James Farentino. You're their leading lady. The other movie, *Carnival of Souls* is being filmed in Lawrence, Kansas backed by some local businessmen. No stars! No nothing! Ever been to Lawrence?" His tone was reproachful.

"Nope."

"No one important goes to Lawrence. Originally it was a stopover for western settlers on their way to someplace else. That's Lawrence in a nutshell."

"There's something about *Carnival...*"

"You're not really considering it!" His face screwed up into a terrible frown. *Carnival of Souls* has no love scenes, no humor, no plot. The only thing that happens in this plotless B-script is the girl ends up dancing with dead people—ghouls in a pavilion somewhere."

"I'm choosing *Carnival of Souls.*"

"Jesus Christ, why?! *Black Autumn* is more commercial—a detective story with suspense and murder. That's the kind of movie that attracts an audience. People will go see you in this one. You're the beauty everyone falls in love with. Give me one damn good reason why you don't wanna do it?"

"Nudity–there are two nude scenes in it."

"What? You're turning it down because of that, in this modern day and age? Some of our greatest stars do nude scenes. The director shoots nude scenes on a closed set. It's all filmed with good taste and artistically done. No one's asking you to do porn movies here."

"Sorry, I can't. I promised I'd never take off my clothes for a job."

"What fool made you do that?"

"My Aunt Margie."

His voice lifted in surprise. "Oh, well, let me call her. Where does she live?"

"Huron, South Dakota."

"Christ almighty, that's worse than Lawrence, Kansas."

*****

My plane was halfway from New York to Kansas when the pilot announced, "Prepare for an emergency landing. We are forced to land due to engine trouble." After four hours in a small plane without air-conditioning, I braced myself as we seemed to be dropping quite fast. The startled look on the stewardess's face was not comforting as she quickly buckled herself into a seat. Was she muttering to herself or saying a prayer? Either way, it was not a good sign. I told myself that the gods were punishing me for going to the Midwest to make a low-budget horror film. Why oh why did I agree to do this? The only thing I knew about the director, Herk Harvey, was that he was part of some film company in Lawrence. Herk and I will be meeting for the first time.

However, I'm not sure any more if that will happen. Oh, dear goddess, the plane just skimmed a field of corn stalks! We're nowhere near the Kansas City Airport. We're rocking about in a small DC-3 with about thirty passengers. The plane lurches sideways. I feel the plane touch down then *bump, bump* as it slides several feet, screeching to a miraculous stop in front of a private flying club. The stewardess, with a note of relief in her voice, asks everyone to wait in the one-room clubhouse until the plane's engine is repaired.

The grumpy passengers and I march into the clubhouse. The temperature is around ninety degrees. There's no air-conditioning in the clubhouse, either, but there is one candy machine and one soda machine. They will be our source of food and drink for the next four hours.

Years later, Harvey confessed that the night my plane finally landed in Kansas City he was so disappointed when he saw me for the first time. I didn't look like what a Candace Hilligoss, the actress, should look like to him. I appeared dowdy, disheveled and hippie, too, plain-looking. It was important to him that the girl be pretty. He spent a sleepless night thinking how he would tell me to go home. It never occurred to him that after twelve hours of flying in a plane with no air-conditioning, my makeup melted away with perspiration. The sweat of my brow caused my damp hair to hang over my face. I lost my comb, lost it in a diverted plane crash. It is hard to look your best when you travel under these conditions.

The next morning he waited for me in a hotel lobby. As I stepped out of the hotel's elevator, he went into shock at what he called an amazing transformation. I showed up with makeup, and my hair curled softly about my face. According to him, my appearance changed like a butterfly emerging from a cocoon. Now I looked like exactly what he wanted. This was the first time I saw Herk smile. The night before he had met me with a very glum face. His assistant director and cinematographer were there, also, and they had stared at me expressionless. The three men had seemed rather solemn. I chalked it up to how serious and dedicated they were to making *Carnival of Souls.*

Herk explained that our black-and-white movie will be shot in sequence, and the first scene will be a drag race between two old jalopies. One is filled with boys and the other, two girls and myself. We're to drive through the countryside, then across an old wooden bridge. In the neck-and-neck race, the girls' car hits the railing. It gives way, and the car falls into the water below. The car disappears, dragged away by the river's currents. As the sheriff questions the boys, someone shouts. In the distance a single figure clambers out of the river onto a mud bank. She is dazed and remembers nothing. Someone recognizes her as Mary Henry. She's a local girl, a church organist. Herk's synopsis sound easy enough. I assumed stunt people did the required action.

Herk and his crew of five (a sound man, a cameraman, an assistant cameraman, an assistant director and a volunteer gaffer) set up for the first action scene. Then I learned that in low-budget movies there *are* no stunt people. We do the required stunts by ourselves.

The bridge was between two counties, Douglas and Jefferson. Herk talked to both of them about running a car through the railing and into the river. Douglas County said they wouldn't be interested but if Jefferson gave permission, they would go along. Herk went to Jefferson and told them he had Douglas' permission, and they said, "Then fine, it's okay with us, too"—as long as Herk paid for the damages to the bridge. Later when he received the bill it was for twelve dollars.

Herk didn't tell me that under the bridge was a gas line. If our car didn't hit the markings in the right place, the bridge might accidentally explode. The Kansas University coed who was driving the car with me had no fear. Giggling, she drove like a madman scrapping and banging into the side of the boy's jalopy. Puffing on a cigarette, she steered onto the bridge and, at the section of the marked railing, she smashed into it. It didn't occur to us that if one wheel slid off the edge of the bridge, our jalopy could have flipped over with the two coeds and me trapped inside.

As we scrambled from the cars, the director and the crew replaced us with three mannequins. The girls and I, along with the boys, waited a safe distance away as the car crashed through the railing then slowly sank into the Kaw River. Herk told me that he had an "understudy" car painted the same in case they messed up the shot.

I was put into a boat, which motored out near a sandbar. Following direction, I dived over the boat and remained submerged under the murky water until Herk called, "Action!" That was my cue to come up, swim then crawl through the mud until I could stand on the sandbar. I did retake after retake for eight hours. If I looked pale and wasted after a near-plane crash, nothing could compare to swimming in mud with one's face covered in slimy silt. Every part of my body was caked in muddiness. Herk was lucky that I wasn't scared of deep water. No one back in New York informed me about spending eight hours in the Kaw River's murky water. This ugly name was befitting like Kaw-ful as in awful.

I asked Herk why he made my character of Mary Henry a church organist? He said that the writer had suggested they film a scene in the Reuter Organ Factory in town. The factory manufactured church organs and agreed to let Herk film inside for free. He said, "Wait until you see the interior of the organ factory. The atmosphere is spooky, just right for us."

Herk's ingenious idea was: by making Mary Henry a church organist, they could use an organ sound track for music. A church organist in Lawrence volunteered to compose original music for them. It was then I learned about the small investment from the 13 businessmen in Lawrence. As Herk said to me, "Anyone can make a movie with $20 million and a crew of 200. But how many producers could do a feature film with a crew of five on a budget of $13,000?"

Herk was in a quandary as to whom to cast in the part of "The Man," who represented the ghoulish specter of Death. One day while shaving, he looked in the mirror and said, "Why not me?" It was really a matter of economics; also, the fact that there were no lines, and he didn't have to memorize anything. There was no time to spare, as he and the film crew were going to go fast and furious. He experimented with The Man's face by smearing his with egg white then pasting salt over that so he would look like a soul rising from the salty lake. Eventually he gave in to white greasepaint and black painted around the hollow of his eyes. He took wet salt and squeezed it through his hair in an unruly effect and, he hoped, a phantom image.

For the long car trip to Salt Lake City, Herk and Maurice spoke to me about taking a chaperone with us. They both wanted me to be comfortable, as I was the only female traveling with five men for more than two thousand miles in the upcoming two weeks. "Oh, I don't need a chaperone. I'm okay with just you guys." I had been around them long enough to know they were perfect gentlemen where I was concerned.

The following morning, in character, I am filmed strolling along the bridge. Mary Henry's behavior is dazed and distracted, and she remembers nothing though drawn to the river. The shock of the accident is too much. Next, Mary Henry is hired as a church organist in Utah. She drives most of the night to get there. While traveling, she passes the famous amusement park and pavilion of Saltair. As she peers out, a reflection of a man's ghostly face with frightening black-hollow eyes appears in her car window. Terrified, she swerves off the road.

Late at night, on the outskirts of Salt Lake City, Herk and the crew waited on a deserted road for me to drive past the amusement park. We're in a world of salt beds as chalky white as snow and, in a way, just as blinding. The assistant director was positioned in the back seat of my car focusing through his camera. I saw Herk waving at me, so I began to steer the car toward him.

Herk gave me a signal to turn off the road. I warned the AD to prepare as I was turning toward a ditch, which I thought was on the same level with the white highway. I didn't have any depth perception. Everywhere I looked a solid world of white loomed up ahead. I let out a scream as the car plunged some four feet on its nose. The AD howled as the camera smashed into his face. For a few seconds the car was teetering on end in the salty ditch.

Herk said he almost had a heart attack because if the car had rolled over on its hood, we would have wrecked the car. And there's no money in the budget for another car. (Remember this is a low budget film. Actors can be replaced more cheaply than a car.) The trunk of the car slowly fell back, and I was able to crawl out. No one bothered to ask if I was all right.

Not since my plane flight to Kansas was I this shaken and scared. The crew ran over to help the AD out who dropped to his knees, rolling back and forth in pain. It took the crew and Herk an hour to free the car stuck in the ditch. Once the car was in place again, I turned the ignition on, and the engine started right up. The guys applauded in relief. However, they didn't seem very happy with me, anymore. It wasn't my fault that I went blind in the whiteness of the salt beds. I tried to apologize, but everyone ignored me. Talk about feeling like a wall flower even though I'm their leading lady.

Early in the morning Harvey took me to an insurance agent. "What on earth for?" I asked. Harvey ignored my question as he purchased a life insurance policy on me and a policy for any accidents, such as loss of limbs or any hospitalization as a result of illness for the rest of the month. He wanted to make sure that if something happened to me, he could still pay back his investors their $13,000.

In the script Mary Henry has arrived at her destination in Salt Lake City. She meets her landlady, a quirky old duck who runs a boarding house. She shows Mary Henry her room, and as Mary peers out a window, the ghoulish male face shows up in the reflection. Of course it disappears when she glances again.

She reports to work at a church, where she will be playing the organ, which the pastor explains to her is the pride and joy of the congregation. When she refuses to greet any members, he huffs and puffs in righteous indignation as if his nose were out of joint. Somehow Mary manages to persuade him to accompany her to the abandoned amusement park. As she tries to open the gate to the park, he asks, "What attraction does this place hold for you?" She can't answer, but it is clear to the audience she will return.

I asked Herk "What was my motivation for going to the amusement park with a stuffed-shirt like the pastor?" He said, "Don't turn into a method actress, just do it. Don't think. You're just a dead girl fighting unseen spirits coming after your soul. Dead girls do strange things. That's your motivation."

Back at the boarding house, the landlady introduces Mary Henry to another boarder, John Linden, a lecherous slimeball played by Sidney Berger. He spies on Mary Henry by peeking through the keyhole of her door. Sidney later tells the director and the crew that at the time they filmed the sexy-look of his eyeball, it was actually his fake glass eye. Who would have guessed?!

In our travels around the mountains of Utah, we stayed in cheap motels. Our crew and cast (me) rode in one car, and a panel truck loaded with cameras and sound equipment followed behind. When five men and I registered at the motel, I wondered what the clerk thought as not one of us had a matching name or a matching address. It was like Snow White and her seven dwarves, only now I have five guys trailing me through downtown Salt Lake City. Each time Herk found a location, he would say, "Stop here. Light this." Maurice aimed one camera while the assistant director shot from another angle. Herk stopped a cab driver with an offer of 25 bucks if he could drive away in the pretense that he didn't see me as I struggled to open the cab door. The driver was more than pleased to oblige. The same thing happened with a policeman who pocketed the $25, then strolled away from me as I begged him for help. Mary Henry's soul was temporarily invisible.

In a train station Herk filmed a porter slamming a gate in my face. A couple minutes later, an executive from the office of the train's depot ran toward us. "What's going on here?" Herk took him aside and, in explaining our movie, he told the executive that he had made a Centron documentary on train travel, and it had featured the Northwestern Railway. Herk had a great speaking voice and, as a teacher, was used to handling classrooms of recalcitrant teenagers. The executive's expression altered. By the end of the conversation, he was pleased and asked Herk, "Let me know when your movie comes out. I wanna see it."

Sometimes I try to press for a further explanation of my character's motivation. Herk just raises his voice. "I don't have time to explain, just do it! We're doing 'grab' shots."

A half-hour after filming at the railway station, the six of us are riding an escalator in a department store. We wander around the ladies' dress department. Herk finds a saleswoman and asks, "Excuse me, ma'am, but for $25 would you let us film in a dressing room? Give us thirty minutes. Just make sure no one else comes inside."

The saleswoman, who had a "You must be nuts" expression on her face, smiled: "Of course, I will. I'll make sure."

My crew and I crowded into a partition as I tried on a new dress. They sat on the floor. This meant there were ten legs spread about as the men balanced a camera and sound equipment. As I stepped over them, I started going crazy as the character of Mary Henry was losing her grip on reality. In my black slip I threw open the dressing room door to call to the saleswoman who can't see me anymore as I'm in that fifth dimension space between life and death. Changing back into my clothes, I hurried out screaming at the saleswoman who continued to ignore me. The camera crew followed. Then Herk spied a female customer. He asked her to let me approach her, but no matter what I said, pretend she doesn't hear me. He slipped her $25. She played her part like a pro as I yelled and shrieked in her ear.

Now Mary Henry is really losing her marbles as she can't hear sounds or voices anymore. Our next grab shot is inside the Greyhound Bus Station. Herk asks someone who is in charge if we could shoot there for a few minutes. We are given permission. No one here seems concerned. Herk decides we need a bus for our next scene. We hurry after him to the departing area for buses. He sees one with a sign that says, "Salt Lake to Los Angeles." He speaks sotto voce to the driver who nods happily as Herk hands him the money.

As the bus driver backs up for several feet, Herk comes to me and indicates a certain spot in the alley. "When that bus reaches this point, you're to run in front of the bus. Remember he can't see you. Let him almost hit you." The camera crew and sound man position themselves, and Herk gives the driver the signal. The bus comes barreling down the alley as I run in front of it, but Herk is not happy. "You didn't get close enough to the bus! Do it again!"

Herk calls to the driver "Sorry. We need another take."

The driver complies and backs his bus up again. This time the passengers are craning their heads out the windows straining to see what is wrong. The bus starts forward, and I wait until just the right place and, with a shove by Herk, I bounce into, then off, the front of the bus. A few feet away in the alley, the driver brakes to a stop, then leans out the window to ask, "Need another take?" Herk says no and "Many thanks" for the driver's cooperation. The driver waves back merrily as he speeds along the street. I'm amazed that I didn't break any arms or slip beneath the wheels of the bus. I'm not even black-and-blue. That's the advantage of being very young: you believe you're immortal.

Poor Mary Henry's world has gone haywire. When she takes her car to a repair shop, the mechanic's face becomes the frightening face of the spectral Man. She dashes from the garage, then into a park, where she bumps into a kindly doctor. He escorts her to his office where she tells him about her unworldly experiences, which he attributes to her shock from the car accident in Kaw River. Still, she is upset. It preys upon her mind. When she practices on the church organ, her inner darkness transforms the music, which becomes wild and discordant. Naturally, the pastor fires her for playing sacrilegious music, music as if from Hell. She continues to be drawn to visit the Saltair Pavilion.

I ask Herk for the reasons why my character would roam through a deserted amusement park then end up wandering inside the pavilion? Herk answers, "Don't turn method actress on me! Your character is reverting to the limbo of the dead! She can't react or react to what is happening to her. Mary Henry is cold and unfeeling."

"How can an audience stay with my character for an entire movie if they don't care about her?"

"I don't want them to care as she's coming to a bad ending."

"But I want to know—"

"All you need to know is Mary Henry's body dies in a car crash. Her soul strives to hang onto life. Having not recognized life's potential, she cannot accept death. The drowned souls attract you to Saltair. They're gonna capture you here. Take you back to the murky salt water—a metaphor for death. That's all there is to it."

There was tension between Herk and me. My instincts cry out that he is wrong, wrong! No matter how sexless, how pathetic, how strange Mary Henry seems, I will portray her in a way that the audience will care by the end when she descends into the clutches of her tormentors, the haunted souls waiting for her in the deep, saltwater.

We're going to be filming in the Saltair Resort for two weeks. Herk says that he got permission when he spoke to the Utah Board of Tourism. They were surprised that anyone would be interested in that rundown place. They offered to send workmen to clean up the place, but Herk said, no, that the resort was fine just the way it was. Then the Board asked if he would be insulted if they charged him $50 for the two-week rental? Herk said, "If you have to, I understand."

The crew and I are in awe. Only a director like Herk could find the most fabulous location and pay a minuscule amount for rental of a world–famous resort. We explored the amusement park. I went through a spooky fun house, which still had the trick mirrors inside. We filmed most of the afternoon there. A strange feeling came over us. There was a sense of eeriness as we moved among the empty carnival rides.

After shooting inside the pavilion, we were ready to leave when the sound-man cried out, "Don't leave me alone here. Someone wait with me!" The six of us clung together as if separated we would be in danger of real ghosts. Grown men are scaring themselves. Let's hope the movie does the same for audiences.

Even though Mary Henry deteriorates into madness, she is lonely and accepts a date from the letch, John Linden. He says lines like, "You're gonna need me in the evening. You just don't know it yet." However, he is such a sleazy creep that the future audience accepts it instead of laughing at the corny dialogue. When he tries to kiss her, she pulls away and sees the reflection of The Man's face in the mirror of her bureau. She screams her head off. This dampens the ardor of John Linden who says, "You're off your rocker!" He bolts from her room in his haste to get away from this crazy girl.

Pity Mary Henry. Previously, her landlady claimed, "You let your imagination run away with you." The pastor shook his finger at her and said, "Profane!" She did what anyone of us in her place would do. She ran back to the kindly doctor to tell him how baffled she was. When he spun his chair around, it was not the doctor, but the specter of death, the figure of The Man whose macabre smile terrified her. Where did Mary escape to, but of course, the Saltair Dance Pavilion?

Herk sets up the cameras for the filming inside the pavilion. He explains that we will be here the entire day and evening. He plans to film into the wee hours of the next morning. I have worked every day since we began. A few times we have filmed twenty-four hours without stopping. "Gosh, Herk, I'm starting to look tired. The dark circles under my eyes are for real." His response was, "Perfect. The worse you look the better for the character. We're nearing the end of your soul's fight to exist."

Tonight's filming is the most important for this movie. This is the final sequence at the pavilion. The souls of the drowned will waltz to eerie music like a ritual of death. Through the Yellow Pages, Herk has contacted the Mormon School of Modern Dance. There are 20 boys and 20 girls coming. I asked Herk how he managed to pull this one out of his hat. He said he made a donation to the dance school. Actually, the dancers were more than willing to come; they were quite thrilled to be portraying ghouls in a movie. This had never happened to them before. They are providing their own costumes of black leotards and skirts; also, they are excited to paint their faces phantom-like. Copying Herk, they smeared black greasepaint around their eyes.

Herk found that the bulky lighting equipment he'd borrowed from Centron was not enough to light the ballroom sufficiently. This was a big problem. He put in a call to the Salt Lake City Electric Company. Could they help him? It seemed there was an old electrician who had installed the original power lines some 30 years earlier. What a miracle he was still alive. When the electrician arrived, he said, "I remember where the main switch is. I hope it still works." He took the lines Herk brought with him and tied them into the still-intact junction boxes. The electrician then walked down the steps of the pavilion and disappeared into a bathhouse underneath. Within seconds, the lights came on in the ballroom. The men chorused, "It works!"

That night during filming with the 40 dancers swaying, their arms embracing one another as they waltzed, the lights were switched on again in the ballroom, and, against the blackness of the night, a gorgeous cascade of lighted lanterns and glistening silver and gold streamers rose high across the ceiling. It was so grand, so very beautiful and, simultaneously, so spooky that at first we paid no attention to distant sirens blaring. Then the madness of the sound drew closer.

Out of curiosity, Herk and I went to the pavilion's balcony. Six police squad cars with red flashing lights were racing along the highway toward the Saltair. To our surprise the squad cars skidded into the amusement park. We had no idea the number of phone calls the police had received from people living in the mountains around the Salt Lake. They wanted to know what was happening to the pavilion that had been dark for these many past years, but now was lighting up the entire lake in a red blaze that spilled across the mountains? Maybe the place was on fire!

A dozen or so policemen piled out of the cars. They ran toward the pavilion. Once again Herk has to placate authorities who are not familiar with movies being filmed in their territory. Herk in his nightmarish, ghoul makeup and black frock coat, descended the staircase in a hurry as the cops drew their guns. Forty dancing ghouls appeared on the balcony. Their white faces with blackened eyes peered down in silence at the scene below. It looked as if a graveyard had come to life.

Talking to the bewildered police, Herk pointed toward the Morman dancers. The police in unison looked up. Soon there was some good-natured chuckling from Salt Lake City's law enforcement. Despite his strange made-up face and costume, he convinced the men of our artistic endeavor to bring great cinema to the masses. The police retreated like a caravan in a John Wayne movie. Herk, our hero for the hour, returned by calling to the dancers, "Places, please. Places everybody. Prepare to waltz again when I say 'action'."

The climax of the dance comes when Mary Henry—who has been staring from the sideline of the ballroom— realizes that the ghoulish face with black eyes on the partner of The Man who glides past her is she, her lost soul captive in his arms. Oh, the climax of all anticlimaxes, her mind is shattered as the last vestige of hope escapes. She dashes from the scene, but to no avail as the ghouls chase her. She flees toward the barren salt beds only to be overpowered by the ghouls whose outreached ghostly white arms snake at her like tendrils. She falls then fades away, back to that impenetrable darkness from which she fought to leave. No trace of her existence is left, except for a few of her footprints and an impression of her body in the sandy salt-beds.

In the movie's next-to-last scene, the doctor, the pastor, and a policeman search for her. How did they guess she disappeared at the old Saltair Dance Pavilion? The pastor, in his Anglican wisdom, puts together clues, as Mary Henry seemed drawn to the old resort. The three men shake their heads in confused wonderment. They study the imprint in the salty beach of what seems to be the last clue. There is no evidence of her physical body, as if she vanished into thin air. Of course, they have no knowledge of Death calling her back, that Death is represented by the water, the river, the salt lake, and finally, the spectral Man who says to her, "You have no right to life." (Somewhere in the background majestic organ music will swell as the picture fades to black.)

At the crack of dawn, Herk dismissed the Mormon dancers. "That's a wrap." There was a round of "Thank you's" from him and the crew. The dancers didn't seem fazed by the long hours. They were still energetic and cheerful as they bid us good luck and goodbye.

It took a couple more hours to load the cameras and the sound equipment in the panel truck. We were tired of filming in Saltair and anxious to return to Kansas. After we checked out of the motel, we were back speeding on the highway. We drove nonstop for two days until we reached Kansas. Herk said that I had one final scene left to do. He needed to film me in the sunken car. I almost forgot that the movie actually ended when Mary Henry's earthy body was discovered in the car as it was rescued from the Kaw River.

We arrived in the middle of the night in Lawrence. I was given permission to sleep until eleven o'clock in the morning. I thought how kind of Herk to give me a break from filming what seemed to be every second of every day. The last thing he said was, "Wear the dress you wore in the first scene when the car crashed." It hung in my hotel closet having been dry-cleaned for me.

Around noon, my driver, one of the local gaffers, came to fetch me. "Sorry, I'm late, but the set-up for your final scene was more difficult than we anticipated." In ten minutes, he drove from the Main Street onto a country road. We passed through a dense forest until we arrived at a clearing. I could see the crew waiting on a muddied beach of the river. Maurice in a down jacket, a cap with ear flaps and leather gloves, was adjusting the lens to his camera. The rest of the men wore heavy jackets and gloves, too. Herk was in a sweat shirt and bathing trunks.

A huge spindle was parked on the beach. Wrapped around the spindle, a heavy iron chain fed into the Kaw River; then I saw that the chain trailed underneath the water to a car far out in the middle of the river, partially submerged. Small waves lapped inside the car through the opened windows.

I was not prepared for any of this. As I stepped from the gaffer's car, the shock of a Nordic wind hit me. What happened to Indian summer? Why did it feel like winter? "Because," Herk said, "winter comes at the end of September in Kansas." As he spoke his breath turned into visible wisps circling in the cold air. He led me down to the shoreline. I became colder with each step. From growing up during winters in South Dakota, I guessed that we were filming in a 45-degree temperature when winter's sun seems weak and almost gray.

Herk said, "Better take your shoes off."

"Why?" I said, growing more fearful, but I took them off anyway.

"Well," he said patiently as if speaking to a small child, "I want you to go into the river and wade out to the car."

"Do what?!" This was preposterous. I glanced over my shoulder at the waiting crew who stared in silence at me while they appeared to shiver in their warm coats and fleece-lined boots. I made one brave attempt. I waded into the water as far as my ankles, but I could not move any farther. My feet turned into ice blocks. "Herk, I can't do it."

"You have to go into the water and get into the car, or we don't have an ending for this movie!"

"Can't you fake it, Herk? Maybe take a picture of me by a car window and superimpose it somehow."

"No, I can't. I have to shoot you physically in the car. It's too important. Without that shot, I don't have an ending!"

"Where are the other two girls who were with me in the car?"

"We did their shot early this morning. They didn't give us any problems."

In today's world an actress could just let a computer put her inside the car. But this was still the twentieth century, and George Lucas had yet to develop his computerized *Star Wars* films. My teeth were chattering. The goose bumps on my arms were as large as hives. "Herk, if the water's this cold—what, what about hyper-hyper-hyperthermia?"

"I promise to pull you out if that happens." He stood in the shallow water next to me. His hand on my elbow. He gave a slight nudge.

I inched forward. The water splashed upon the calves of my legs. "I can't stand it! Please, Herk, I'm sorry. I don't want to do this!" When the icy air meets glacial water, a human being can turn into an iceberg. There was no way I could survive the cold long enough to reach the car, which seemed to float even farther away.

Herk didn't say another word. He shoved me forcibly. I screamed worse than a stuck pig. Anyone from Dakota or Iowa knows that sound. Maneuvering behind me, he grabbed a hold of my shoulders. I screamed louder than at any time I was portraying Mary Henry, and I kept on screaming.

A highway patrolman heard my screams and drove his car at full speed through the country road just in time to see Herk pick me up in his arms as he waded out to deeper water. Then he threw me into the air. I fell kicking and flailing into the opaque deep.

"Hey! What's goin'on?!" The concerned cop was on foot, his hand on his holster, ready to pull out a gun. Ready to make an arrest.

"We're just filming a movie, officer." Maurice hollered back, pointing to his camera.

Herk reached for me underwater. He lifted me up into a lifeguard's choke hold, where I'm on my back unable to move as his arm encircled my neck and shoulder. Towing me, he swam toward the car. Frozen with fear and the Arctic air, I can't move anyway.

The wary cop came closer until he stood behind Maurice and the camera. The cop said, "Say, I donno' about this. Better stay right here and watch."

By this time, the assistant director was in a small boat with another camera. He rowed to the opposite side of the sunken car. I'm in a state of paralysis. I can't lift an arm or a leg—couldn't even squeak in protest. I kept my eyes closed in terror. Luckily for me Mary Henry is now dead as a door nail (to coin a new phrase).

I didn't have to worry about saying lines. Somehow I floated through the opened window of the car, and somehow Herk managed to crawl through the swirling current of the river into the back seat. He still hung onto me as he shoved me into a seated position, tilting my head just above water level. Kneeling in the boat, the Assistant Director focused his camera on me. "Herk, her lower lip is trembling. She doesn't look dead."

"Candace, don't let your mouth tremble." Herk commanded. "Don't be frightened. I'm right here. If the car breaks loose, we'll get you out safely." As if this would provide me any consolation.

I struggled to keep my lips from moving. I could feel Herk's hands underwater, pushing my shoulders down so I won't bob up. In a couple of seconds, my mouth felt frozen, and my lips went still with numbness. Could any corpse be colder? Success! Mary Henry has finally joined the Carnival of Souls. The End. Fade Out.

*****

After a year passed, Herk called me in New York to apologize. Much as he had hoped to invite me to the premiere of the movie in Lawrence, there was no more money left in the budget to purchase an airline ticket for me. Nonetheless, he promised to let me know how it went. In fact, it wasn't until years later that he finally admitted to me what actually happened at the premiere.

The premiere was held at a large Main Street theater, renovated for this occasion. Due to his reputation as a director (more than 400 industrial films) and a professor, it was a full house. To celebrate his (and writer John Clifford's) foray into feature films, everything was done like a Hollywood opening night: klieg lights, movie posters hanging outside and inside the theater, and so on. It was a thrill to think that even the chilling organ score was composed by a local organist in town. Many folks in Lawrence were cast as extras in the movie. Should Herk's movie be successful, this would be the beginning of many feature films made by him at Centron Studios. Jobs would be created. The excited audience waited in breathless anticipation. They knew that *Carnival of Souls* was supposed to be a horror movie and expected something like the old Lon Chaney and Boris Karloff movies.

Ninety minutes later, the movie ended. The audience remained silent. They were puzzled. Where was the blood? Where was the gore? There was not one scene of violence! Who in the hell and what was this strange girl doing? Was she dead or wasn't she? Mary Henry seemed stuck between the living and the dead. She was non-religious yet she embarks on a career as a church organist. She's haunted by a ghoul and drawn to his dancing lair in an abandoned ballroom and former carnival grounds. What on earth is the meaning or theme of this arty movie?

The theater curtain came down on *Carnival of Souls*. The houselights went up. Herk waited in the lobby as the disquieted audience trekked out. It was obvious that this far-out horror film with the symbolism of Death coming back to reap his reward, had left the audience confused. He knew he was in trouble when the best compliment he heard was someone saying, "Interesting. Very interesting." One by one his investors approached him. They managed weak smiles as they chimed in, "Interesting, Herk. Like a Cocteau or Bergman movie, you said. My, my, very interesting. Well, good luck anyhow."

Herk felt a chord of panic strike his heart. Could the audience's cool reaction to *Souls* be a harbinger of future audiences and, more importantly, of studio executives?

Herk made a trip to Hollywood to arrange a screening of the movie, but no producer came or even sent his secretary to see it. He screened the film in New York City to executives from United Artists. Their read on it was very neutral, as people in show biz say.

My agent, Marty, and I went to one screening. The prospect of starring in a movie for the first time is about as thrilling as it can be for a young actress, and I was in every scene, too. Marty and I sat together as we watched the movie. I couldn't be objective, but I thought my agent would jump for joy at the prospect of this much film for submission to casting agents.

The movie ended, and Marty was silent. We stood as the lights in the screening room came on. He said to me in disgust, "Jeez, are you weird!"

"What do you mean? Can't you tell that's the character? Not me?"

"You're too weird. I can't represent you anymore. I have a reputation to protect."

Without another word to anyone, he walked away and, literally, walked out of my life. I was shocked. Judging from my agent's behavior, *Souls* will ruin my movie career before it has started. Feeling as lost and unreal as the ghouls in the movie, I said my goodbyes to Herk Harvey, never dreaming that it would be many years before we would meet or be in contact again.

*****

On Broadway near Times Square, I shoulder myself through the throngs of noisy people. I can feel and hear the rumble of subways beneath my feet. The sickening smells of fast food shops with their barbecued chickens and pizzas fill the air. If I were a man like John Barrymore or Jason Robards, I would go to the Algonquin Hotel and drink myself under the bar. But I can't even afford to do that. My payment for *Souls* came to two thousand five hundred dollars. I was the only one in this venture that received any money for her or his efforts. It was the most money Richard and I ever deposited into a checking account. We considered this a small fortune, and, because of it, Richard rejoiced as he quit his night job as a waiter at The Hickory Pit.

Up in our apartment, I flop onto the bed becoming more depressed if that is possible. I stare dry-eyed with constant grief out the window. I can hear a hearse parking in the driveway of the funeral home across the street. Soon the ding, ding, and the wail of a fire truck draws near our block. The firemen make as much noise coming back to the station next door as they do leaving for an emergency. They cause this racket about five times a day. In a few minutes there is the thump of Richard's footsteps climbing the five flights of stairs. His keys jingle as he opens the front door.

He leans into the bedroom. "Well, how did it go?"

"It was a tragic fiasco. You'll never believe this. When the screening ended, Marty said I was too weird to handle. That I'd ruin his reputation if he continued to represent me. He literally bolted out the door. He didn't even stop to thank Herk Harvey for the invitation to the screening. I may never work as an actress again."

"Look, you made a low-budget movie. No one important will ever see it. Maybe in a drive-in like in Texas. Who cares? Memory is short. The South has no taste anyway. Especially Texans."

There is a look of misery etched in Richard's face. While I spent a month filming in Kansas, he opened and closed in an off-Broadway play. He had jumped at the chance to be the last minute replacement for the leading man's part opposite a well-known female star. He had no idea she was a selfish diva whose acting style had consisted of upstaging him. The critics panned the play, and the New York Times critic said that Richard Forest played his role as if he were sleep-walking. Several important theatrical agencies attended opening night, as a result not one agent would return his phone calls throughout the ongoing fall and wintertime. In fact when Richard ran into an agent on the street, he said, "Richard, do you still fall asleep when you're on stage?" The agent gave a short laugh. Richard felt as if a dagger had been thrust through his heart.

Both of us sit at dinner barely able to speak, piling a kind of misery, disappointment, yearning upon heartache as we try not to think about our hopeless futures. What a feeble parody is the life of an actor. The gods have swept away our hopes and dreams. We are ruined. Tears spill into my soup.

"Don't cry, sweetheart." Richard's hand squeezes mine. His eyes are downcast. Through a blurry veil I gaze at him, but he glances away, hoping I can't tell that his eyes are glistening, too.

Five weeks later a Broadway stage manager phoned Richard to come that afternoon for an audition to stand-by for Sir Laurence Olivier in 'Becket,' plus a small speaking part as a guard. It was just six o'clock, and I knew by the way Richard came running up the five flights that the news had to be good. He flung open the door. "Sweetheart, I got it! I got the part!" My fun-loving, charming, witty, handsome husband was back.

I swing into his arms. We dance around the living room. Our lives are restored, then Richard says, a hint of doubt in his voice, "What if Olivier gets sick? I mean, can you imagine what an audience would do if I came on stage instead of him? The greatest actor in the English-speaking theater! People would storm the box office to get their money back."

"Oh, honey, that's not going to happen. Olivier never misses a performance. Be positive. You're not just an understudy but a stand-by for the greatest actor in the world. Think how this credit will look on your résumé for the rest of your life."

"You're right." Richard is smiling again. Since we don't own a television set, he flips on a radio. An orchestra plays Cole Porter's music from the ballroom in the Hotel Pierre as we continue to dance in rapture, for all the glory that is bound to come our way.

*****

Herk Harvey went back to Kansas, without finding any interest in *Carnival of Souls*. A friend of his recommended him to Herts-Lion, a newly formed Hollywood distributor. Herk signed a seven-year contract with them but retained the television rights. Distributor Kenneth Herts wanted to pair *Souls* in a double bill with *The Devil's Messenger* starring Lon Chaney Jr., primarily for drive-in theaters.

In order to fit the movies together, he chopped ten minutes from *Souls*. Now the two movies were billed as "*A Fiendish Double Feature*."

The real fiend turned out to be the distributor who did not want to release *Souls* as an art film but to make it a B-movie via sensationalistic posters of a half-naked blonde being chased by the Devil. Herts-Lion switched the emphasis from psychological horror to sex. They tried to persuade Herk to add a couple of nude scenes. "Can't ya at least have her clothes ripped off in the car accident? Show at least a breast—or two? Maybe, she's naked in the bathtub scene?"

Herk was adamant that any nudity would destroy the feeling and intent of his film. He was then led to believe that a good piece of the gross profit would come from Herts-Lion when they released the movie as a drive-in horror film since there are 18,000 drive-ins in this country alone. Herk went off to make documentaries in South America.

After he returned from his film assignments, he finally received a first check from Herts-Lion. Although they previously had reported grosses, Herk wasn't getting' any money. After many threats that he would go to L.A. to get the money, he learned that it didn't matter. The check bounced anyway.

Herk discovered that Herts-Lion had folded and had not paid the lab bill for 75 prints of *Carnival of Souls* used in distribution. The lab had put a lien against the film. The lien, compounded by contract stipulation with Herts-Lion, resulted in the film being turned over to another lab, Du-Art Laboratories in Los Angeles, and it would remain there indefinitely.

Herts became a fugitive when he ran off to Europe where no one could locate him. Herk couldn't just walk into Du-Art Lab and take the movie, as legally it didn't belong to him anymore. Worse than losing the film was Herk's embarrassment when he had to tell his investors that Herts-Lion had taken the film, all the receipts, all the foreign and television sales, and had absconded with the money. Until Du-Art Lab's bill was paid, the original print would sit in their vaults. Eventually, the film sank into oblivion, as lost as the soul of Mary Henry. Then came more bad news for Herk with the discovery that Herts-Lion had never copyrighted *Carnival of Souls*. Pirated videos were being sold in bookstores, food markets, drug stores—the list seemed endless. There was nothing Herk could do about *Souls* anymore.

Herk and writer John Clifford considered the movie dead. A couple of years later, a teacher from Lawrence, who spent her summer vacation in Sweden, brought Herk a review of *Carnival of Souls*. It was a smash hit in Sweden where audiences compared the film to Ingmar Bergman's including the actress who resembled a Bergman star, too.

Late one night Herk received a call from a friend in Florida, who said, "It's one a.m. here. Guess what I'm watching on TV in the middle of the night? *Carnival of Souls!*"

When Herk investigated further, he learned that Herts had sold the movie to 187 television stations. Herk did not have the money it would take for legal action in a breach of contract suit or for the accounting of monies made by the movie. Then he found out that in 1970 Du-Art Lab sold the movie to National Telefilm Associates for television showings. A few more years passed and neither Herk, nor his writer, nor his crew, nor I were aware of the underground swell of interest *Souls* as it went from one college campus to another.

One day in New York City I opened the *TV Guide* and discovered that *Carnival of Souls* was that week's *Million Dollar Movie*, which meant every night at eight o'clock the movie was shown for a week. The Upper West Side movie theater, The Thalia, which featured art and foreign films, ran ads for coming attractions on Halloween for *Souls*.

Manhattan's local TV Channel 11 booked *Carnival of Souls* twice a year. The television station bragged that *Souls* was one of their two most popular movies. Fans would write to Channel 11 asking for the dates for the next showing of this cult classic film.

I had no idea of the odyssey of my movie or the travails Herk Harvey had been going through. I was a mother of two small daughters, trying to balance a life between raising them, taking care of a husband, and still working as an actress on stage.

Once I was riding a subway with a group of teenagers from Harlem. Usually teens like them are very boisterous; they never stop hitting, jumping and laughing but, all at once, they were strangely quiet. I glanced over at this motley gang, and everyone's head was turned toward me. They were staring with mouths open. I knew exactly what they were thinking: Is this the girl from *Carnival of Souls?* What's she doing on our train? Nah, it's impossible! It couldn't be Mary Henry, the spooky Utah organist, who scared the living jeebies out of them. Or could it?!

That same year I was strolling across 49th Street and Broadway when a group of Hell's Angels on motorcycles headed our way. The leader of this pack drove right up to me and stopped, "Are you Candace Hilligoss?"

I was so frightened, I shook my head no. The biker, covered in tattoos, silver chains and black leather, continued, "*Carnival of Souls* is my favorite movie. We're demanding that it be shown at the Bleecker Street Cinema in the Village. You're a great actress!" Then he and the rest of the Hell's Angels roared off. It was remarkable to know that the Hell's Angels were my fans and, instead of stoning me or calling me too weird as an actress, they were genuinely enthusiastic fans.

Around 1980 while I was living in California, a writer, David Zinman, called me from back East. He wanted an interview about *Carnival of Souls* for his book *FIFTY GRAND MOVIES OF THE 1960s AND 1970s*. He selected Polanski's *Rosemary's Baby* and Herk's *Carnival of Souls*, chronicling the two films as the best for the 1960s. He said, "I've never had a problem locating any actor or director, but I couldn't find you. I made many calls, but it took a phone call to someone sitting on a yacht off the Bahamas who knew where you were."

About this time, Herk Harvey was invited to the Munich Film Festival, which was featuring *Carnival of Souls*, a favorite of German audiences. Herk said that the night his movie was scheduled was the same night as the European soccer tournament. He didn't expect anyone would want to give up soccer for a low-budget American movie. To his great surprise, the theater was sold out. In fact, there were people sitting in the aisles and standing in the back. At the end of the movie, he went on stage to answer any questions. The audience kept him there until two a.m. The movie was a great success in Germany. Herk also was invited to Italy as *Carnival of Souls* was a hit with the Italian audiences, too.

In the mid-1980s the producer of the USA. Film Festival in Dallas invited Herk to be a guest as *Souls* was the opening movie for the festival. Herk planned to go, but first he needed to find the original negatives of the movie.

Doing his own investigation, Herk at last located the film negatives in a New York City laboratory and bought them back for $500. At the same time, The Foundation for Moët Champagne contacted Herk for a print, too. They were going to donate it to The British Film Society who wanted to include it in their 100 best movies of all time. The British Film Society planned on showing *Carnival of Souls* in perpetuity with the other movies. In the restoration of his movie, Herk put back the scenes that Herts-

Lion had cut years ago. This time he secured a copyright. The Foundation for Moët Champagne paid Herk for the expenses.

Many newspaper reporters, most of them unfamiliar with *Carnival of Souls*, attended the USA. Film Festival. Their glowing reviews sent the film into orbit. Across the country the movie opened almost everywhere as though it were discovered for the first time. It re-released to rave reviews from the *New York Times*, to *Siskel & Ebert* and *Entertainment Tonight.*

In a feature in the *New York Sunday Times* the theater critic recommended that on this hot summer day if you couldn't go to Jones Beach and listen to Guy Lombardo's orchestra, then stay at home and watch *Carnival of Souls* on TV. *The New York Post* ran this headline in their Weekend Movie Section, *The Movie That Refused to Die.* The story went on to say that *Carnival of Souls* had influenced George Romero's *Night of the Living Dead*; the dance of the dead in *Souls* was copied by Brian De Palma in *Carrie*, and how about the dancing ghouls that inspired Michael Jackson's *Thriller* Video?

A distributor and producer in Kansas told Herk that he talked to a distributor in Vienna, who said, "Oh yeah, that's a great picture. That's the one made in Lawrence, Kansas." Everyone in the University thinks of KU basketball as well-known, but worldwide, it's *Carnival of Souls.*

Due to the success of the restored *Carnival of Souls*, I went to the 1989 cast reunion and screening in Lawrence at Liberty Hall, which sold out four hundred seats for $25 apiece. Herk and I met for the first time in 26 years. "Well, well," he said, "how does it feel to be an icon?" It was important to him that I agreed to come to Lawrence as *People* had reporters covering the event.

I sat through the movie seeing it for the first time on a big screen. At the end I was directed by *People* reporters to go back stage. There were a number of press representatives waiting there. Herk reached for me and said. "Get ready."

"Ready for what, Herk?"

"For your speech."

"What speech?"

Once again Herk shoved me. The two of us entered the stage to a thunderous applause. He whispered, "We're a hit. How does it feel now?"

The acclaim came 26 years too late. All of us suffered because of the failure of *Carnival of Souls* to get proper distribution. The dreams of starting a film center in Lawrence, Kansas were lost. Maurice Prather, the wonderful, imaginative, artistic cinematographer, along with the assistant director and the rest of the crew who took shares in the project, would never recoup a dime.

In 1996 Herk Harvey passed away from cancer. His legacy is *Carnival of Souls*, a testament to how talent can compensate for the hurdles imposed on independently produced, low-budget films. His advice to future young filmmakers was: Go for psychological terrors instead of the physical one. Real terror lies within the abstract. You can do anything you set your mind up to–to make a film. Stress and strange luck will always come together on your side.

Carnival of Souls has often been imitated but never surpassed. Fans point out that *Carnival* influenced *Let's Scare Jessica to Death*, *BeetleJuice*, *Ghost Dad* with Bill Cosby and *The Gathering* with Christina Ricci.

The *New York Times*_recently, reviewed a new German film called *Yella* and said that it was inspired by *Carnival of Souls*.

Our movie was a true indie movie before most people knew the meaning of the word for independent films. It is a tribute to Herk Harvey that *Carnival of Souls* will never be just another low-budget tale, but an inspiration to new filmmakers everywhere. The fan mail I have received this month from France, Greece, Sweden, Germany and Canada is proof of the intriguing power of *Carnival of Souls* that continues on for today's audiences and future audiences, too.

Here's what some of the country's front-line critics said about *Carnival of Souls*.

> *The New York Times*
> Herk Harvey's cult horror movie succeeds in being mildly tingling without visceral explosions. It's a portrait of a lonely rationalist besieged by spirits carries an eerie chill.
>
> *The New York Post*
> Gives you the creepy crawlies… Hilligoss is crucial to the movies power.
>
> *The Village Voice*
> Genuinely creepy… The most powerful scenes are Hilligoss's attempts to articulate her alienation to a series of hostile or non-comprehending characters.
>
> *New York Daily News*
> Lost *Souls* return to haunt us. The ultimate triumph of talent, care and a sort of sinister serendipity over budgetary constraints. Few who've seen this genre gem can forget it's at-once-scary, sad and genuinely unsettling imagery. *Carnival of Souls* is nothing less than the best genre movie of 1989.
>
> *Rolling Stone*
> …Now, gloriously undead, this eerily atmospheric chiller about a church organist (Candace Hilligoss) who escapes a car wreck not quite alive-returns to claim its place as a horror classic.

The Boston Globe

Its mix of art-house ambiguity and genuine creepiness make it a must-see.

The Daily Texan

Harvey's film has become a cult favorite because it expands such existential angst into drama and so allows the audience room to laugh. *Souls* has captured a unique moment and history and stumbled upon a genuinely horrifying aspect of our world.

Washington Times

...*Carnival* needs no gore to induce terror. Refreshingly lacking in special effects and blood baths, it spooks you instead with images and quirky little moments... Harvey's only horror film is uniquely and memorably creepy.

Los Angeles Times

...*Carnival of Souls* is a genuinely creepy movie. Made on a budget of $30,000 it's a demonstration of how evocative a scar picture can be even when the production is strictly bargain-basement.

The New Yorker

...*Carnival of Souls* has the power to detach you from your surroundings and put you in the middle of its own distinctive nowhere. For eighty-eight minutes you're immersed in it; and when you come up, the world looks stranger.

Jo Bob Briggs Drive-in Movie Critic of Grapevine, Texas

...*Carnival of Souls* had its *real* premiere at the drive-in. For all the people who watched it at drive-ins of America and didn't need some Goonie Professor to tell 'em it was a great movie, let's reclaim this one for the good guys. First of all, it's a zombie movie. It's not about 'existential angst,' "a bizarre concoction of Cold War idealism and paranoia. It's a zombie movie. In fact, the star of the movie, Candace Hilligoss, is the most beautiful zombie ever to appear in a zombie movie...in the Drive-In Hall of Fame. Four stars.

In *Souls* finale, Mary watches the dance of the dead and comes face-to-face with *The Man* in the ballroom of the Saltair Dance Pavilion.

Mary Henry peers downstairs to see "The Man" stalking her.

The lecherous, neighboring boarder (played by Kansas University actor Sidney Berger) tries to seduce Mary Henry in *Carnival of Souls*.

Mary Henry seeks psychiatric help, but even in the doctor's office, she isn't safe from "The Man."

Mary Henry's cross–country ride becomes a trip into horror with repeated sightings of a special character, "The Man" played by *Souls* producer-director Herk Harvey.

After a drag race ends in tragedy, Mary Henry wades out of the river and into a new existence in a world between life and death.

A montage photo created to represent the lost Mary Henry and the haunted Saltair Pavilion.

Famous as a resort in the 1930s through the 50s, the Saltair Pavilion in Great Salt Air, Utah, was used for scenes in *Carnival of Souls*.

INTERMISSION FOR PHOTOS

My first leading role as Lina Szczepanowska in G.B. Shaw's "Misalliance" at the University of Iowa, Iowa City in 1956.

Candace as Helen of Troy opposite Michael Higgins as Hector. Actor in center is Robert Milli as Paris. Jean Giraudoux's *Tiger at the Gates* Arena Stage, Washington D.C. 1962.

Candace with Burgess Meredith in *The Remarkable Mr. Pennypacker* at the Cape Playhouse in Dennis, Massachusetts, 1958.

As Cherie in *Bus Stop* Candace got to sing "That Old Magic."

Candace with the *Bus Stop* cast at Neff Mills Playhouse in Pennsylvania.

Another scene from *Bus Stop* when Cherie falls in love with Bo. A couple years later, Candace repeated the role at The Candlelight Dinner Theater in Washington D.C.

At the Cape Playhouse in Dennis, Massachusetts Candace played Raina in G.B Shaw's *Arms and the Man*. Her costume was donated by actress Gertrude Lawrence, who had been married to the owner of the Playhouse. Lawrence wore this costume when she starred in *The King and I* on Broadway.

Sam Wanamaker and Candace in Ionesco's *Rhinoceros* at the Olney Theater in Olney, Maryland 1962.

One on the Aisle

Candlelight Opens Season

By Richard L. Coe

OUR THEATER-RESTAURANT, the Candlelight, opened a season of summer comedies last night in the air-conditioned Presidential Arms, 1320 G st. Arnold Stang, who starred last season in George Axelrod's "Will Success, etc.," became the second summer's first star with another Axelrod comedy, "The Seven Year Itch."

The bright particular news this morning is an unfamiliar, beautiful and clever light comedianne named, so help me, Candace Hilligoss. Mark the name well—THAT shouldn't be difficult—for this girl could give you the notion she's slumming while perched on a cloud.

Miss Hilligoss is playing role Marilyn Monroe did in the movie version and like Arthur Miller's lady, has a deft, trimly timed sense of humor. She has ashblonde hair, biggish features, an ideal figure but above all wit. To a now familiar comedy, many witticisms of which are withered, she infuses welcome freshness.

Miss Hilligoss was called on last Friday to take over, three days later, the role originally assigned to Micki Marlo, whose forte evidently is songs not words. Though Miss Hilligoss has played the role before, she rates another A for whisking up the part so quickly.

One on the Aisle

Olney Hits 'Rhino's' Eye

By Richard L. Coe

ONCE MORE Olney brings us top-of-the-season quality in midsummer. The play is Ionesco's provocative comedy, "Rhinoceros," its first local hearing, and Sam Wanamaker stars in a production I would match with any summer theater's best. This is a rare evening in the theater.

The play is of that rare genre which is both farcical and thoughtful. It is a blend the commercial theater fears but ultimately embraces, as in the cases of "The Skin of Our Teeth" and "The Matchmaker." America's Thornton Wilder has had a clear influence on what has been called "The Theater of the Absurd."

evolution scene. Candace Hilligoss, as beautiful a leading lady as our stages have seen in some time, returns with her highly individual style to make

of Daisy a lovely but impressionable female. The nuances of light comedy suite her expressive face and Waring has guided her unusual appeal more imaginatively than in any of her previous appearances here.

THE WASHINGTON POST

One on the Aisle

Farce Makes Pretty Package

By Richard L. Coe

ARENA STAGE'S "Volpone" is rather more what Arena should be and less than rare Ben Jonson. Still, it is sumptuously caparisoned, adroitly staged and boasts several first-class performances.

Here is glamor and class, too, in the whimpering Celia of Candace Hilligoss. Her hair and costuming are sights to behold, her performance has a freshening originality and let the producers stop screaming that they can't find an individualistic, eye-catching blonde. Also very good is

46—THE WASHINGTON DAILY NEWS, WEDNESDAY,

A Welcome Tiger

By TOM DONNELLY

ARENA STAGE is back in form with a mettlesome production of Jean Giraudoux's "Tiger at the Gates," in the Christopher Fry translation.

The fabulous Helen has been designed by the playwright and his adaptor as a kind of prehistoric Lorelei Lee, and Candace Hilligoss is delight-

Newspaper Review C
Critic Richard Coe.

Theater reviews submitted as evidence to the judges that Candace had a career as an actress.

John Ericson and Candace in a scene from *A Streetcar Named Desire*. Vivian Blaine starred as Blanche.

In another scene from "*A Streetcar Named Desire*" with Vivian Blaine as Blanche and Candace as Stella.

Vivian Blaine Rides Kenley's "Streetcar"

By Fred Childress

"A Streetcar Named Desire" is, of course, a great play, and the Kenley Players have treated it with great respect. Vivian Blaine and John Ericson star in the Tennessee Williams drama, which opened last night at the Packard Music Hall in Warren. If Miss Blaine is a bit difficult to picture as Blanche DuBois, I can assure you her interpretation of decaying southern aristocracy is sincere and moving.

In getting the point across, Ericson gets notable assistance from Candace Hilligoss as the wife, Stella, who is also Blanche's sister. Miss Hilligoss, an actress who is new to me, plays Stella with great charm and conviction, giving the role dimensions that are equally new. I never cared much for Stella, but Miss Hilligoss makes her understandable, and even appealing.

John Ericson Star Vivian Blaine, In Fine Production O. 'Streetcar'

By JACK DARROW
Tribune Amusements Editor

Tennessee Williams' "Streetcar Named Desire," 1948 Pulitzer Prize winner and the Kenley Players' 12th production of the 1961 season, is an absorbing drama that is extremely well done by a strong cast.

Acting Has Warmth

Candace Hilligoss as Stella, is an understanding wife and sympathetic sister. Miss Hilligoss's acting has a warmth, sincerity and a needed balance to offset the emotional outbursts of Blanche and the flaring temper of Stanley after he gets drunk.

CLOSE-UP OF A STARLET: Candace Hilligoss is the ingenue discovered for the movies in "Once in a Lifetime," the Kaufman and Hart lampoon on the early talkies, which continues at Arena Stage through Nov. 18.

Reviews for *A Streetcar Named Desire* and a photo of Candace from Arena Stage's production of *Once in a Lifetime*. Submitted by Candace's lawyer in the divorce proceedings as Petitioner's lawyer testified she had a fantasy of being an actress and needed psychological testing to find out what her true vocation should be.

Candace dancing with Robert Webber in "*Idiot's Delight*" at the Hinsdale Theater in Hinsdale, Illinois 1958.

Candace and husband with Kurt Vonnegut discussing his play, *Happy Birthday Wanda June*. First produced off-Broadway at Theatre de Lys in 1975.

Candace's mother in her 20s touring Piazza San Marco in Venice.

Candace's eighteen year-old father, Leonard Hilligoss, in his World War I uniform.

Chapter Nineteen

From Reel Life to Real Life – 1980s

How surreal it seems that last week in New York, my cult classic film and I were being celebrated at Fangoria's Film Convention. I signed autographs for three days. It was like a cherished dream but, right now, I have to grapple with the real nightmare. Ron Litz and I are in court again. Six months have passed since we were in Judge Herbert Klein's courtroom. My support has now been reduced to one dollar a year forever unless my tiger-attorney can reverse Klein's decision. This time Ron is also asking for my community interest in Richard's residuals and pension plans. Richard called me to threaten if I did this, he would force me back to court and run up my barracuda lawyer's bills so high I'd be forced to live in the streets.

David Stitz, filed his motion: SECOND SUPPLEMENTAL FILING TO PETITIONER'S ORDER TO SHOW CAUSE TO TERMINATE OR MODIFY RESPONDENT'S SPOUSAL SUPPORT AND SECOND SUPPLEMENTAL FILING IN RESPONSE TO RESPONDENT'S ORDER TO SHOW CAUSE FOR MODIFICATION.

What this means is that Richard's contract with the *Santa Barbara* TV show has been terminated. He is now unemployed and respectfully requests that my spousal support be reduced to zero as his income also is approximately zero, too. He has been forced to sell his two cars to keep a roof over his head and to pay for the rent on two apartments for our two daughters. He claims child care expenses of $36,000 a year even though one daughter has graduated from college. (He doesn't mention that their ages are 21 and 24.) He lives in a small house and now faces a tax liability of $50,000.

My attorney files his motion: BRIEF RESPONSE TO PETITIONER'S SUPPLEMENTAL FILINGS, TO PETITIONER'S ORDER TO SHOW CAUSE TO TERMINATE OR MODIFY RESPONDENT'S SPOUSAL SUPPORT AS IT PERTAINS TO RESPONDENT'S ORDER TO SHOW CAUSE FOR MODIFICATION.

Now this means that Richard is lying and wherever his attorney cites documentary evidence or court rulings, they are taken out of context and are incomplete. At our hearings Richard claims that he has lost his job and is now an out-of-work actor, or that due to his cardiovascular episodes he must pursue a much less stressful and low-paying career as a boat captain. As soon as our last OSC was concluded, he filed his

OSC for modification on the grounds that his television role in "*Santa Barbara*" was about to end. However, he had to keep continuing the hearing dates because of employment obligations.

Ron made a list of ninety-one TV shows from which Richard is currently receiving residuals. In our pleadings, Ron stressed to the court that Richard's income is 250 percent more than he was making when the case was first filed before Judge Shafer, who stated that my support was not to be terminated unless I remarried or either Richard or I died.

"Why is it that each time we're in court, he always says he owes fifty thousand in taxes? Is this the same old tax bill or a new one? You can't owe taxes unless you make money!" Ron was quite frustrated. "Look at the pity card he's playing. In his Declaration he states that though he is a Coast Guard Ocean Operator with a rating of 'Captain,' and also with hundreds of hours to study–the boat is not a luxury but a source through which he can obtain satisfaction by helping others. Due to finances he has put the boat up for sale."

We are supposed to be impressed with the sacrifice of his vessel, a custom 52'9" Huckins Oceanic. According to marine surveyors the replacement value is estimated at $275,000.

*****

During our marriage Richard owned a total of around six or eight boats. I couldn't keep track of them. They were wood tubs that required hours of scraping, caulking and painting. At that time I learned that if a boat was made of Fiberglass, it was ready to sail without any of the back-breaking hours he spent on a wood one. He claimed he couldn't afford the luxury of an expensive Fiberglass boat. He kept his boats in the City Island Boat Yard near the Bronx. The owner of the boat yard told me that every time someone defaulted on his storage bill for a boat, he and his crew would cut it up in pieces and sink them in the ocean. Then Richard came along. So now the saying in the boat yard is, "Let's see if we can get Forest to buy this wreck before we sink it."

To be married to a boat owner is worse than being a golf widow. Richard spent most of his weekends away from his family working on his boat. As soon as the snow melted in the spring he began his summer love affair with his boat. By the following Labor Day his boat was usually the last one to leave dry dock. Once his boat was moored in a slip, Richard would spend a couple of nights sleeping on it to make sure there were no leaks as this was always a potential hazard of a wood boat.

The most memorable boat he owned was a 34-foot cruiser, "The Aloha." He bought it from a widow who only sailed it on weekends. One day in the middle of July, he and our neighbor Larry decided to take the boat out to go fishing for Blue Fish. The best time to catch Blue Fish is around six a.m. The plan was for them to go to City Island in the evening, and sleep on the boat so they would be ready to catch the fish that start jumping about the ocean in the early morning hours.

I have never known Richard to be interested in fishing, but any excuse to use the boat he was ready, willing and able. Since Larry owned the fishing tackle, Richard was happy to try his hand at fishing. They left in the early evening. The plans were to sail through the in-land waterways, the East River and around City Island.

What I didn't know was that by eleven p.m. the two fishermen got bored sailing back and forth waiting for morning when the jumping Blue Fish appear. In their brief journey, they discovered a tavern called "The Pink Pussy Cat Bar" built out on a barge under a bridge at the foot of Fordham Road in the Bronx. They were able to tie the boat up to it. Due to the crooked barge, the Pink Pussy Cat Bar tilted so when Richard and Larry entered, they walked at a sideway slant. "Like being two sheets to the wind," Larry said later. This hideaway place was jumping with jukebox music and married Puerto Rican men who were partying with their girlfriends. After chatting with Richard, they asked if they could go for a midnight joy ride before he and Larry set off on the fishing trip. Of course, Richard agreed as he loved every chance to show off "The Aloha."

Four Puerto Rican couples clambered on board with drinks still in hands. There was great merriment upon the high seas. After a short while Richard asked if anyone knew how to steer a boat as he needed to go down into the galley to check on the engine. Paco spoke first: "I can do it. I'll steer." He and his girlfriend took over the wheel.

A few minutes later Richard was leaning over the engine when he heard a loud crack. The boat lurched, and he was thrown against the pilot house. He leaped up the stairs into the cabin. In the darkness, Paco had struck a submerged telephone pole, which opened a gaping hole in the hull. The point of entry was through the head where a couple was making passionate love. Richard said, "Hey, why were you in the head? You could have used one of my berths!" The guy answered, "Oh, man, I didn't wanna mess up your sheets. My hands were too dirty."

Richard quickly assessed the damage. At the rate the water was entering, the boat would sink in a matter of minutes. He asked the Puerto Ricans if they could swim. To his dismay, all eight confirmed they didn't know how to swim. How could they have grown up on an island in the Caribbean and never learned to swim?! He made everyone put on a life jacket. Another boat was passing "The Aloha." Relying on his Coast Guard training, Richard took a lighted lantern and flashed the emergency signal SOS. He flashed the distress signal several times, but the boat mysteriously increased its power and sped away. Richard shouted for help! The Puerto Ricans broke out into a chorus of, "Help! Help us! Help!" Obviously, the captain of that boat did not have any Coast Guard training.

Larry and Richard agreed that they were in dangerous currents. In fact, they were in the very spot known as Hell's Gate where the East River twists mercilessly into the ocean. If they all jumped overboard, everyone would be swept away into the black sea. The lights on the boat went out, pitching Richard and his passengers into a dark abyss. Some of the Puerto Ricans were shaking in fear. One heavy-set man developed lockjaw from the sheer terror of sinking. His mouth froze open in a big, capitalized O.

Richard spotted some fifty yards away an abandoned barge that was sticking partially out of the water. He tied a ship's line to his waist and swam for the barge. A lifeline was then stretched from the sinking craft to the barge. He swam back to the boat. There he cautiously lowered each passenger down the boarding ladder where Larry, treading in the water at the bottom, caught one Puerto Rican after another. Larry showed the Puerto Rican couples how to grasp the lifeline, pulling themselves through the currents toward the barge.

Senor Lockjaw became so terrified that he could not descend the ladder into Larry's waiting arms. Instead he dropped on top of Larry's head, sinking both of them. Larry, who had been a sailor in World War II, was able to break the strangling grip of the man under the water. Then Larry put one arm around him and swam to the barge. The rescued Puerto Rican couples helped pull Senor Lockjaw onto the barge. Even though they reassured him he was safe, he still could not close his mouth. He fell over on his back, unable to move. Like a beached whale, his eyes bugged out and his mouth remained stuck in a permanent O shape.

Somehow they were all safe atop of the barge just in time to see The Aloha sink to its bubbly grave. They crowded together in hopes that another boat might come their way. At one point Richard heard youthful voices in the darkness on a distant bridge by the Queens shore. They seemed to be two teenagers on bicycles. Richard called out, "Hey there! We need help! Call the Coast Guard! Or police! Our boat sank!"

The teenagers laughed. One yelled, "Jeez, it's too far to find a phone." Then they pedaled away. Richard, Larry and the Puerto Rican couples were stranded for more than three hours when Paco reached into his pocket and found that he had the presence of mind to wrap a match booklet in plastic. It was still dry. "Look what I got! Matches."

"Wait a minute, let's see if we can start a fire." Richard and the rest picked out dry kindling from the top of the barge and set a match to it. A blaze caught. Everyone scrambled for more dry wood. A crackle of flames were shooting up higher and higher. A few apartment lights turned on from the shore. In minutes a Coast Guard rescue ship appeared flashing spotlights in the direction of the barge.

Around four a.m., my phone rang at home. I answered it, and a strange voice said, "Your husband and a party of ten just sank in the East River."

"What do you mean 'party of ten'? My husband is on a fishing trip."

"Is your husband's boat The Aloha?"

"Yes, but I don't understand?"

"There are no survivors."

"How dare you scare me like this. I'm going to call the police."

"Ma'am, I am the police. Here's our phone number."

He proceeded to give me the number. I sat in shock. I couldn't believe it. No survivors! It was then that I heard our front door open, letting in a rush of bonfire smell followed by a wayward Richard in torn clothing. He was quite hoarse as he said, "What I'm about to tell you, don't worry as everything that happened tonight turned out okay."

My mouth fell into the same shape as Senor Lockjaw. After Richard's mariner's tale of the night's tragic sinking of his boat, he said between coughing spasms, "I just hope the survivors don't find out I'm on TV in a soap opera and sue me. They're apt to think I'm as rich as Johnny Carson or Lucille Ball or a mega star like that."

How will the Puerto Rican survivors find out Richard's true identity? It was quite easy. The next day the entire New York population knew about Richard's seamanship as the headline of the New York *Daily News* read: TV STAR, 10 SAFE AS BOAT SINKS. On page three was another headline: SOAP OPERA STAR'S BOAT SINKS AND CHANNELS TEN. The feature story went on that Richard, who has moistened many a viewer's eye with his portrayals, yesterday swamped his friends when a cabin cruiser he was piloting hit a submerged obstacle and sank in the East River. There was the whole story with the names of the Puerto Ricans alongside the names of their illicit girlfriends. The feature ended with the questions: Will Richard be able to salvage the expensive boat he has owned for only a couple of months? Will he ever make that fishing trip? Tune in tomorrow, folks, for the next exciting episode.

Richard was mortified. The *Daily News* even used an old photo of him. A reporter called and asked if he could take a picture of "The Aloha" when it was salvaged. Because of the lifeline Richard tied to the barge, the Coast Guard found the boat easily enough. In a couple of days, The Aloha was back in dry dock. Richard took the reporter for the photo shoot. The reporter expected to see the remains of a yacht. He couldn't believe what he saw belonged to a TV star. "Are you telling me this old wreck is yours?"

Richard was taken aback at the reporter's reaction. "This boat is a classic of its kind. I completely restored it myself."

"Hell, this is a piece of shit! No self-respecting sea captain would sail it. I'm not gonna take any pictures."

Richard was mortified for the second time. He complained bitterly to me that the reporter didn't understand why anyone bothered to restore an old boat. It's the same reason some people love antiques and care for them; the same way a sea captain loves and tends to his wooden boat. The reporter had the gall to ask why a Wasp-looking actor like Richard had so many Puerto Rican friends.

Richard's past adventures on the high seas have no bearing now as we wait in Department Two. It's another room in hell where truth is neglected; where the wheels of justice grind slowly over an ex-wife simply because her former husband does not need her services any more. He's the one who violated the covenant of marriage, not me.

Ron interrupts my thoughts: "What will you say in court when Stitz asks why you never took any aptitude tests?"

"Because of my limited alimony, I can't afford the expense. You know as well as I do that this psychobabble about testing is meaningless." I wanted to tell him that Jacqueline Onassis took an aptitude test at Miss Porter's School and learned her most suitable career path was that of a waitress. If she were divorcing Richard today, she would end up waiting tables at the Charthouse in North Hollywood with Stitz as her customer.

Ron raised another question: "Stitz wants the court to note that the selection of paralegal school was done without benefit of vocational testing–as urged by Commissioner Jill Robbins. What's your answer?"

"What if a test shows that my career is meant to be in a theater? Or that I should be an astronaut? Why doesn't the court take note that I'm not eighteen anymore? I've given my youth to a jerk!"

"The judge is going to ask why you're in a two-year program for paralegals when you could go to Los Angeles City College and be done in one semester."

"A judge and maybe a lawyer should understand that LACC's paralegal program is not approved by the ABA. I've given you the evidence from human resources at law firms who say that they won't hire anyone from a school that is not approved by the bar."

"Your case can be heard right away if you elect to return to Judge Klein."

"Why would I want to see him? He's the one who reduced my support to one dollar. He's the one who made fun of my temp jobs. You and I know that a woman my age is not going to get permanent employment when agencies tell me that they can hire women half my age and pay half as much for healthcare."

Ron asked for a new judge. The judge in charge checked the court calendar on his desk, then spoke to Ron, who repeated to me, "Now we've been assigned to Judge Montez."

"No, no, I can't have my case heard by him. He's the same judge that told Susan Goldstein that I'd have to be a hell of an actress to be granted twelve hundred dollars a month in support."

"You don't have a choice any more. You're only allowed one veto. That's the rule."

I reiterated my argument, but he raced ahead of me, throwing over his shoulder a caustic remark, "You've already alienated three judges."

It was right after lunchtime when we went before Judge Montez, whose attitude was still a dismissive coldness. I leaned into Ron to ask a question before we began. Ron suddenly turned and said with vituperation, "Get away from me!" His voice was filled with anger as though he had always hated me.

I leaned back in tears of shock, aghast at the waves of panic flooding me. If he had struck me I couldn't have been more hurt. What happened to my tiger?!

"Go sit in the back of the court!"

I moved a few feet farther so I could still hear the judge as he spoke to Ron. "I don't have enough time this afternoon to try your case. You'll have to continue it."

"Your Honor, this woman's support has been reduced to one dollar. I can't keep coming back to court with her. She doesn't have any money."

"Well, then, get rid of her," Judge Montez shrugged. It was a simple as that. How many women, as a consequence of Judge Montez's callous decisions, have been left penniless, left to live in homeless shelters? I almost tripped after Ron as we exited into the hallway. I said as calmly as possible. "I never said a word to this judge. Are you going to claim that I alienated him too?"

My tiger refused to answer. In silence we went to the parking lot. He found his car first, a brand-new white Jaguar. He opened the front door then sat, speaking with restraint: "I can't represent you anymore. You're a business loss to my firm."

"I'm sorry about that." I felt quite sad as if a love affair just ended. We have been together for three years. I have poured out my heart and soul to him. He knows more about me and my marriage than a close girlfriend does.

He tried another tack, forcing phony enthusiasm into his voice: "Listen, you can represent yourself. When you appear Pro Per before the next judge, he, in a way, will become your attorney, your advocate. He'll be obligated to help as you're without representation."

"If you say so." I do know that a judge can also be annoyed to be put in a position to act as my attorney. How can I recover from the blow Ron dealt me? I said with some effort, "What's the date of my continuance?"

"Thirty days from today. Come to my office tomorrow. I need you to sign me out as your attorney. I'll advise you what to do."

If I refused to sign the substitution form, he would be forced to file a motion for a hearing to get rid of me. Then I'd explain to a judge that I have paid Ron about $14,000 in the past. It's not as if he has never received money from me. That's why I'd tell the judge I want Ron and only him to represent me. He could be ordered to represent me. I doubt he realizes that I know that much about the law.

As he slammed the car door ending the conversation, I walked away, never looking back. I found my parked Chevette and waited a couple of minutes in the underground garage so I wouldn't end up driving behind him. I drove home in a stupor. Later, I took Whiskey for a stroll around the block. We sat on the back steps of our apartment house and watched the sunset. I dreaded the moment it will be night, and we will both be alone again.

Later I phoned a friend and explained what happened. He was as upset as I was over my legal battles and offered to wire Ron the money to stay with my case. I said it was really no use. It would be like throwing good money away as my attorney was too hostile toward me as a client. In my eleventh hour, when I needed him most, he chose to abandon me.

*****

In the morning I sit in the reception area of Ron's firm. I'm the only one thumbing through the magazines. His unsmiling secretary opens the door to the inner offices. She nods that I'm to come with her. The day I first became a client, she offered me coffee, tea or soda. Today I'm not worthy of a glass of water.

In her cubicle she shows me the substitution form waiting on her desk. I'm to sign at the line with the big X marking it. She seems nervous, a bit anxious, as if I might change my mind and refuse to sign. Once I put my pen to the paper and, with shaking fingers, write my name, she whisks the form away, then runs victorious into Ron's office.

How do I say goodbye to a lawyer who has treated me at the end so barbarously? Sitting behind his desk, Ron glances up at me. "Sorry, that things didn't turn out better for you."

"I feel as if my life is in ruins."

Ron considers then says as if in defense, "Many of the guys I know won't represent women anymore. They can't pay the legal fees, and the courts don't award enough to any lawyer to make it worth his time. Women are a business loss for most firms. With an ex-husband who's working, a lawyer knows he'll get paid in the end. But with an ex-wife, a lawyer has to think twice if he wants to represent her."

"Well, it's a shame that California can't be like New York where the working husband has to pay for the wife's defense. Governor Cuomo states that no woman should be forced to represent herself when her husband can afford an attorney. Which reminds me, do you have some pleading papers I can use as Pro Per?"

He hesitates before he throws the last arrow. "Oh, ahm—ahm you can get pleading papers at the court in Santa Monica."

What an asinine statement! How patronizing of him when his secretary has cartons of pleading papers in her cubicle.

Then Ron says, "One of our handymen is bringing a special cart to pick up your files."

"There's that much?"

"Yes, I believe about twenty boxes."

As if on cue, his secretary pokes her head in the doorway. "He's here—waiting in reception."

"Goodbye, Ron." I don't smile.

He doesn't smile either but remains seated. "Goodbye. Drop in sometime and let us know how you're doing."

That's one of those empty statements that means as much as air kisses, or "Let's have lunch soon."

In the garage the handyman stacks boxes in the back seat of the Chevette until they reach the roof of the car. He fills up the car trunk then takes a couple more boxes and puts them on the passenger seat and on the floor of the car. This represented the beginning and ending of my divorce, years of agony. It makes me look like a professional divorcée.

Early in the evening, Gertrude and I take our dogs for a stroll along the street past the Beverly Hills Tennis Club. Gertrude is almost as upset as I am. "Jesus," she said alarmed, "do you have any money left?"

"I have twenty dollars to my name."

"Oh, my god, what will you do?" Gertrude's huge brown eyes fill with tears.

"I can't even think what's going to happen to me."

"Somehow, somewhere, you must write about this actor–husband. Forget about a book on that Dakota stuff, the Depression, the dust bowl–this is the story, your story, your humor that will make the difference in your life!"

"I guess I could call it the Odyssey and the Idiocy—Marriage to an Actor."

"Perfect! That's it!"

*****

After we parted, I carried Whiskey over one shoulder as his weak heart had worn him out. When we reached our apartment house, I let him lie on the front stoop to rest for a few minutes. I said a quiet prayer, "Dear goddess, if I'm to continue writing, give me a sign."

Whiskey waited as I went to my mailbox, then opened it. There was a letter from a law firm in Mitchell, South Dakota. Not another lawyer! What have I done now? I tore the letter open and read it as quickly as possible. It took some time to digest the contents as I felt a rush of dizziness. Even though I have been estranged from my father for thirty years, his lawyer wanted to inform me of my father's passing and that I was his sole heir. He had left me one hundred thousand dollars. What heavenly irony. Dear goddess, you were listening after all.

"The poet, to the end of time
Breathes in his works and lives in rhyme:
But, when the actor sinks to rest,
And the turf lies upon his breast,
A poor traditionary fame
Is all that's left to grace his name!"

– William Combe

Chapter Twenty

Even though my inheritance came, there was no reason to quit paralegal school as I was about halfway through the program. Upon graduation I would have two specializations, one in litigation and the other in corporations. I chose corporations thinking it must be about white collar crime, which might interest me.

Tonight our instructor, a corporate lawyer, is lecturing on registration procedures as stated by the 1933 Act that prohibits the sale of any security subject to the Act unless a registration has been filed with the SEC. The instructor drones on and on by listing forms for different types of issuers. She warns us to pay attention carefully as we will have to remember all the contents of the forms for the upcoming semester test. She lectures in depth about Form S-1—Form S-2 and S-3—forms 11, S-18 beside S-8—then she says, "Oh, I almost forgot Form-4." In my school bag I have one hundred eighty index cards of different corporate rules committed to memory. Like Chinese water torture, I review them about ten times daily.

Behind me I hear soft snoring from a legal secretary whose face is lying in the middle of her textbook. The instructor won't admonish her. This is night school, and most of the students have dreary or weary day jobs. The worst and most tiring position is as a legal secretary who has spent eight hours a day typing at ninety words a minute to finish a complaint in time for submission to the courts.

We have a brief class break then we run to a community room where we munch on popcorn from a microwave oven or drink diluted coffee or sodas from a vending machine. A classmate, Gina, says under her breath to me, "I just heard. Take my advice, do not appear Pro Per in court. If you think it was bad with an attorney, the next judge will crucify you as a woman daring to represent herself."

"What am I going to do, Gina? Where do I find a new lawyer I can trust?"

"Come meet my boss, Michael Kelly. I've worked for him for the past ten years. He is well-known as a divorce and family attorney. Kelly's a top gun. For the past twenty years he's handled many celebrities in show biz. He is currently the Chairman of the California State Bar Custody Committee. He even is admitted to practice before the courts of the District of Columbia and Florida as well as California."

"My, my, that's impressive. Since you recommend him, how can I contact him?"

"I'll speak to Mr. Kelly first. He's very particular about whom he represents. Your handicap is that a few lawyers have already represented you. He doesn't like to take cases that are messed up with other attorneys' hands."

My panic button went into overdrive. I'm damned or cursed. It hadn't occurred to me that new lawyers might not want to champion my case again.

Gina said with implacable conviction, "I'll urge him at least to see you. I'll tell Mr. Kelly how your previous attorney abandoned your case. That you were put under a court order never to act or to write again—that the last judge reduced you to zero support because you were caught writing a novel on weekends. I'll win him over."

She was true to her word. Before the week ended I was waiting to meet Michael Kelly in his firm's reception room, the downstairs of a duplex building in Santa Monica. The carpeting was wall-to-wall on both floors and the color was, of course, kelly green. From the display of posters, decorative plates of four-leaf clovers and leprechauns and coffee-table books from Ireland, I knew that Kelly was proud of his Irish ancestry.

Do I dare mention that I'm eighty-five percent Irish since in my background I have the O'Briens and Dinneens hanging on my family tree? "Top of the mornin' to ya! Begorra, me lad, as one Irishman to another, keep the bill on the wee side of low, if ya might."

A young secretary in a mini skirt strolls by as she asks just like an airline stewardess, "How about a soda, tea or coffee? Glass of water?"

"No, thanks." I know the drill as this is my number six lawyer's initial consultation. The first visit, one receives complimentary drinks. As the legal bill escalates, the offers of drink shrink to where if necessary, you have to plead for a small glass of water, which is not given any more.

Gina leans over the banister from the second floor: "Hi, Candace, come up here." I hurry up the stairs. She leads me to a doorway of an office, "Mr. Kelly, meet my friend, Candace." She steps away.

At his desk Michael Kelly, wearing a headset as he speaks on the telephone, sits in a leather swivel chair that he tilts back and forth or sideways. As he talks into a tiny microphone in the headset, he reminds me of a singing rock star or a TWA airline pilot running the engine controls.

There are two other, younger attorneys in the office. They also seemed to be waiting there like a meet and greet committee. One of them seated on a couch says, "Hi, I'm Arnie." He wears a short sleeve T-shirt, showing off a tattoo of a Vietnam Navy Seal on his arm whenever he flexes his biceps. The other attorney, in an overstuffed, green armchair, says with a salute, "Robert here."

My dry mouth feels like a wad of cotton is stuck inside, and my hands are sticky with perspiration. Arnie pats a cushion on the couch. "Why don't you sit down?" I obey. We wait in silence until Michael Kelly ends his phone conversation. He never removes his headset as he rotates his chair so he can take a better look at me. Right away he exclaims, "I hate messy cases like yours. They stink. Too many hands. Too many lawyers mess it up for me. Why didn't you come to see me first?"

"I didn't know about you, Mr. Kelly. Originally, my husband brought me out to California. Three days after my arrival, I was served divorce papers. I didn't know a soul who could recommend lawyers. I literally used the yellow pages to find someone to represent me."

The three lawyers seemed to roll their eyes in sympathy. I continued, "As you can see, Mr. Kelly, from one attorney to the next my case seemed to go downhill."

"Call me Michael," he said with a wave of his hand. "Earlier today, Gina gave us your files of complaints and your OSCs from some of the lawyers you retained. How in your many travels did you miss out hiring Marvin Mitchelson?" Arnie and Robert chorused, "Yeah, how come? You could have gotten the 'red bathrobe' treatment." At their own imagery, the men burst into locker room laughter. Arnie decided to answer, "At the same time she'd get to hear Mitchelson sing an aria from Wagner's *Tristan and Isolde!'* Their three heads fell back as they roared louder with laughter.

Anyone who lived in California during this time who did not know about the most famous, controversial, flamboyant, successful lawyer of international and national repute, Marvin Mitchelson, must be lost on Mars. His clients were a virtual who's who of celebrities, including Joan Collins, Bianca Jagger, Rhonda Fleming, Zsa Zsa Gabor, Mickey Rooney, Robert DeNiro and many ex-wives of errant playboy sheiks.

In Mitchelson's Century City office, he had a chair once owned by Rudolph Valentino and an illuminated ceiling of Botticelli's Venus, which matched his belt buckle. This year four female clients who did not know one another and were not famous stars, but could afford his retainer of $5000, testified to the Grand Jury that from an adjoining bathroom in his office, Mitchelson would jump out in a red bathrobe. He raised his hands like an opera conductor as he directed an imaginary orchestra while humming a melody from *Tristan and Isolde*. Then he would attack the women. He proceeded to rape them beneath the gaze of Venus in the illuminated ceiling. He warned his victims to forget any rape charges as they were never going to be believed. He bragged he knew every secret about every important lawyer or judge in Los Angeles and Hollywood. He was right.

Even though the Grand Jury voted there was enough evidence from these women to indict him, the Los Angeles District Attorney declined to mount a prosecution. There were a number of other rape victims whom Mitchelson paid off. Eventually, his fall from grace came not from his abuse and assault of women but from his conviction for not paying taxes on some two million dollars in income. He was like Al Capone who got away with murder but finally went to prison for income tax evasion. While Mitchelson was serving his prison term, he started an opera club.

I explained further to Michael and the other attorneys, "I didn't bother to meet Mitchelson because my husband was not that big a star. There was no real, tangible community property to divide either. I'm sure once Mitchelson knew that, he wouldn't have wanted me as a client."

The men stopped laughing as they seemed to take under consideration what I just said. Michael slapped his hand across one of my legal files on his desk. "Do you know what's the real problem with your case?" Before I could blink, he answered his own question. "The women's movement has shafted women like you in court. You can thank Betty Friedan and Gloria Steinem and the rest of those women libbers for that. The only people they liberated are men! Any man who has the money for legal fees—like your ex-husband—can whip his former wife into the streets if he wants. He'll continue to file for termination of support until he finds a sympathetic judge who agrees with him. Used to be, I'd try to find a female judge for my women–clients. Not anymore. Too many female judges are so anxious to be part of the boys' club that they sometimes give out the cruelest judgment of all to women. Take what Commissioner Jill Robbins did to you. Technically she put an end to your support. The other numbskulls just followed her lead."

I felt as if I were defending myself in a criminal's dock. I tried to sound as erudite as possible. "Didn't Betty Friedan in her last book reverse the feminist thinking? She wrote that when the divorce reform was passed, what feminists wanted was equality of right and opportunity, therefore, alimony was not necessary. But that they did not realize the trap they were falling into—a trap when they said no alimony because divorced housewives were in terrible straits. She also said they fell into another trap by accepting no-fault divorce without provision for mandatory economic settlements. They came to the realization that most of these women not only needed alimony, they had earned it."

Michael protested, "Friedan's argument came too late to help your case. There's no evidence the California courts are aware of the economic turmoil that has been created for women like you. Women, who spent twenty years of their life nurturing a family, who gave up a career and now have no pension, no health insurance. The cruel joke is that women of your generation assumed they had a contract in marriage, both implied and expressed: their husbands would share their income with them. After a woman has fulfilled her share of the bargain, it's not fair to change the rules in the last quarter of the game. But the courts don't consider that. Judges don't care that you're in an age group that is the first to be fired and the last to be hired in the work place. I warn young women today that the clear implication is that they had better not forgo any of their own education, training and career development to devote themselves to families. The law assures that they will not be rewarded for their devotion. The courts still give orders stating that it is healthier to go out, get a job rather than live off the lap of alimony. Your ex's attorney, David Stitz, loves that phrasing. He uses it quite often in Richard's Declarations."

"What about the change in the standard of living from when I was married?" My voice was growing husky. If Richard were here, I would take a gun and shoot him then claim insanity as he drove me into madness. I could say I overdosed on Twinkies. I learned about the Twinkie defense in paralegal school. Dan White on the Board of Supervisors shot Mayor Moscone of San Francisco and gay rights leader Harvey Milk then pled insanity due to the sugar rush from Twinkies. He succeeded, too.

Michael remarked, "Forget about standard of living. Even though the California appellate court warned that wives should not be forced to live on substantially less than their husbands or to live at the level of welfare, the judges in our Superior Court do not care. The women's movement, in their rush to embrace equality, thought that alimony was a sexist concept that had no place in a society where men and women were to be treated as equals. Alimony was an insult! That's what the judges listened to. What the women needed to do is to go to work. Get themselves liberated. So even if a judge in the LA Superior Court feels that a husband can afford to support his former wife, the judge rarely requires a man to help a wife sustain a standard of living half as good as his own. Judges still decide that it is often better to leave most of the family's post-divorce income with the husband, viewing it as his rather than hers."

There was a moment of silence as Michael seemed to study me. Perspiration was dampening my hair like glue against my forehead. A drop or two trickled along my cheek. I felt like a frantic child who is about to be punished. Will I be chastised for being foolish enough to marry an actor? Or worse, to have stayed married to an actor for twenty years?

Instead, Michael said simply, "I'll need a check for five thousand dollars. That's my retainer. We'll straighten out this messed-up case of yours. Trust me. I'll never abandon you like your last lawyer."

Robert and Arnie applauded. "Go get 'em, Mike! Watch out for the Irishman!"

"Give her a contract, Robert," Michael said abruptly as his phone was ringing again. He spun around in his chair so his back was to us as he took the new call. We left the office.

I went with Robert into his office, a much smaller space. He handed me a three-page-contract. "Take this home. Read it over. Return it with a check. Next week is fine."

I opened up Michael Kelly's standard agreement for new clients. Besides the hourly rates, there was a consensual lien incorporated into the retainer agreement. Next to every paragraph was a line for me to initial. Each paragraph stated that it hereby gives said attorney a lien upon any money or property. Kelly had the right to my house or any other real estate I might own. There were three pages that stated he would have the legal right to take automobiles, bank accounts, jewels and so forth. I decided not to initial the list of contingencies. I just would hand it in with my five thousand dollar check and pray that Kelly and his crew would be too busy to notice.

Gertrude and her dog Skip met Whiskey and me on the corner as we began our nightly walk for the animals. She snorted with laughter as I explained my legal contract with a new lawyer. She said, "Two weeks ago, you were about ready to give up an apartment, be forced into a woman's shelter. Today you're an heiress who has hired a well-known lawyer to represent you. Isn't life a bitch? Maybe now you can take the time to write a book about the ex-husband, the actor, and your legal eagles."

"Oh, Gertrude, I'm too close to it. To live it and write it at the same time is too painful."

"You just have to do it. Your book about the actor-husband will be your success. I can sense it."

"I'll give it some thought. Maybe in the near future. Right now I have to prepare for my next trial."

"Jeez, another trial? Do you need me to testify again? I'm more than willing to be a witness for you."

"This trial won't have witnesses unless they're accountants. Kelly is going to settle my community-interest in pension plans and television residuals. He is filing an order to request alimony again."

"How many times have you gone to trial?"

"Gosh, Gertrude, I lost count. There were so many continuances, so many trials. Richard has no shame. He drives me into court to terminate support on the grounds that he's an out-of-work actor. Then he's so busy working as an actor that he can't make the hearings."

*****

In Michael Kelly's office I read over the documents he has prepared for me: THE ORDER TO SHOW CAUSE, THE APPLICATION FOR ORDER AND SUPPORTING DECLARATION, my six pages of DECLARATION, Kelly's nine pages of his MEMORANDUM OF POINTS AND AUTHORITIES. Some of the documents I must sign under penalty of perjury.

Attached to Michael Kelly's DECLARATION was Exhibit "A." I couldn't believe what he had uncovered regarding Richard's income for the two years he took me to court six times to terminate support. In that time the total of the actual amount Richard received in residuals alone came to $174,022.10. This was not taking into account the salary he received for starring on a popular soap opera. Kelly discovered after that Richard has a yearly income just from residuals of more than $50,000.

At the time Richard testified before Judge Montez at our last appearance, he claimed that as an out-of-work actor he had no income. He testified further that he had donated his $97,000 boat to charity. Yet he filed an INCOME AND EXPENSE DECLARATION that indicates $850 per month to fix the boat as well as $281 per month for the slip for the boat.

Kelly found out later that the charity that received the donation of the boat was Los Angeles City College, but they returned the boat to Richard. They didn't want it. They must have realized what expense it would be to maintain a boat with a 53-foot-long hull.

"What's this with his tax bills?" Michael asks as if I would know. "Your ex alleges a tax bill of $50,000, then he gives oral testimony to Judge Montez that this amount is over $90,000, without any proof."

I shake my head helplessly.

Michael continues, "At the income level your husband was making, your alimony award should have been around $7,000 a month. Never less than $4,000 per month, which I'm asking for this time."

Robert joined us. He said to me, "I called Ronald Litz today. We wanted to ask what happened from his viewpoint."

Did Ron tell him I alienated judges? That he couldn't stand to have me near him? That he ordered me to get away? Sit in the back of the court room? In a cross-your-fingers moment, I asked, "What did Ron Litz say?"

"He said that in his twenty-four years of family law he had never met a husband in this length of marriage—with children—that was as big a son of a bitch as your husband. He said he couldn't get him. He hoped we would do better for you."

"Oh, really? He really said that?" I couldn't help smiling.

*****

A month later we're back in Department Two of LA Superior Court. The assembly room for the department is crowded today. I know that whatever side of the room my lawyer and I sit, Richard and his lawyer will choose the opposite side. There is a low hum of voices as lawyers check in with the clerk. As the lawyers greet one another, there is the meaningless play and interplay between them. They're suited up in the dark gray or black like funeral attire. It is befitting because here is where the death of a marriage happens.

While waiting for Michael, I looked around until I realized that I was sitting exactly four rows behind Ronald Litz. He was seated next to his client, a man. Naturally, he's with a man as I ruined him from ever handling a woman again. The distance between us is impassable but if he turned, we might make eye contact. We would never exchange greetings. I wanted to bolt from my seat, run to the farthest side of the room and hide. I used my pocketbook to block half of my face from recognition. He would be either furious or dying of curiosity to know where I found the money to hire a top gun, family lawyer like Michael Kelly.

Without warning, Ron's client let out a loud gasp like a death rattle. This was followed by a terrible groan as the man's arms flung up in the air then he slumped down into his seat, his bald head banging on the back of the chair. His jaw dropped open, exposing gray gums which matched the pallor of his skin. Immediately a fashionably dressed woman with her lawyer in tow came running toward the man. Obviously, it was his soon-to-be-ex-wife. She put her arm around his head as she bent over him in a manner of a tolerant mate who still cared. An unsmiling Litz rose to his feet, his arms folded in front of him as he stared coolly at the man as if he were a despicable criminal. It was the same stare that I got when he represented me.

A security guard rushed to assist the man, who was too sick to stand. How well I know from the familiar look on Ron's face his annoyance. He has blocked out this day on his calendar for a trial, and the man has the indecency to go into an epileptic seizure or let the stress overcome him. Ron will have to file for a continuance. A step he abhors as he will have to start the inevitable process of a new motion again for at least thirty days henceforth.

Michael tapped me on the shoulder: "I need to confer with you." We stepped into the hallway. At the other end Richard was sitting alone on a bench, his face averted from us.

In a confidential tone, Michael said, "Stitz is no longer representing your ex-husband."

"What! Why?" I couldn't quite believe that Richard fired an attorney who kept winning for him in court.

"Most likely he didn't want to pay Stitz's high legal bills any longer. I can't tell you how confusing it was separating the files from Stitz's or Litz's. The names drove us crazy. It was like Stitz said such and such and then Robert would say, you mean Litz not Stitz. It was like 'Who's on First'? Your ex-husband's new lawyer, George Milman, does international law, not family law, which is odd. Why would Richard use him?"

"Oh, Milman's a personal friend of Richard's. I bet he's representing Richard for free." I spotted the lawyer, who was now sitting next to Richard.

"Milman wants a continuance since he's new to the case. As a professional courtesy, we'll grant him that."

I wanted to wail, "Not another continuance!" This means my legal bill will escalate for yet another court appearance. By then Richard will again find an excuse for another continuance as he usually gets a TV guest spot within thirty days of a hearing. If this were a movie, lugubrious violin music would play in the background as I mentally chip away at my inheritance for the escalating legal bills.

"Milman wants to know if we'd be interested in a settlement—a lump sum payment."

"For what?"

"A buy out of your spousal support rights."

"What do you think I should do?"

"Take a look at Richard. He doesn't look so good to me."

I study Richard, whose expression looks like a sad-sack; the lines around his mouth seem to tremble with intense misery. He never once glanced in our direction. His attitude did not change as Attorney Milman whispered into his ear.

Michael said, "The guy appears sick to me. There's no color in his face. Didn't you say he had heart trouble? Hospitalized in London for it?"

"Sure, but that was a few years ago."

"This man's days are numbered. He's probably still got heart trouble. That's why he looks like a corpse warmed over."

I had to agree. Richard did look bad. His face was unusually pasty pale as if he were recovering from a night of boozing. "How does his health affect my case?"

"Your support order ends with the obligor's death. However, on the other hand if there's a spousal settlement, a buy out, it doesn't matter if he dies. His estate will have to finish paying for it."

"How much are we talking about for a settlement?"

"That has to be negotiated. Let me speak to Mr. Milman and find out how much."

The next day at our powwow, my team of lawyers laid out the facts for me. If I accepted a buy out of my spousal rights, I would have enough money to spend the rest of the year in paralegal school without taking temp jobs. I could graduate in peace without the constant worry of Richard's threats to take me back to court every time he was an out-of-work actor.

In the associate's office for the Kelly Firm, Robert said, "Their offer is for $24,000. Your ex-husband refuses to pay you in a lump sum. He wants to pay out at two thousand a month for the next year."

"What does Michael think of the offer?"

"We agree that with your ex-husband's health issues, you should accept it. I thought he looked terrible in court. What a mess. He's a shadow of his former self. When I use to see him on TV, he was a handsome dude. Well, anyway, don't be surprised if he kicks the bucket before the year is up."

At paralegal school I asked my professor of family law his advice on waiving my rights for alimony—forever. What if I got sick or had an auto accident? I explained how much time and money my legal battles have taken away from me for more than eight years. He said, "You know that your daughters have passed the age of majority. Even if one of them decides to live with you again, the court won't consider it any more. In fact, there is no record of the Superior Court in Los Angeles awarding women alimony five years after she's been divorced. Have I answered your question?"

*****

I sat opposite Robert as he placed the buy out agreement on his desk. Since technically my case is over for them, Michael has handed the reins to his associate. The agreement is about two and a half pages long. I read it quickly. I didn't want to sound nitpicking as I tried to keep the reproachful tone out of my voice: "There's a clause here that I didn't agree to–this is not kosher."

"Hmm? Let me see." Robert twisted the paper around as he reads with my finger still pressed against the abominable sentence. "Ah, you mean where it states that the dollar amount will be called alimony."

"Exactly. A buy out agreement of my rights is not alimony. The fact that Richard wants to call it that so he can take $24,000 as a tax deduction is unfair and not legal. If I agreed that it was alimony, then the IRS expects me to pay the taxes. My calculated guess is that I'd have to pay five or six thousand dollars in taxes."

"Ah, don't worry. The IRS will go after the person with deep pockets. They'll jump on Richard, not you."

"Are you sure?"

"Of course," Robert said, amicably enough.

"Okay, if you say so." I scribbled my name on the signature line. Richard and his lawyer had already signed the document. No more lawyers meant no more outrageous legal bills. This was cause for celebration. I will never have to appear again in LA Superior Court where I felt like Alice in Wonderland. The last chapter of Alice's story, she appeared in trial. The only difference between her nonsensical judges and mine is that her judges wore wigs.

> "I don't want to be a doctor; and live by men's diseases, nor a minster to live by their by their sins; nor a lawyer to live by their quarrels. So I don't see there's anything left for me but to be an author."
>
> – Nathaniel Hawthorne (to his mother)

Chapter Twenty One

Two years flew by. Richard was still alive, and fortune smiled upon him. His Great Aunt Dorothy died at age ninety-four and left him her entire estate of $1.5 million. This consisted of her home in Pasadena, Blue Chip stocks, antiques and jewelry.

During our marriage I was required to pay homage to Aunt Dorothy for Richard's sake. The raison d'etre was that as Auntie was a widow with no children, Richard stood the best chances of anyone in line as her heir. At the time we thought her quite old at seventy-one. Richard assured me that she was very frail with a toe practically in her Forest Lawn plot. He promised that to sacrifice a couple of summers visiting her in Pasadena, I would share in his just reward. Our brief appearances in her life were like an insurance policy to protect his so-called inheritance as Aunt Dorothy liked to brag that at least two gentlemen callers a year proposed marriage to her. We knew they were fortune hunters (unlike Richard, of course).

Like waving a red flag in front of Richard's face, she said in a veiled threat that Pasadena College offered her a huge sum of money for her Tudor house with its verdant gardens of peonies, roses and gardenias. The College wanted to purchase it for a professor's home. They promised to engrave her name on a brass plate. An honorarium like that pleased and flattered her. This last statement gave Richard chest pains. He insisted it would be unwise to pass another summer without a quick visit. Particularly since at this time, she had just turned eighty, much to Richard's disappointment. She attributed her good health to a course taught by a world-famous vitaminologist in 1930 at Pasadena College. She should have been made the poster child or have been followed up in a scientific study on how to outlive everyone else.

We rehearsed our eight and eleven-year-old daughters on etiquette before each visit to Aunt Dorothy, whom they came to know and dislike as Auntie Pruneface. She was tiny at four-foot-ten. Her gray hair was styled weekly at Elizabeth Arden's. Often she attended luncheon fashion shows at I. Magnin's where she complained that she would never buy a dress modeled by a Negro. She also was a conservative Republican and a staunch supporter of President Richard Nixon until she learned that in his White House tapes, he had said F-U-C-K. She knew the parents of that nice boy who grew up to be Nixon's chief of staff, Bob Haldeman. She boasted that she had known anyone important in society as many years ago, her husband and she often had been chaperones for Pasadena's debutante balls. She said she was a personal friend of Julia Child's father and mother who were always taking young Julia and her sister to doctors to see if anything could be done to prevent them from growing so tall.

Upon our first visit to Auntie Pruneface's house, our daughters held out their white-gloved hands for her to shake. The décor of the living room was locked in the time warp of the 1930s and appeared as if no one had lived there since then. It was quite immaculate, like a movie set. Two magazines rested on a coffee table at a certain angle as in a photograph. Every book in the bookcase had the same black cover. Auntie Pruneface and her housekeeper made sure nothing was out of place. As guests were admonished that when sitting in a chair or on a couch, we must not allow our backs to touch the furniture. Auntie Pruneface didn't want grease spots from any human beings. Jennifer and Tina made sure to keep their backs straight, hands folded in their laps.

At breakfast time she always served us soft-boiled eggs, which we hated. The minute she turned away, the children and I flung the eggs out the window. Our second course was oatmeal with no sugar, which we tolerated.

A week later, as Richard, the children and I happened to pass a tree outside Auntie Pruneface's kitchen, we glanced up and there hanging in the branches were white blotches of our soft-boiled eggs. Tina counted out loud, "Twenty-one eggs!" My hand curled around her mouth as we hastened away.

In the evening we dined in her formal dining room. At each place setting was a finger bowl with one of her gardenias floating inside. Auntie Pruneface rang a dainty bell for a uniformed maid to take away the dishes. She was quite proud of her silverware since her late husband's family fortune had been made in silver. She liked to remind us that William Randolph Hearst bought all his silver flatware, vases, chandeliers, picture frames and candlesticks from her husband. "In fact," she said, "if you ever visit the Hearst Castle, notice the silverware displayed there. It was designed and made by our silversmiths."

Auntie Pruneface hated more things than she liked. She was jealous of any and every woman, regardless of shape or age. Her gray blue eyes would crinkle into scorn as she said, "You know, Candace, in California we don't need as much makeup as we have sunlight here." If I was not in the room, she made statements to Richard such as, "When Candace wears that white pantsuit, she looks much taller than you. Doesn't that bother you? Why does she always ask to be excused to lie down because of a headache? Is she seriously ill? She's so pale, she looks like a sickly apparition."

Even in her nineties, Auntie Pruneface still took walks for a half-hour every day following her afternoon naps. It was amazing that she didn't have to wear eyeglasses except for very fine print and her hearing was uncanny. She could hear a whisper a room away. After we moved to California, my daughters and I took turns accompanying Auntie Pruneface on her daily walks. When it was my turn, I always waited for her in the foyer rather than take a chance that my shoes might leave a mark on the Oriental rugs in the living room. The routine was always the same. From an upstairs hallway, I heard the pop of a lipstick tube. Then she carefully undid her hairnet, which kept her curls in shape as she napped. She put on earrings and a black silk dress as if she were invited to a tea party. Her spindly, bowed legs came marching downstairs. She struck a pose in her leather flats from Salvatore Ferragamo's. I knew that it was my cue to compliment her. "Oh, how beautiful you look today, Aunt Dorothy. And younger than springtime, too."

After we exchanged our usual amenities, one day she said, "What are you going to do for a living? Richard certainly can't be expected to pay you alimony forever."

"You see, it's this way, Aunt Dorothy: If Richard had any community property to split, I wouldn't have asked for alimony." It was preposterous for her to give advice, since she had never held a job. She was barely seventeen when her mother sent her to a French finishing school to learn how to snare a rich man. Before the year was over, they were successful. Mother managed to live in this house with daughter and husband for thirty-five years. Tensely, I waited for Aunt Dorothy to continue our chat as we went strolling along Arden Drive.

"Richard says you're trying to write a novel."

"Yes, Aunt Dorothy."

"Give it up."

"It's about what happened in South Dakota in the—"

"No one wants to read about that dull state. Not enough population there to make your book a best-seller anyway."

"What about the theater, Aunt Dorothy? I'm best qualified as an actress."

"Impossible, you're too old now for motion pictures. Why don't you become a theater critic? Get a job on a newspaper."

To mollify her, I answered, "What a super suggestion. As soon as I'm home I'll research the opportunities."

We circled the block. A few residents recognized her with a wave. She didn't really care to respond as she pointed out a house that belonged to a widower who sends her flowers once a week. "Did you notice my bouquet? By the front door."

I didn't really, but I quickly recalled there was in the entry a wilted floral spray that left a faint funeral scent in the air. "Oh, how thoughtful of the gentleman."

"He wanted to know, if we married, could he move his grand piano into my living room? I would never stand for that. The nerve!" She winced at the thought.

Once Richard announced the date of his wedding to the librarian, I no longer felt obligated to call upon Auntie Pruneface. Let the librarian pay her dues, so to speak. A couple of years after that, Auntie Pruneface passed away.

About the same time, my precious Whiskey went into heart failure as was predicted when he was just a puppy. His lungs were filling with fluid. The veterinarian drained the fluid once a month, then it became once a week. On my last visit to the vet, Whiskey let out a strange sound that I had never heard before. The vet explained that Whiskey was crying. I have heard whimpers, howls, but never an actual sob as if crying like a person. I cradled Whiskey as he was injected with whatever a vet gives to put an animal down. Before I could count to five, the vet said, "He's gone." I sat in a chair, my face nuzzled in his white fur. My tears splashed over both of us for a long, long time.

Whiskey took the divorce worse than the rest of us. From day one, he hated living in California. The minute I left him alone in my apartment, the neighbor said he never stopped barking at the door. Whenever I returned, I would discover his revenge. He undid the telephones, took the kitchen garbage sack out of its container then spread garbage across the living room rug. In the bedroom, he jumped on top of the desk where he leaped at the glass panes of a window and broke them.

I made Richard take Whiskey part of the time. I thought he might be happier in a house with a backyard to run around. However, Whiskey didn't like Richard. He ran away from him three times. Whiskey wore a collar with tags for identification: one tag had Richard's phone number, another had Richard's talent agency's number and the last was the phone for the veterinarian. Whiskey was rescued overnight twice, once by a gay couple who lived in a penthouse overlooking Sunset Boulevard. They offered to keep him as Whiskey hid under the bed when Richard showed up at the door. The third time was stressful as Whiskey was lost for a week. We put up signs everywhere along Sunset Boulevard near Richard's house.

One rainy night a truck driver stopped at Denny's on Sunset Strip to get a hamburger. He had left the door of his truck open. When he returned with his food, there was a dripping wet Whiskey waiting in the passenger seat. On Whiskey's tags he saw Richard's address, and he drove the three blocks to Richard's house. Richard immediately called me to pick up Whiskey. "I can't take this dog anymore," he said as though laying down an axiom. "I could have a heart attack."

After Whiskey died I arranged for him to be cremated. Almost a week later a man knocked at my apartment door and hand-delivered a parcel from a pet crematorium. As I undid the wrapper, inside was a box with a small tin container. Wrapped around it was plain blue paper. The top opened like a pint-size paint can. How could my Whiskey fit inside this little thing? Where to bury him? He hated California so on my next trip to New York City I took his ashes with me. In New York I couldn't find a proper burial place either as we had moved away too long ago.

Today Whiskey's ashes rest inside my closet on a shelf beside my shoe boxes. I have instructed my daughters that upon my demise, they are to blend my ashes with Whiskey's. If it is too expensive to put us in the family plot, in South Dakota, then bury us in some foreign but unpolluted sea. They are *not*, and I repeated, *not* to let their father take out one of his boats and toss Whiskey and me into the putrid waters of Marina Del Rey.

*****

Gertrude found out she had breast cancer. I raced to her bedside at the Motion Picture Hospital in Woodland Hills. She was recovering from a mastectomy. She discovered the lump a few years ago but, as a devoted Christian Scientist, she refused to see a doctor until it was too late. "I'm really worried," she said.

I put her thin hand in mine. "About the cancer?"

"Oh, no, not about that. It's my memory. A while ago, I was reading a paragraph in a magazine. A half hour after I put the magazine down, I couldn't remember what I read. There are other forgetful symptoms that I haven't mentioned." Her voice caught as if she were trying to swallow the tears.

What could be worse for a writer than to have her cognitive abilities decline? Gertrude lived to write, even if her last two books were rejected by publishers. She never gave up. If you stood on the sidewalk beneath her apartment window, you could hear her typing away on an old upright typewriter. She refused to switch to a computer. She kept a posted sign on her apartment door, "Writer at Work, Do Not Interrupt."

Gertrude sat up in bed. She reached for a pen from a dresser then a sheet of stationery. "I have to write my will. This is what I want to leave you–the rights to my unpublished books. Take any of the plots and use them in your scripts if you like.

"I'm giving you six file cabinets for research. It's better than going to the library. It's all the material I've accumulated in a lifetime. For instance, look under C, and there's my research for Elizabeth Taylor's *Cleopatra* from a locked exhibit on Cleo's life stored in the archives of the Pasadena Museum. I was the only writer at the time the museum allowed to view and to touch the authentic Egyptian documents. Under P, you'll find every kind of poison known to man. Find the best one to use on your ex, the kind that leaves no trace." Gertrude wrote with a fury as though her time were short. "I'm going to leave you the screenplay rights to my book, *So Deadly Fair.*"

"Where did you come up with that title? It's so intriguing."

"It's by Lord Byron." She closed her eyes, her forehead wrinkled in thought, she then recited as dramatically as any professional actress, "Such is the aspect of this shore. T'is Greece, but living Greece no more! So coldly sweet, *so deadly fair.* We start, for soul is wanting there. Hers is the loveliness in death. That parts not quite with parting breath. But beauty with that—that…"

She opened her eyes. "I can't remember any more."

"Why, Gertrude, you remember a lot. Your memory still works."

An inexplicable sadness came over her. "I may remember Lord Byron's poem, but I can't remember yesterday. Or what I ate for breakfast today." She kept scribbling and talking at the same time. "This is a holographic will, which is legal in California. As long as the testator has dated, signed it in her handwriting. I lived off so many damn options for *So Deadly Fair*. Maybe in your career, you might do something with my book. It's still the best damn noir story around. Bette Davis and Joan Crawford both wanted to star in it for the movies. But somehow Warner Brothers let my bestseller fall through the cracks." She paused; her eyes were now shrouded in pain. "Call the nurse for me. I want her to sign my will as a witness. It's not necessary. But I added the witness for precaution."

After the nurse came in to sign the will, Gertrude handed it to me. "You keep the will. I trust that when my time comes, you'll know what to do."

Now that I had graduated from paralegal school, I explained about my upcoming trip to New York to find work as I hadn't been able to in L.A. It was the last time I spoke with her. Six months later, when I realized the unemployment in New York was just as bad as in L.A., I decided to return. I went to Gertrude's apartment and found it vacated. Her neighbor told me that Gertrude's relatives moved her to an assisted home for the elderly in Palm Desert.

"Do you know what happened to her book collection, the file cabinets or her manuscripts?"

The neighbor said quite casually, "Gert's relatives hired one of those junk trucks that picks up stuff. They took it out to some garbage dump site."

"What about her original Garbo movie posters?"

"Oh, they threw them away, along with some others, too."

"That's a shame. Gertrude said they were worth a great deal. In an emergency, she'd sell the posters to a memorabilia shop in Hollywood."

The neighbor nodded. "Trust me, her relatives didn't care. They seemed well-off." She handed me a slip of paper with the phone number for the Chateau Gardens in Palm Desert. I tried calling a couple of times, but one of those robot-like employees answered in a matter-of-fact tone, "Miss Gertrude Walker no longer speaks. She's been silent ever since she arrived at the Chateau Gardens."

I knew that Gertrude was dying inside first like her old Studebaker. She was shutting down—descending into the dark of nothingness. So this is what can happen to a writer at the end of her life. I imagined those laborious hours she spent writing thousands of manuscript pages that were left to decay in a tomb of forgotten garbage.

Within a month, I received a letter from Gertrude's cousin. Gertrude had died. The relatives couldn't find her will. Did I know anything about it? I wanted to write back that they already threw away her estate. Technically, her will was useless, but I would Xerox it for them anyway.

A paperback copy of *So Deadly Fair* lay on my bookshelf. I crossed my palms on the book in prayer: "Dear goddess, free Gertrude of any misery. Take her to that heavenly place for writers. She's a good Christian Scientist who doesn't believe in bad endings and death. She believes the stars wink at her. Don't let her soul linger on this earthly realm. When she makes an entrance in paradise, introduce her to the poet she admires so much—Lord Byron."

> "But words are things, and a small drop of ink,
> Falling like dew, upon a thought, produces
> That which makes thousands, perhaps millions think."
>
> – Lord Byron
> Canto III

Chapter Twenty Two

In reviewing one of my executed legal agreements, I noted that Richard was to begin paying my share of the actor's pension plans when he reached the age of eligibility: fifty-five. For two years after he reached 55, not a word was heard from him. His usual mantra had been, "I'm so broke. I'm an out-of-work actor." It must be hard for him to complain how destitute he is now that he's rolling in his million dollar inheritance from Auntie Pruneface. Surely he might feel more generous. Rather than involve lawyers, I left messages for him but no response came henceforth, as they say in court. In these past two years, I have spent most of my inheritance as I moved to New York for a year, then back to Los Angeles where I bought a car. I simply don't have the money to hire a new lawyer.

According to my next-to-last attorney Ronald Litz, even if Richard had not retired himself, I am entitled to monthly payments. This sum of money would be quite helpful as I am doing temp legal work, most of it is writing banal deposition summaries.

In a neighborhood market, I ran into one of my former law professors, Clifford Dicker, one of the best teachers at U.W.L.A. He taught the introductory course on the American Legal Environment, which he made interesting as well as enlightening. While I was attending paralegal school, he happened to say that he went home to lunch one noon, turned on the TV, and there I was in some television production. He asked me what in the hell was I doing wasting my time becoming a paralegal when I was an actress?

Mr. Dicker and I exchanged pleasantries. I brought up the difficulties of the paralegal job market, then I mentioned the latest problems with Richard and my community interest in the pension plans. He pushed his glasses up his nose as he spoke confidently, just the way he did when lecturing in class: "Well now, Candace, you are entitled to sue him."

"Sue him! A new lawsuit?!" The phrase alone was enough to turn my heart inside out, my stomach to cramp with the pain of a thousand teeth. To go back to court was like guerilla warfare that never ends.

"How else will you get the payments as they accrue each month?" He waited a moment, then in his professional voice said, "Candace, my private practice is family law. We need to meet to discuss this matter further. Don't you agree?"

“Oh, certainly, yes, yes. That would be good—very wise—sure, sure.” My voice sounded reluctant, while my head kept bobbing in agreement.

“Why don’t you come to my office in Culver City tomorrow? Bring your last legal documents, the Agreement, OSCs, and the Judge’s Orders and Findings. Is two o’clock okay for you?

“That’s fine, Mr. Dicker.” I waved goodbye as he left the market swinging a sack of bananas. He was quite distinguished looking with his thick silver hair and a polite, engaging manner. Thanks to my lucky stars I bumped into him today. As my former professor, he of all attorneys would understand my struggles to find work at my age as a new paralegal. He would be aware that I’m not a rich divorcée living off the unhealthy lap of alimony as Richard’s lawyer, Stitz, liked to argue. Maybe if I had used Mr. Dicker in the beginning of my legal rat race, I wouldn’t have had to suffer so much. I wouldn’t have to live on substantially less than Richard or to live at the level of welfare. Perhaps Mr. Dicker was the jurisprudent knight, the fighting tiger I had been hoping to find! Hope! For the first time in a long while, I felt hope again and, why not, hope springs eternal in the human breast. So I was taught to believe.

*****

Ten minutes into my conversation with Mr. Dicker, he pulled from my files my Buy Out Agreement for alimony. He let out a sigh of resignation that meant, "How could you have been so stupid to give up your rights to alimony?" He shoved the Agreement aside as though he couldn’t bear to look at such a travesty of justice. He is not quite yet aware that for the past eight years I have been in constant court battles with Richard, or that Mr. Dicker is number seven in the line-up of lawyers who have represented me; that I am beyond my wits’ end with Richard.

As Mr. Dicker read the Agreement for the Pension Plans, he grew more irritated. “This is a mess! I don’t understand what you’re to receive in payments from three different actor unions that don’t agree on the same age for retirement. We’re going to have to file a motion in court for a judge to figure this out. If you had seen me within the first year of this Pension Agreement, I would have filed a malpractice suit against the lawyer who drew it up!”

Oh, wouldn’t that have been fun! On top of Richard’s divorce lawsuits, I could have added a malpractice one as well. It never stops. For someone who is not a run-of-the-mill criminal, a heroin-addicted gang member, a movie star shoplifter, or even a scheming murderess, these past eight years I have seen more courtrooms than the total times of each of those evildoers. I am clearly the winner!

I wrote out a check for two thousand dollars for Mr. Dicker to settle my new case. We shook hands. Our next meeting would be in Department Two of LA’s Superior Court. He promised that this hearing before a judge would not be adversarial. All we were asking for was a legal interpretation of the Agreement for the pension plans.

Thirty days later, Richard and I sat on benches about a city block apart in the hallway of Superior Court as our attorneys met with a judge inside one of the courtrooms. Their conference lasted ten minutes. The door opened, and the two attorneys came out smiling at each other in a relaxed manner. Just as Mr. Dicker reached me, he said, "The reason Richard hasn't paid your community share of the pension plans is that he didn't know how much to pay. Mr. Milman asked for a continuance so that they can retain an accountant to figure out what money is owed to you. This is a reasonable request. I said that was fine with us."

"Mr. Dicker, for two years I have been asking Richard for an accounting. Since it takes a court appearance to make him do something honorably, did you request your legal fees?"

"Oh, his attorney agreed that Richard should be responsible for my fees. The attorney is mailing me immediately Richard's check for eight hundred dollars."

Nonetheless, over time Mr. Dicker granted several continuances to Richard and his attorney. Finally, Mr. Dicker grew frustrated and went to court anyway without the other side appearing. The judge read through the Agreement for Pension Plans and the accountant's statement and was furious. "How could her attorney, her very own attorney, do this to his client? She is tied to a penalty payment as if he retired at fifty-five, and that means when he retires at sixty-five, she won't receive the increase of fifty percent of the monies at that time. From the calculations here, she is only entitled to $263 a month. However, at his age of sixty-five, he will receive around six thousand dollars a month. Half of that should have been hers!"

Could I receive any more bad news? Of course I could. The Internal Revenue Department sent me a letter. They stated that I received income of $24,000 for one year and didn't file taxes for this sum. My tax expert said, "Oh, you will have to pay the IRS about $5000. That's not including the penalty or interest fees."

Richard had deducted from his income taxes as alimony the $24,000 for the buy out of my spousal rights. The advantage of being a recent graduate of paralegal school was that I knew as well as any attorney how to fight this. It is against the California law for a husband to declare any monies as alimony if his wife's alimony has ended for at least two years. I researched the legal precedents for the cases that supported mine and listed them. I included Judge Herbert Klein's Order that my alimony was reduced to zero more than two years ago. The IRS accepted my excuse that this was a buy out of my spousal rights, not alimony. I hoped that they ran back to Richard, who fraudulently claimed the money as a big tax deduction for himself. Let the IRS punish him!

From his current bill, I noticed that Mr. Dicker was charging $250 an hour to review correspondence from me, to write to opposing counsel and to write to me. My bill was now $6000 excluding my retainer payment. The only correspondence from me was one letter protesting his fees, which I didn't consider to be a proper billing subject.

I wrote him that I think it is improper to bill a client for the time it takes to render a bill. I asked for any copy of the correspondence to opposing counsel.

Mr. Dicker did not bother to answer me but billed me for that letter, too. My latest shining knight was beginning to lose his luster. I wrote back that I was not aware that his hourly rate had gone to $250. In regard, please send me copies of any attorney fee contracts, which I may have signed since I retained him. I can find none in my file. I have some substantive concerns about his past billings.

I still did not get any answers from Mr. Dicker but received an additional bill for that letter. This time in my follow-up letter, I listed my grievances in a way that could be read aloud in a court.

1. The $800 from the ex-husband has never been credited to my account.
2. This matter has taken four years due to the numerous continuances granted my ex-husband. I protested these repeated continuances, and question if I am liable for the extra fees incurred.
3. The sums already paid you constitute reasonable compensation for the legal services, and I do not believe I owe you any additional compensation.
4. If you disagree, please inform me of the following: the identity of any and all contracts, which support your position that I owe you more money; copies of such contracts, and or the availability of any alternative dispute resolution procedure that would be applicable to our disagreement concerning the legal fees and the services rendered.

Continuing on in my paralegal style, I wrote: "Please be advised that I consider it a breach of your fiduciary duties to charge me attorney fees with respect resolving this dispute; billing me for my inquiries about your bills has a chilling effect and is contrary to the fiduciary duties, which you owe me. I trust that we will be able to resolve this dispute in an expeditious and reasonable matter. I look forward to your reply."

What would he charge me to read this letter? It is much longer than my other ones. I waited for my next monthly statement from Mr. Dicker. I waited and waited. It seemed my shining knight rode off into the sunsets without so much as a fare thee well. I never heard from Mr. Dicker again or ran into him at the organic banana stand in the market.

Life kept moving on without some of my closest friends. As Blanche DuBois said in *A Streetcar Named Desire*, "The Grim Reaper put his tent up on our doorstep." I went from one legal temp job to another. There were a couple of paid options on my screenplays, as well as some enthusiastic meetings or luncheons with young wannabe producers who never seemed to have enough clout to reach the development stage.

There were other baby-faced producers whose claim to fame was always a relative who was married to a girl who had a nephew whose cousin had a wife whose brother had millions of dollars to make a movie.

Somewhere along in this chain of relatives, my script always disappeared. "Who lost it? Why can't you find my script?" This seemed to become my battle cry, which was often met by a blank stare with a finger up his nose by someone who looked like a fetus in a business suit.

*****

The quotation on this page is my favorite. Sandy Meisner, who was head of the Neighborhood Playhouse, had it framed and hung on the wall of his office. Not only did I have the opportunity to study with him in his private professional class, but I worked with him as an actress, too.

Sanford Meisner and Candace are a married couple in a tense TV scene from *Naked City*.

"I wish the stage were as narrow as the wire of a tightrope dancer, so that no incompetent would dare step upon it."

– Johann Wolfgang von Goethe,
"Wilhelm Meisters Lehrjahre" - Book 4, Chapter 2

Epilogue

Early one morning, I wandered through the Beverly Hills Library wishing and searching for ideas for a new project. Nothing came to my mind. What was I doing anyway spending a gorgeous day in the library? I sauntered around the bookcases until I came to the last one before the lobby. I noticed the shelves with the sign, "*New Biographies.*" I hesitated for a few seconds, then decided to take a quick look as I enjoy thumbing through the pictures in famous biographies. On the shelf above my head, I reached for a book. It was stuck. The librarians really stuff the shelves with new books. I pulled at the book, causing the entire line of books to shift. At the end of the shelf, a book started to fall. My hand caught it just in time. I was about to replace the book when I noticed the title *The Hidden Life of Otto Frank—The Biography of Anne Frank's Father.* Since I had already read *Anne's Diary*, and the play based upon it, I was not that interested. Nonetheless, this biography had many pictures I had never seen before. I decided to take it home.

I left the book on a coffee table in my apartment. I forgot about it until four days later when I was sleeping, Otto Frank came to me in a vivid dream. He wore a stylish chesterfield coat of the fifties and carried a felt hat. He seemed quite happy that I found his biography. In his charming Germanic manner he ordered me to get busy. Read the book right away! He wanted me to adapt it for a play. Don't resist. Don't be intimidated. He would guide me.

I asked him, "How should I write your story? Where do I begin the play?" He smiled in enthusiasm as he started to give me instructions. Then I realized there seemed to be a glass–like partition between us, and I could no longer hear him. He put on his hat and, after a courtly bow, waved goodbye. I called emphatically to him, "Don't go! Wait! I didn't hear what you said! Please, don't go!"

The sound of my voice awakened me. To my shock I was standing next to the bed with one arm outstretched as though I were reaching for him.

I mentioned my Otto Frank dream to my colleagues in our writers' workshop. They reacted with about thirty seconds of laughter in disbelief. This didn't daunt me. My main concern was that *The Hidden Life of Otto Frank* probably had been scooped up by some Hollywood studio. This new biography provides the answer to one of the most heartbreaking questions of modern times: Who betrayed Anne

Frank and her family to the Nazis? How could a producer not be intrigued about a book with never-seen before documentation on Anne's father?

The Pulitzer Prize-winning play of her story had promised immortality and the only book that had outsold hers worldwide had been the Bible. Almost no one knew about the struggles Otto Frank went through to get her diary published. He was the only one of his family to survive Auschwitz.

When Otto returned to Amsterdam after World War II, he learned of the discovery of Anne's journal. For two years he pursued publishers who rejected the diary as the public wanted to forget the war and saw no benefit in the words of a fifteen-year-old girl. He refused to give up as her book became one of his primary reasons for living.

Then into his life came the man who betrayed him and his family to the Gestapo. This person threatened to kill any chance of selling *The Diary of Anne Frank*. This was the one remaining enigma of the story, which was to lead Otto into a nightmare of blackmail, fear and betrayal.

Surely by now a Hollywood producer had writers turning Otto's story into a screenplay. But then I knew that producers don't like to read; in fact one well-known producer bragged that he never read the screenplay of any movie he produced. I never have bumped into a producer at a city library. This is foreign territory for a producer. Producers prefer to take time off to swing a racquet at the Beverly Hills Tennis Club or get a little sun and turf at Pacific Coast beach clubs or join poker parties in Sherman Oaks or Encino.

Why not take a chance and find out if the biography was available? I reminded myself that Otto Frank was on my side. Through the magic of the Internet, I contacted the author, Carol Ann Lee, by sending an email to her Swiss agent. Carol had acknowledged the agent in the book. I have learned that almost anyone can be found on the Internet somewhere or someplace. The agent responded almost immediately. She forwarded my information to the author, who would contact me directly if she was interested.

Two days passed when, from halfway around the world in Amsterdam, I received an email from Carol. She wrote that I was the first person to express interest in doing her book as a possible film or play. She asked me to contact her American publisher, Harper Collins, as they have to approve of any dramatic deals arising from the book.

A woman in Harper Collins' legal department sent me another email wanting to know about my previous screenplay projects; do I have relationships with specific producers or an actor in mind who would be interested in Otto Frank if I adapted the book?

I responded in the negative to every question. I offered to send Carol my first twenty pages of four screenplays as a sample of my work. As soon as Carol received my writing samples, she said she thought all four were terrific and was in the process of passing them on to her cautious agent in Switzerland. They didn't keep me waiting in suspense for very long. Carol's agent gave her approval. My California agent wrote up a brief option for Carol and me. This sounds so simple, but the two-page option became as complicated as an international treaty for a Hague Convention. The option was forwarded to Amsterdam, Switzerland, and New York, then returned to California. If one line was changed, the option went back and forth between two continents again. More changes, more waiting time for Harper Collins' legal department to review, then back to all parties concerned here and abroad.

Finally, after almost six months, Carol and I were able to sign the agreement between us. In a year of research and writing drafts of my play, I fell in love with the character of Otto Frank and the type of man he was.

Through a chance acquaintance, I learned that one of Otto's closest and most trusted friends during the 1970s lived in a town just an hour's drive from L.A. This was a Catholic priest, Father John Neiman, who agreed to meet with me. What a rare opportunity to check my facts and research on Otto.

At our appointment, Father Neiman and I met in the parish house. He explained how he first read Anne's Diary in the fifth grade and wrote to Otto Frank to tell him how much the book meant to him. After nine years of correspondence, Otto invited Father Neiman to visit him at his home in Basel, Switzerland.

Opening his personal album of pictures, Father Neiman said, "I was most impressed by Otto's humanity, which he had retained after the most terrible of experiences. He changed my life. I was thinking about the priesthood but had some doubts. Otto said to me, 'Your love for Anne is a wonderful thing, but use it, turn your love into doing good for others.' It was then that my decision became clear." He turned to photos of him with Otto. Looking at me with a smile, he added, "In your play, I hope the audience will come away with a reverence and understanding of Otto Frank. He was truly a wonderful man."

It was my intention that my play showed the courage it took Otto to save his family by hiding them for two years in the secret annex of his spice factory, and his determination to keep the loyal workers in the factory employed. Father Neiman and I were in agreement that I had to be absolutely circumspect about the villain in my drama, the betrayer. I knew that he had to be portrayed in a way that the audience would understand Otto's secret decision in regards to blackmail.

I asked Father Neiman if he would light a candle for my Otto Frank play. He answered, "Later today at Mass, I will offer a special prayer for you and your play."

*****

Almost a year later, my play *The Unfinished Story of Anne Frank* was given a staged reading by professional actors in a Beverly Hills theater. This was the beginning of a new odyssey for me. There is something magical about the theater.

Do I hope for success with this play? At the close of Act II, my character of Otto Frank says to the audience, "I know you were expecting a sad, maybe even a tragic ending. But as someone once said, 'Hope springs eternal'. And I found mine. If the end of the world were imminent, I'd still plant a tree."

And so would I, Otto. And so would I.

"If it be true that good wine needs no bush,
tis true that a good play needs no epilogue."

– Shakespeare ('As You Like It')
(Epilogue, 1.3)

THE ODYSSEY ENDS

www.ingramcontent.com/pod-product-compliance
Lightning Source LLC
Chambersburg PA
CBHW080538090426
42733CB00016B/2617

* 9 7 8 1 5 0 6 9 1 4 3 5 0 *